AIRSHIPS

A popular history

of dirigibles, Zeppelins, blimps and other

lighter-than-air craft

AIRSHIPS

A popular history
of dirigibles, Zeppelins, blimps and other
lighter-than-air craft

Robert Jackson

DOUBLEDAY & COMPANY, INC.   GARDEN CITY, NEW YORK

1973

First Published 1971 by Cassell & Company Ltd.
ISBN 0-385-00761-2
Library of Congress Catalog Card Number 72-84920
Copyright © 1971 by Robert Jackson
All Rights Reserved
Printed in the United States of America
First edition in the United States of America

Acknowledgements

I have received assistance from many quarters in the preparation of this book; there is not space enough to mention the dozens of people who delved into their files or their memories to bring to light half-forgotten snippets of invaluable information. I should, however, like to thank the following in particular for their help:

Miss Ann C. Tilbury, Photo Librarian of Flight International, whose lengthy research on my behalf turned up much rare illustrative material; Squadron Leader A. A. ('Bert') Evans, RAF (Retired); Flying Officer Rick Phillips, RAF; Frank Yeoman, who spent much time searching through his copious files on First World War aviation; the Officer Commanding and Flight Lieutenant P. E. Plowman of the Royal Air Force Station, Cardington, who kindly provided several photographs of all types of airship; Mr P. Jarrett of the Royal Aeronautical Society, who also helped to find a large number of pictures; Captain L. G. Traynor, USN, who generously supplied information on the US Navy's lighter-than-air activities up to 1962; the staff of the Etablissement Cinématographique et Photographique des Armées, Fort d'Ivry, who supplied material on French airship operations; Mr J. White, Assistant Publicity Officer with Short Brothers and Harland Ltd, who went to great efforts to provide me with information on the airships built by his company; and Mr Max Rynish, Managing Director of Cargo Airships Ltd, for his far-reaching suggestions about the future of airships.

Contents

List of Illustrations

A tank at Pulham Airship Station, Norfolk (via Flying Officer R. A. Phillips)

1 Birth of a Dream

One day in the year 1268, a messenger delivered a bulky manuscript into the hands of Pope Clement IV. Entitled *Opus Majus*, the work was divided into seven parts: the first dealt with human failings and their causes, the second and third with theology and languages, the fourth with mathematics and its relationship with philosophy, the fifth and sixth with optics and experimental science, and the seventh with religion.

Written in meticulous Latin, the manuscript was the work of one man: a troublesome English scholar named Roger Bacon. Troublesome, because for years he had been openly defying many accepted theories in the fields of science and philosophy—theories which were generally supported by the Church. Born near Ilchester in 1220, Bacon had been a pupil of the eminent scholar Robert Grosseteste, Bishop of Lincoln. He studied and taught at Oxford and Paris, rapidly establishing a reputation as an original thinker and devoting all his effort to the advancement of science. He believed that scientific truth could be found only by experiment, contradicting the traditional schools of thought which held that the real key to all scientific problems lay in learned discussion. 'During the twenty years that I have specially laboured in the attainment of wisdom,' Bacon wrote later, 'abandoning the path of common men, I have spent on these pursuits more than two thousand pounds [a fortune in present-day terms] on account of the cost of books, experiments, instruments, tables, the acquisition of languages, and the like.' Time and again, he stressed that the true student of science 'makes no account of speeches and wordy conflicts but follows up the works of wisdom and remains there. He knows natural science through experiment.'

The contributions made by Bacon to science—in terms of original thought, as well as invention and documentation—were manifold. Moreover, they provided a badly needed stimulant for the small band of scholars who, in the thirteenth century, were slowly beginning to search beyond the narrow confines of science hemmed in by religious dogma. But Bacon was destined to suffer the same fate as so many other medieval scientists who looked down the years ahead towards remote and fascinating possibilities: he eventually came up against the all-powerful and impenetrable bastion of the Church, and broke himself against its walls. In the end, weary and disillusioned, he became a Franciscan monk and went into almost complete seclusion, forbidden by his superiors to carry out any further experiments. Then, in 1267, there came a brief flash of light in the darkness when Pope Clement IV himself asked Bacon to undertake the enormous task of collating and recording all known scientific law and theory under one cover. The scholar set to work with a a will, labouring during the hours of daylight—and often far into the night, by the flickering light of torches—to complete the work as quickly as possible. It took him a year; a year during which much of his former zeal returned. At last, *Opus Majus* was finished and delivered to the Pope—who, apparently, ignored it.

It was a pity. Not only was *Opus Majus* a masterpiece of known scientific fact and analytical thought, detailing vital contributions to science such as research into optics and the formula for the composition of gunpowder; it was also a book of scientific prediction in which—among other things—Bacon envisaged machines 'for walking in the sea and rivers, even to the bottom without danger' and flying machines 'which can be constructed so that a man sits in the midst of the machine revolving some engine by which artificial wings are made to beat the air like a flying bird'.

Bacon had always been fascinated by the possibility that one day men would fly; there are many allusions to it in his writings, and he dealt with the subject at some length in his treatise *De Secretis Operibus Artis et Naturae*, which preceded *Opus Majus* by several years. Like others before him, Bacon at first dropped into the pitfall of believing that, in order to fly, man had to emulate the flight of a bird as closely as possible, which meant beating the air with artificial wings. His knowledge of languages

2

enabled him to study non-ecclesiastical records containing accounts of the few attempts at manned flight made prior to the thirteenth century in the Middle East and elsewhere, such as that made by George of Trebizond before the Sultan of Turkey at Constantinople a hundred years earlier—a short gliding flight that ended in death for the unfortunate Saracen. Bacon was shrewd enough to realize that the disastrous outcome of this and other flights had nothing to do with the will of God, which was the verdict of the Church; through his scientific knowledge of the human body, he knew that the real reason behind failure lay in the inability of man's puny muscles to sustain the weight of his body in true bird-like flight—hence his references to 'engines' as a motive force. The references were vague, but they showed that Bacon had at least some grasp of the principles required.

It was at this point that Bacon's originality led him into a new channel of thought. Essentially, he saw the problem as a simple one: if the attempts at manned flight so far had failed because of weight, then the solution was obviously to build some kind of apparatus light enough not only to lift a man clear of the ground, but to sustain him in the air. He discussed how this might be achieved in his two major scientific works, envisaging a gigantic globe of extremely thin metal that would be 'filled with the thin air of the upper atmosphere, or with liquid fire, thus rising high into the heavens'. It was beyond even Bacon's scientific genius or vivid imagination to elaborate, but his writing gives us the first recorded instance of serious thought on the lighter-than-air principle.

It was to be nearly four centuries before there was a return to the embryo idea of a man-carrying balloon. This time, the scientist involved was a Jesuit priest named Francesco de Lana. Born at Brescia, in Italy, in 1637, de Lana—like many other followers of his Order—took an active interest in natural sciences, and gave considerable thought to the application of the latest scientific discoveries. After studying the experiments of Pascal and Torricelli, who found that the density of the atmosphere could be measured and that it decreased with altitude, and the discovery by Otto von Guericke that a vacuum could be artificially created, de Lana worked out a design for a flying ship that was to be carried into the air by four big globes of thin coppér, from which all the air had been exhausted. Again, although the principle was sound enough, the Jesuit's design could not possibly have worked in practice for the simple reason that his copper globes would have been instantly crushed by atmospheric pressure. A drawing of the craft was, however, published in 1690 and caused some consternation among the Jesuit hierarchy, already under some suspicion because of the Order's dabblings in matters of which the Church did not approve. De Lana immediately claimed that he had designed his 'flying ship' only to prove that any attempt by man to fly would bring down the wrath of God and end in disaster! Other scientist-priests did not, apparently, share de Lana's fear of the Church's anger: one such was Father Bartholomeo Lourenço de Gusmao, who submitted a number of flying-machine designs—including one based on the lighter-than-air principle—to King John V of Portugal in 1709, and who received a royal award of 600,000 reis for his efforts.

By the middle of the eighteenth century, scientists were beginning to make the discoveries which, ultimately, would enable men to turn the dream of de Lana and the others into reality. In 1766, the scientist Henry Cavendish, a Fellow of the Royal Society, discovered a gaseous agent which he called 'inflammable air', later to be named hydrogen by Antoine Laurent Lavoisier in 1790; while in 1774 the Birmingham chemist and physician Dr Joseph Priestley continued his research into his new discovery of 'dephlogisticated air', or oxygen as Lavoisier was subsequently to call it, and published his findings in a work entitled *Experiments and Observations on Different Kinds of Air*.

The book aroused considerable interest among Europe's scientists, but it fired the imagination of one man in particular: thirty-six-year-old Joseph Montgolfier, who obtained a copy when the French translation appeared in 1776. Joseph had more than a passing interest in the possibilities of flight, and his brother Étienne—five years his junior—was, if not quite so enthusiastic, at least an interested observer. Later, Étienne was to become as passionately interested in the subject as was his brother, but it was Joseph who was encouraged to carry out his own experiments after reading the work of Priestley and other scientists. Joseph's first tentative experiments involved the use of hydrogen, which he produced himself. He made a small paper balloon—a natural choice of material and one available in abundance, thanks to the traditional Montgolfier family trade of paper-making—and filled it with the gas, expecting it to rise into the air. But the experiment was a failure, and so was a subsequent one using a silken balloon; the reason was simply that the hydrogen passed easily through both silk and paper.

Joseph consequently abandoned the use of hydrogen and began to experiment with hot air as a potential means of producing lift. There are conflicting stories about how he stumbled on the idea; the most plausible is that he saw a paper bag, thrown on the fire by his wife, fill with hot air and sweep up the chimney. Whatever the truth, Joseph did not grasp the real principle behind the hot-air balloon, which is that when air is heated it expands with a consequent increase in volume and a reduction in its weight per cubic foot: instead, he believed that combustion produced some kind of gas, which could sometimes be seen in the form of smoke. He also believed that the quality of the gas varied according to the type of material that was being burnt, and he wasted considerable time and effort in experimenting with various unlikely combinations such as wool, wet straw, old shoes and even cow dung. For months, the Montgolfier home at Annonay reeked unbearably as Joseph endeavoured to hit upon the combination that would, to his way of thinking, produce the lightest form of gas. Eventually, he settled for wool clippings and damp straw.

During this time, he also wrote down his observations on the potential uses of balloons, pointing out that they could be of great military value. He admitted that his thoughts on the matter had been influenced by the battle for Gibraltar, which in 1782 was being attacked by the French and Spanish forces in an unsuccessful attempt to dislodge the British garrison. Joseph pointed out that no matter how thick the walls of a fortress might be, they could not prevent troop-carrying balloons

5

from flying over the heads of the defenders and landing in their rear.

Joseph's thoughts on lighter-than-air flight were finally translated into practical form in November 1782, when he built and tested his first successful model balloon at Avignon. He held the silken envelope over a fire until it filled with hot air, then let it go and watched jubilantly as it rose straight up and hit the ceiling, where it hung for half a minute until the air inside it cooled and it came spiralling down. Étienne Montgolfier was also present during this first practical experiment, and when the two brothers returned to Annonay a few weeks later they worked together to build a new and better model balloon. This was tested out of doors and appears to have reached a height of about seventy feet. It was followed by three more balloons, all of much larger capacity; the first attained a height of 550–600 feet. No details of the second balloon's performance have survived, but it was of approximately the same size as the first, with a capacity of 650 cubic feet. The third model had an envelope 35 feet in diameter and the Montgolfiers had fixed 3 April 1783 as the date for its first test flight, but this had to be postponed because of unfavourable weather. A free flight was eventually made on 25 April, the balloon drifting downwind at an average height of 800 feet until it finally descended a little under a mile away.

Joseph and Étienne now felt that they had acquired sufficient expertise in the technique of balloon-building to enable them to carry out a public demonstration with a fair chance of success, and with this in mind they began construction of a new balloon which emerged as an almost perfect globe. It was far larger than anything they had attempted previously, with a capacity of 22,000 cubic feet and a total weight of 500 pounds. The envelope, which was made of cloth and lined with paper, had a circumference of 110 feet and was reinforced by a spider's-web network of strings, the bottom ends of which were attached to a square wooden frame surrounding the aperture.

On the morning of 5 June 1783, the market place at Annonay was crammed with hundreds of people who had streamed into town from miles around to watch the Montgolfier brothers' demonstration. A few of the more sporting among the nobles present tried to lay wagers that the flight would be a success, but there were few takers. Tradesmen and peasants laughed and joked among themselves as they gaped at the still-deflated envelope of the balloon; it was not often that they were treated to a spectacle as fine as this—entertainment which, they felt certain, was bound to end in disaster.

Suddenly, a hush fell over the assembly in the square as the envelope—held fast by two men—began to fill with hot air from the fire kindled beneath its aperture and to swell into a bulging, spherical shape. As the balloon grew steadily bigger, six more men—who had been hired by Montgolfier and who had been standing by on his orders—ran forward and hung grimly on to the frame, holding the balloon down as the ropes that moored it snapped taut. Joseph looked at the faces of the crowd, many of them filled with superstitious fear as well as with awe: this was his moment of triumph. He gave a signal, and the eight men clinging to the balloon's frame let go abruptly. Slowly, in complete silence, the balloon rose majestically to a height of about six thousand feet, where it was caught by a gentle wind and carried southwards. The crowd streamed across the fields in its wake, crashing through fences in their excitement. After ten minutes, the balloon drifted slowly to earth and came to rest in a field about a mile and a half away from its starting-point. Breathlessly, those of the crowd who had kept up the pursuit gathered round the collapsed envelope. They were not laughing and joking now; even the most dull-witted peasant somehow realized that he had been watching an event that would be remembered long after he and his fellows were dust.

The news that two unknown brothers from the Provinces had successfully built and flown a large balloon, when it broke in Paris, rocked the Academy of Sciences to its normally unshakeable foundations. According to all accepted theories, based on the latest scientific knowledge, such an achievement could only have been made with the use of hydrogen, which was the only known agent light enough to lift a balloon into the air—but according to all the available information it appeared that the Montgolfiers had stumbled on some new and revolutionary type

7

of gas. This assumption was strengthened by Joseph himself, who had still not realized that hot air would grow lighter and expand no matter what materials were used in the burning, and who genuinely believed that the secret lay in his foul-smelling combination of straw and wool.

Within a matter of weeks, however, the Academy's faith in hydrogen as a practical means of obtaining lift was to be vindicated by the flight of another balloon; one whose performance far overshadowed anything the Montgolfiers had achieved so far. When the brothers made their first public demonstration at Annonay, plans for building and flying a hydrogen balloon were already being discussed by some of the Academy's younger members, and one of the staunchest advocates of such a project was a thirty-seven-year-old scientist named Jacques Alexandre César Charles. As soon as news of the Montgolfiers' success reached Paris, Charles determined to go ahead with the idea. Shortage of money presented no problems, for the project received great publicity in and around the French capital, and funds to cover the cost of building the balloon were quickly raised when the Academy of Sciences offered ringside seats at the eventual launching in return for contributions.

The balloon rapidly took shape in a small workshop off the Place des Victoires. The envelope was made of silk, coated with a rubber solution to prevent the leakage of hydrogen; this process was the invention of two brothers, Ainé and Cadet Robert, who were to remain Charles's close collaborators throughout his involvement in lighter-than-air flight. The envelope was small in comparison with the Montgolfier balloon, having a diameter of only 12 feet and a capacity of 940 cubic feet. On 23 August 1783 the completed balloon was taken out of the workshop into a small yard, where a high wall concealed operations from curious eyes, and was suspended from a rope stretched between two masts directly above the hydrogen generator. This generator consisted simply of a barrel filled with iron filings, on which sulphuric acid was poured. The resulting gas entered the balloon through a pipe running from the barrel into the aperture. In the event, inflation proved to be a far more complicated process than Charles had envisaged:

the gas passing into the balloon was so hot that buckets of water had to be continually thrown over the envelope to prevent it from catching fire. There was a further setback the following morning, when it was found that the balloon, although apparently fully inflated, showed no inclination to lift; it was some time before the men discovered that this was due to a large quantity of ordinary air which had entered the envelope through a faulty stop-cock at the neck of the balloon. There was nothing for it but to deflate the envelope and begin the process all over again.

This time there were no serious snags, and by dusk on that same day the balloon was fully inflated and straining against its mooring-ropes. After checking that the stop-cock at the neck was fully closed and that there was no way in which the gas could escape, Charles and his colleagues left the balloon where it was for the night. The following day—25 August—was spent in checking the balloon's lifting capacity, and the men were somewhat worried to find that this gradually decreased as the day went on. The reason was that the hydrogen was slowly leaking away through the fabric of the envelope, but the prospect appeared brighter when Charles found that the balloon could be kept in a fully inflated condition by the addition of small amounts of gas from time to time.

Charles had decided to make the first public demonstration of his balloon on 27 August, and the site he chose was the Champ de Mars. This choice was influenced by two main factors: first, the yard in the Place des Victoires was too small, and second, the crowd outside was growing bigger every day. News of the activities of Charles and his team had spread quickly, and the people were becoming restless—especially since they had caught a tantalizing glimpse of the balloon during a brief captive ascent on the 26th. To throw crowds off the scent, the balloon was loaded on to a horse-drawn cart and taken to its new location in the early hours of the morning with a cavalry escort.

Lack of sleep, coupled with anxiety, was already taking its toll of Charles and his helpers, but there was to be no respite. The crowds were already beginning to assemble in and around the Champ de Mars at dawn, and Charles knew that there was

9

no time to be lost if an unpleasant scene was to be avoided. It was no use explaining to the crowd that a considerable amount of gas had been lost while the balloon was being transported to the Champ de Mars, and that the process of re-inflation was a laborious one lasting several hours. All Charles and his men could do was to toil manfully to get the balloon ready for flight as quickly as possible, trusting that the military escort would prove strong enough to keep the crowd at bay. At last, shortly before five o'clock in the afternoon, a greatly relieved Charles was able to announce that the preparations were complete. A few minutes later, the angry roars and jeers of the crowd were silenced as the mooring-ropes were cast off and the balloon rose majestically to a height of almost three thousand feet, drifting in and out of cloud on a flight that was to end forty-five minutes later and fifteen miles away, not far from the village of Gonesse. By the time Charles and his assistants reached the scene, all that remained of the balloon was a mass of shredded fabric, scattered over a field—the work of local peasants, who in their superstitious fear had attacked the writhing envelope with scythes and pitchforks.

In all probability, the record flight of Charles's hydrogen-filled balloon came as something of a shock to Joseph and Étienne Montgolfier. Although they had been keeping a close watch on their rival's preparations, they had not thought to see their own efforts outclassed by so great a margin and they must have experienced something closely akin to despair. If Charles had accomplished so much with his first balloon, what might he achieve with the second? The brothers immediately decided that no time was to be lost in building and flying another of their hot-air craft if they were to have any hope of recapturing their lead. The new balloon was the biggest project undertaken by the Montgolfiers, measuring some 74 feet from top to bottom with a diameter of 43 feet and a weight of roughly 1,000 pounds. Construction followed similar lines to that of the first balloon, layers of paper being reinforced with linen. The new craft gradually took shape in the workshops of a man named Reveillon, a close friend of the Montgolfiers, who was also a paper-maker. Reveillon placed almost the whole of his labour force at the Montgolfiers' disposal, and the men slaved to get the balloon ready for the week preceding 19 September. The brothers had not only committed themselves to a public demonstration on that date, but had invited a royal party including Louis XVI and Marie Antoinette to attend.

On 14 September, despite a number of setbacks, the work was complete and the balloon was taken out for its first inflation, suspended over a wooden platform with its neck tied down over a circular hole. Beneath the hole was the furnace, fed with the usual evil-smelling mixture of wool and straw. Within a matter of minutes, the balloon—brilliantly painted in blue and gold—had inflated successfully and was straining at its ropes.

It was at that moment that disaster struck. Without warning, a rainstorm, accompanied by violent gusts of wind, burst over Paris. Rain lashed the balloon, turning its paper into sodden pulp. One by one the mooring-ropes tore loose, ripping great gashes in the envelope. There was nothing that could be done. Tears rolled down the Montgolfiers' cheeks as their majestic creation collapsed on the platform in a heap of saturated ruin. Lesser men would have abandoned the whole project, packed their bags and gone home: but not the Montgolfiers. There were still four days before the deadline; four days in which they might at least attempt to salvage something from the wreckage. One thing was certain: they would have to start from scratch, for the original balloon was totally destroyed. A frantic race against time developed as the Montgolfiers and their helpers strove to build another before the day of the royal demonstration. They did it with less than twenty-four hours to spare. Smaller than the first, the balloon was spherical in shape, fifty-seven feet high and forty-one in diameter, with a capacity of 37,500 cubic feet. Its paintwork—blue and gold like that of its unfortunate predecessor, with the Royal coat of arms of France emblazoned on its side—was hardly dry when the first captive test flight was made in Reveillon's spacious gardens on 18 September. This time, the weather was kind and the flight was made without incident. Fearful in case any further mishap should destroy their work all over again, the Montgolfiers made immediate arrangements to take the balloon to Versailles, where the demonstration flight was to be made before the royal guests.

At Versailles, a platform sixty feet square had been set up for the balloon, which was suspended above it in the usual way and concealed by curtains draped from a scaffolding. As an added precaution, soldiers of the Royal Guard were posted around the platform to provide a deterrent to anyone who might inflict damage on the balloon, whether maliciously or otherwise. After dining at a banquet held in their honour, the Montgolfier brothers set about inflating the balloon, watched by Louis and his Queen. The assembled crowd, meanwhile, pressed against the cordon of troops to get a better view of the proceedings—but beat a hasty retreat when the furnace was lit, smothering the whole area with clouds of suffocating smoke from the straw, wool and old shoes which the brothers were using for fuel. Within an hour the balloon was billowing above its platform, fully inflated. In a wicker cage attached to its neck sat three bewildered passengers: a sheep, a cock and a duck. Originally, the Montgolfiers had wanted the flight to be made by a human being; unfortunately, King Louis did not share their confidence and absolutely forbade the idea, believing the venture to be fraught with extreme peril. So it was that the honour of becoming the first air passengers in history fell to three dumb animals.

An expectant silence fell over the crowd as three cannon shots boomed out. Then, heralded by a fourth shot, the mooring ropes were cast off and the balloon rose into the air, climbing to about 1,700 feet before drifting away on the breeze. Eight minutes and two miles away, it came to earth in the forest of Vaucresson—a disappointingly short flight, for the Montgolfiers had worked out that the flight would last for at least twenty minutes and that the balloon would reach a height of 12,000 feet. Later, they found some small holes in the fabric, which they held responsible for the premature descent.

Some of the spectators had followed the flight of the balloon on horseback, racing to be the first at the scene of its landfall. Those who had expected to see only the mangled remains of the three animal passengers were disappointed. The wicker cage had been broken open as the balloon came down through the trees and the sheep was standing nearby, giving its undivided attention to a patch of grass. The duck, too, was waddling around, apparently unconcerned. Only the cock had suffered in any way, having sustained a slight injury to one of its wings.

A matter of days after the Versailles demonstration the Montgolfiers announced a project to build an even bigger balloon, designed to carry two men—for even King Louis could surely no longer deny that if animals could travel safely by air, men could do the same. The King, however, remained sceptical, and it was some time before he reluctantly gave his consent—and even then, it was only on the understanding that the balloon's passengers would be criminals, who would receive a free pardon if they came down safely.

The idea that the honour of making the first manned flight should fall to criminals was received with considerable criticism by the Montgolfiers and their supporters—and one of the most outspoken critics was a young scientist named Pilâtre de Rozier, a staunch advocate of ballooning. He had followed the efforts of the Montgolfiers with avid interest, and in fact had been the first to reach the balloon after the demonstration flight at Versailles. He had immediately approached the Montgolfiers and offered not only to help them in any way possible with their next balloon project, but to be its passenger when the time came. He was a determined man, but he knew that alone he could never hope to persuade the King to change his mind. There was one man, however—a close friend—who might succeed: the wealthy and influential Marquis d'Arlandes, who had contact with many leading members of the Royal Court. The Marquis agreed to help at once—provided that he could be the second passenger in the balloon. What followed then was little short of a conspiracy: the Marquis paid a visit to the Duchesse de Polignac, governess to the royal children, and came away with the knowledge that he had made a firm ally. History, unfortunately, does not relate how the alliance was achieved; but since the Marquis was by all accounts a handsome man and the Duchesse an attractive woman, it is not difficult to draw some conclusions. In any event, it took the Duchesse very little time to persuade Queen Marie Antoinette that Pilâtre and the Marquis would make far more fitting passengers for the Montgolfier balloon than a pair of criminals. The Queen, in turn, went to work on Louis, who in the end—presumably for the sake of peace and quiet—authorized the Montgolfiers to select whosoever they wished to become the first aeronauts.

While the argument went on, construction of the balloon had been getting under way at Monsieur Reveillon's home in Paris. Made from heavier material than its predecessor, the balloon was slightly over 75 feet high, with a diameter of 49 feet. A wickerwork gallery three feet wide was fitted around its neck, below which an iron wire basket was slung. The fire that would be kindled in this could be fuelled by the two occupants to keep the balloon airborne. Total weight of the finished balloon was 1,600 pounds, and its capacity was 79,000 cubic feet.

The first tethered flight was scheduled for Wednesday, 15 October 1783. The balloon was inflated without trouble and Pilâtre de Rozier climbed aboard. Cautiously, the men on the ground began to pay out the mooring-rope—but hastily hauled the balloon down again when it began to sway violently while still only a few feet in the air. The trouble was Pilâtre's weight, which had unbalanced the craft, and it was speedily rectified by the addition of ballast to the opposite side of the gallery. The second attempt went off without a hitch; the balloon rose to a height of 84 feet—the full length of the mooring-rope—and Pilâtre maintained it for four and a half minutes by throwing straw into the fire in the basket suspended under the neck. The only trouble came when, after allowing the balloon to drift slowly down to the launching platform, de Rozier jumped down from the gallery while the envelope was still inflated—which resulted in the balloon shooting up to the end of its rope once more. Fortunately, the ground crew were able to haul the craft down safely again. Several more ascents were made before nightfall, Pilâtre's confidence growing each time as he learned how to control the vertical movements of the balloon by feeding more straw on to the fire. Word of the test flights spread quickly, and on Friday the 17th a huge crowd had gathered in the Rue de Montreuil to watch the next trial ascents. The weather was unfavourable, however, with a strong breeze blowing, and only one short captive flight was made. De Rozier realized that the buffeting of the wind on the balloon as it strained against its mooring-rope could easily tear the craft apart. Conditions were better on 19 October, and this time the crowd was not disappointed. Pilâtre made four ascents, each one higher than the previous one; on the third, the ballast was removed and a passenger, Girond de Villette, climbed into the gallery in its place. With the two men on board the balloon rose to a height of 324 feet, descending to its platform after nine minutes. De Villette then got out and his place was taken by the Marquis d'Arlandes, who accompanied Pilâtre on the last flight of the day.

An attempt to make a free flight had been scheduled for 20 November, but it was frustrated by wind and rain. The weather had improved considerably by the following morning, although the wind was still stronger than de Rozier and the Montgolfiers would have liked, and it was decided to go ahead with the preparations. The Montgolfiers asked de Rozier to make one more captive ascent to check the balloon's lifting power, and the envelope was duly inflated. Suddenly, an unexpected gust of wind caught the balloon and plucked it off the launching platform which had been specially erected in the gardens of the Château La Muette, in the Bois de Boulogne. The balloon was hauled down again with difficulty, but not before several holes had been torn in the envelope.

The Montgolfiers were now faced with the prospect of having to call off the attempt—a far from attractive thought, for the huge crowd that had assembled was beginning to grow restless. However, an unexpected stroke of good fortune came to their rescue when a number of seamstresses came forward from the crowd and offered their services. The women set to work on the torn envelope at once, stitching away without pause. Within two hours, the damage had been put right and the Montgolfiers were once more able to go ahead with the inflation. Even the weather seemed to have turned in their favour: the high wind had been replaced by a light breeze, the clouds had broken up and sunlight glittered on the balloon's paintwork. At ten minutes to two, watched by the Dauphin, who had arrived from the

Château La Muette with his entourage, de Rozier and the Marquis d'Arlandes climbed into the gallery. Four minutes later de Rozier gave the signal to cast off, and the balloon rose steadily into the air accompanied by a great cheer from the spectators. An even bigger cheer went up when, at a height of about 300 feet, the two aeronauts waved their hats in salute just before the gentle north-westerly breeze caught the balloon and took it towards the Seine.

Twenty-five minutes later, de Rozier and the Marquis came safely to earth on the Butte-aux-Cailles, near where the Place d'Italie now stands, some five miles from La Muette. The whole flight had been made at relatively low altitude—less than 1,000 feet—and it had not been uneventful: several times, the two men had been forced to apply wet sponges to glowing holes in the fabric of the envelope, caused by flying sparks. The margin between success and disaster had been narrow: but for the first time, man had cut the thread that bound him to the earth. The conquest of the air had begun in earnest.

The news that a Montgolfier balloon had made a successful manned flight, although universally hailed as a triumph, nevertheless came as a bitter blow to one man: Jacques Charles. Behind the scenes, he and the Robert brothers had been labouring for some time to build a man-carrying hydrogen balloon, hampered for most of the time by lack of funds and relying on public subscriptions. Just how close they came to beating the Montgolfiers into first place may be judged by the fact that the completed balloon, filled with air, was exhibited in the Tuileries Palace only five days after the flight of de Rozier and d'Arlandes. Charles's balloon represented an enormous advance over the hot-air 'Montgolfière' in its design: its basic plan, with only minor changes, would be used by hydrogen balloons for a century to come. Spherical in shape and with a diameter of just over 27 feet, it was made from tapered sections of silk treated with the Robert brothers' special rubber solution. It had an open neck, allowing gas to escape on expansion—so avoiding the hazard of the balloon bursting as a result of the decrease in pressure at altitude—and more gas could be released through a spring-loaded valve at the top of the balloon, operated by a cord that hung down through the interior of the envelope. The upper part of the envelope was covered by a cord net, fastened to a wooden ring stretching round the balloon's equator. From lines attached to this ring the car—a somewhat ornate device, resembling a boat—was suspended below the neck. It was not a very satisfactory arrangement, and on later balloons the boat-type car would be replaced by a more functional basket suspended from a net that covered the whole envelope; but in 1783, the design showed considerable genius and forward-thinking.

The maiden voyage of the balloon took place on 1 December 1783, with Charles himself and Aîné Robert as the passengers. The weather this time was excellent, and a crowd whose number some accounts put as high as 400,000 gathered in and around the Tuileries gardens to watch the ascent. Joseph Montgolfier was among them, and Charles courteously asked him if he would do him the honour of releasing a small five-foot balloon, brought along to enable the aeronauts to gauge the direction of the wind at altitude.

At 1.45 p.m., with the two aeronauts safely on board, ballast was thrown out and the balloon released. It rose at what seemed incredible speed to a height of 1,800 feet. Borne on a south-west breeze, it drifted across Paris for almost an hour, crossing the Seine twice. Another hour went by, the two men held spellbound by the vistas unfolding beneath them and by the sheer serenity. But the idyll could not last for ever: Charles knew that it was time to come down. Looking around, he saw that the balloon was drifting towards an expanse of open ground near Nesle, and he pulled on the valve line to vent off gas. The balloon slanted towards the earth, avoiding a line of trees by a matter of feet as Charles hastily threw some ballast overboard. A few seconds later it touched down with scarcely a bump at the end of a journey that had taken it 27 miles across the French country-side. The balloon was held fast by peasants and a group of towns-people from Nesle, and the two aeronauts settled down to write a short account of the flight while the details were still fresh in their minds and to await the arrival of anyone who had been pursuing the balloon's flight from the Tuileries. Three riders came galloping up just as the sun was setting, and embraced the aeronauts enthusiastically. Charles, filled with the exhilaration of success, immediately insisted on making another short flight—alone this time. Climbing back into the car, he signalled to his volunteer ground crew to let go. The balloon shot upwards in the dusk, and a few moments later a great cry went up from the spectators as the last rays of the dying sun caught it and turned it into a glowing bubble of light far above their heads.

The balloon climbed rapidly to a height of nearly ten thousand feet. The cold was intense, but Charles hardly noticed it; he was alone in golden sunlight, while down below men passed unnoticed in the shadows of approaching night. As the light faded over the horizon, a new wonder filled the aeronaut as he realized that he had become the first man to see the sun set twice in one day. Suddenly, an excruciating pain in his right ear—the result of his rapid climb to nearly two miles above the earth—interrupted his daydream. He pulled the valve-release line and the balloon began a descent that brought it to rest, half an hour after the start of the second dramatic flight, in a ploughed field three miles from Nesle.

Whether Jacques Charles was overwhelmed by the sheer wonder of his experience, or whether his solo balloon flight frightened him deeply, we shall never know. We only know that for some inexplicable reason he never flew again, even though the Robert brothers made several more ascents.

The new year of 1784 had scarcely dawned before the Montgolfier brothers made a determined effort to re-establish the reputation of their hot-air balloon, which had been almost eclipsed by the incredible success of Charles's hydrogen-filled craft. Construction of a new Montgolfière was begun during the first week of January 1784 at Lyon, where the brothers had journeyed from Paris. The new balloon was a monster, with a capacity of 700,000 cubic feet, and a ground crew of fifty men was needed to hold it down during its trial inflations. The huge seven-ton craft made its first flight from Lyon on 19 January, carrying no fewer than seven passengers—including Joseph Montgolfier, making his first ascent. The balloon reached a height of 3,000 feet before making a heavy landing three minutes later.

More ascents followed quickly. On 25 February, Italy saw its first manned balloon flight when the Chevalier Paulo Andreani, accompanied by two colleagues, made a twenty-minute flight from the grounds of his villa near Milan. The rest of the year would see a spate of further ascents in France, Spain, Belgium, Austria, America and Britain.

But even as the ranks of those who had tasted the heady joy of flight grew steadily, there were those who were not content. They knew that a man in a balloon could never be truly master of his new environment; he could rise beyond the clouds and he could come down again safely, but where he came down depended on one thing alone: the wind. Not until an aeronaut had some means of steering his balloon, of directing it in whatever path he chose, would the conquest of the air have begun in reality.

The first attempt to steer a balloon in flight was made on 2 March 1784, by a thirty-one-year-old Norman named Jean-Pierre Blanchard, a man of considerable inventive capability. At the age of sixteen he had built a 'velocipede', an ancestor of the bicycle, and had later equipped it with four flapping wings driven by foot treadles and hand levers in an unsuccessful attempt to get the machine off the ground. Later, following the first balloon ascents, he decided to attach his steering apparatus to the car of a hydrogen balloon; with the problem of lift overcome, he would be free to concentrate on manœuvring. The balloon was launched from the Champ de Mars. His mechanical wings flapping furiously, Blanchard tried desperately to make the craft go in the direction he wished. Needless to say, he failed—as he did on two subsequent attempts later that year. Disappointed, he took his balloon to England, where his skill as a balloonist was quickly recognized. It was the beginning of a reputation that was destined to place him high in the ranks of the great aeronauts.

Blanchard's flapping-wing arrangement was ingenious enough in its way, but it was based on a fairly loose study of the behaviour of birds in flight and was backed by no sound scientific knowledge. It was different in every way from another approach to the same problem, made by a young French army

Lieutenant named Jean-Baptiste Meusnier. While Blanchard was flapping his ineffective wings, Meusnier was putting the finishing touches to a design for a dirigible balloon: a craft with a streamlined, elongated envelope, which was to be pushed through the air by three screws driven from its car.

Meusnier looked upon his dirigible balloon as a kind of ship: a ship that would carve its way through the air as a conventional vessel knifed through the sea, turning with the aid of a rudder at the will of its pilot. His craft was destined never to fly; but in years to come, the sky would know its successors. It would be a century before the airship became a practical proposition: a hundred years before the dream of guided flight became a reality. But it was Meusnier who pointed the way, almost before the cheers of the crowds that watched the first balloon ascents had died away.

2 A Road in the Sky

Jean-Baptiste Meusnier's dirigible balloon design was, in fact, preceded by a paper entitled *Memorandum on the Equilibrium of Aerostatic Machines*, which he placed before the French Academy of Sciences on 3 December 1783. In it, he put forward a revolutionary idea for a device which he called a 'ballonnet'—a kind of inner balloon within the main envelope, into which air could be pumped under pressure by the aeronaut. Such an arrangement, Meusnier pointed out, could result in a considerable saving of gas and ballast as well as giving the aeronaut a measure of control over the height of his balloon. As the hydrogen within the main envelope expanded under the effects of altitude, considerable pressure would be exerted on the internal ballonnet and air would be forced out of it through a safety valve, making it unnecessary to release precious gas; at the same time, any leakage of gas could be remedied by pumping more air into the ballonnet, maintaining the shape of the envelope.

This arrangement lent itself best to an envelope in the form of an ellipsoid—the basic shape of a non-rigid airship—and this emerged in Meusnier's first 'dirigible balloon' design, which appeared in 1784. He made several sketches of the projected craft, and these are today among the fascinating collection of the *Musée de l'Air*, near Paris. They show an oval envelope with a length of about 260 feet, with a long gondola slung from a network of lines attached to a reinforced strip of fabric running round the craft's equator. Mounted on a wooden frame above the gondola were three large propellers, designed to be hand-driven via a rope-and-pulley arrangement by the ship's crew of eighty men. Movement in the horizontal and vertical planes was to have been governed by a primitive rudder and elevator assembly, mounted at the rear of the gondola.

An ellipsoid-type balloon using a ballonnet, designed by

Meusnier, was in fact constructed in 1784 by Jacques Charles and the Robert brothers. It had a length of 52 feet and a capacity of 30,000 cubic feet, about half that of the original design. The craft made its maiden flight from Saint-Cloud on 15 July, manned by the Robert brothers and the Duc de Chartres. However, the ballonnet had been incorrectly fitted and constricted the balloon's neck, with the result that gas was unable to escape following expansion at altitude. A disaster was narrowly averted by the Duc de Chartres, who stabbed the distended envelope with his sword and enabled a safe if heavy landing to be made near Chalais-Meudon. The principle of the ballonnet, however, was sound, and the Robert brothers went on to construct another elongated craft in which Cadet Robert and a M. Collin-Hullin covered the 150 miles from Paris to Bethune on 19 September 1784, the flight taking six hours forty minutes.

Although they employed what was later to become the classic airship shape, these balloons were not in any way dirigible—although both were fitted with parasol devices which, when opened and closed by the crew, were supposed to push them along through the air. Meusnier, an accomplished scientist and engineer, knew that such devices could not possibly succeed; neither would the man-powered propellers of his dirigible balloon have the desired effect. Hampered by the lack of an efficient power source, he abandoned balloon-designing and returned to his original career as an army officer, rising rapidly to the rank of General. Tragically, he was killed while fighting the Prussians at Mainz in 1793. But for his premature death, there is little doubt that he would once again have applied his genius to the science of flight, his agile brain probing towards new discoveries. As it was, the fact that he was the first man to design an airship as such assured his place in the annals of aviation history.

Several more dirigible balloon designs appeared during the latter years of the eighteenth century, the most impressive being the creation of an Englishman, Baron Scott. In 1789, he proposed a dirigible that bore an uncanny similarity in both form and size to the Zeppelin designs of a century later. Although the design owed a lot to Meusnier's earlier project, there was one

22

major innovation in that the ship was to be equipped with two ballonnets, situated fore and aft, which could be inflated or deflated to control the craft's vertical movement. The idea was ingenious enough, but it would probably not have worked, for the simple reason that there would have been no great difference in weight between the inflated and deflated ballonnets—at least not enough to influence the attitude of the ship to any great extent. In any case, the ship—like its contemporaries—would have been doomed to failure from the start for lack of a suitable means of propulsion.

In October 1804, the London-published *Monthly Magazine* carried a report that a certain Professor Danzel had written a fourteen-page pamphlet entitled *Bases of the Mechanism for Directing Hot-Air Balloons*. Who Danzel was, and the exact nature of his theories, remain unknown to this day, but it seems likely that his ideas were based on the sudden expulsion of air from a balloon—the basic reaction principle. Danzel apparently claimed that he had propelled a balloon through the air at twelve feet per second—a claim that brought congratulations through the pages of the *Monthly Magazine* from at least one man who read the report, the British scientist-inventor Sir George Cayley. The report, in fact, inspired Cayley to write his first paper on aeronautics, entitled *Essay upon the Mechanical Principles of Aerial Navigation*. A fascinating document, it contains Cayley's early thoughts on dirigible balloons; thoughts backed by sound technical knowledge. 'The bag or balloon containing the gas', he wrote, 'ought to be in a form approaching to that of a very oblong spheroid, but varied according to what may be found the true solid of least resistance in air, that this must be supported by light longitudinal—and two transverse—axes of wood braced with cord to give stability to the fabric, with such other stays as may nearly preserve the form intended, without allowing the resistance of the air occasioned by the motion to press out the gas too rapidly.'

It was the first-ever proposal for a semi-rigid airship—and the first time that the principle of streamlining had ever been set down in technical terms. Cayley went on to explain: 'To the hinder extremity of the balloon must be fixed upon a universal joint a rudder of considerable length opposing both an horizontal and vertical surface (by the two planes of which it is composed intersecting each other in right angles) to the air. A handle to direct this rudder must communicate with the boat.'

What Cayley had written was a highly accurate description of the cruciform tail steering unit of the kind that would become standard on the Zeppelin airships of a hundred years later. He went on to refer to an engine for his dirigible, promising to give more details of this in an appendix to his paper—but the paper was for some reason never finished, and if Cayley made any sketches of his proposals at this stage they did not survive.

After writing these early observations on dirigible balloons, Cayley turned his whole attention in the field of aeronautics to the study of heavier-than-air flight, and it was not until 1816 that he mentioned the subject of airships in another paper. Once again, he was inspired by an article written by another scientist: John Evans, who in the November 1816 issue of the *Philosophical Magazine* had told of his experiments with model hot-air balloons fitted with large planes. If the planes were tilted upwards, Evans wrote, they deflected the balloon forwards as it rose; while by tilting them downwards, the balloon could be made to descend in a slanting glide towards the ground. Cayley replied to this article in the February 1816 issue of the same magazine, adding his own observations and going on to propose a design for a hot-air dirigible balloon with two hulls mounted side by side. The craft would be 'made of woollen cloth, and kept to its shape by light poles attached to it, and internal cross bracings of wire or cord, opposing the tendency to become circular from the internal pressure of the heated air: this vessel to be 15 yards in elevation, 30 in width, and 100 in length. About 27 yards below this vessel must be suspended a convenient boat-shaped car, by six ropes collecting the cordage of the netting.' Once again, the principle of semi-rigid construction was clearly described.

The boat-shaped car, Cayley explained, would contain the furnace, the hot air reaching the envelope by way of a chimney made of thin metal. Inside the chimney, three nets of fine wire would filter out any stray sparks. The craft's woollen envelope, Cayley pointed out, would not catch fire; 'but it is requisite that it should be made air-tight, and likewise impervious to rain, by some coats of paint or varnish on the outside'.

The scientist then went on to describe how the craft would be controlled. 'As soon as the balloon is inflated,' he wrote, 'let the front ropes be lengthened and the hinder ones shortened, till it stands in an angle of about 30° with the horizon, when it will be found to rise in an angle of about 45°, and the horizontal velocity towards its destined harbour will be about 20 miles per hour. The power of the heated air would be about 17,600 pounds: of this about 6,800 pounds would be required to generate the velocity specified, and the remainder will be consumed in the weight of materials, fuel, passengers etc.' It would need, he said, 880 pounds of fuel to inflate the craft, and about 100 pounds per mile to keep it airborne.

In his next article on the same subject, published in the May 1916 issue of the *Philosophical Magazine*, Cayley dealt at some length with the idea of a hydrogen-filled airship. This, he stated, would not be more than seventy yards in length, and would need only half the power of the hot-air ship to propel it. A larger airship, 144 yards in length, 'would convey 500 men during one hour, 410 men during 12 hours, 290 men for 24 hours, and 50 men for 48 hours, without fresh supplies of fuel or water. The extent of the voyage in calm air would in the latter case be 960 miles.' The craft would be propelled by 'three tiers of wing to be worked by the steam engine, or any other first mover; each wing to be divided into many strips or portions, which are so constructed as to heel up and down by the alternate pressure of the air above and below them at each stroke of the engine, and thus by their oblique waft to propel the balloon.' He also speculated that the wings, if beating powerfully enough, might enable the car to descend safely to earth should it have to be cut away from the envelope in the event of fire.

Cayley persisted with the idea of flapping wings in all his subsequent aeronautical work. He did, however, consider the possibility of using airscrews for propulsion for a brief period before abandoning the notion, and as an alternative to flapping wings he equipped his third airship design, revealed in 1817, with

25

propellers. The fact that he did so was probably the result of another article by John Evans, who wrote suggesting that 'a large wheel with oblique vanes . . . be substituted, which by revolving continually in one direction would attain the desired object, with no more waste of power than what would arise from the additional machinery necessary to obtain a rotary motion from the steam-engine'. Cayley later dismissed the idea in somewhat haughty terms; he had not made a comprehensive study of the principles involved, and he was perhaps afraid that he might be drawn into an argument over a subject about which he knew comparatively little.

It was to be twenty years before Cayley published another paper dealing with airships, or indeed with aeronautics at all. Meanwhile, in 1816–17, two more researchers had attempted to find a practical solution to the problems about which Cayley had theorized at length. Durs Egg, gunsmith to George III, and John Pauly, an engineer—both Swiss nationals residing in England—began construction of an ambitious airship project in a shed in London at Knightsbridge some time in 1816. Designed to be driven manually by oars, the craft was shaped like a huge fish and was appropriately named the *Dolphin*. An enormous amount of money was spent on it—£10,000, according to some accounts—but the ship never flew, and it was finally abandoned after Pauly's death. Ridiculed though it was, the airship—known almost universally as 'Egg's Folly'—incorporated an interesting innovation in the form of a box filled with sand. This was suspended from a cable slung between the stern of the ship and the car, which was positioned well forward; the idea was that the box, when pulled along the cable by means of a rope, would enable the aeronaut to trim the ship for climb or descent. Another interesting point about the unfortunate craft was that its envelope was made of goldbeater's skin, the tough membrane obtained from the large intestines of cattle. This material was to be used in the construction of many subsequent non-rigid airships.

In spite of these repeated failures, the notion that balloons could be propelled through the air by means of oars died hard. In 1832, a French Army Colonel of Scottish ancestry, the Comte de Lennox, and a Frenchman named Le Berrier made an ascent from Paris in a balloon fitted with oars and claimed that they had succeeded in changing the craft's direction in flight. The claim was of course totally false, but when Lennox founded a company named the 'European Aeronautical Society' two years later for the purpose of setting up an air link between Paris and London with the aid of yet another oar-powered balloon, he received considerable financial support for the venture. It has never been established whether Lennox genuinely believed that the project would work, or whether the whole affair was one big confidence trick. Whatever the truth, Lennox apparently did not believe in half measures; he opened offices in both Paris and London, where people could book places on the balloon—named *The Eagle*—when the service was inaugurated.

On 17 August 1834 the balloon was inflated in the Champ de Mars, watched by a huge crowd. Suddenly, the mooring-ropes broke and the craft bounded into the air, where its envelope burst a few moments later with a loud thud. The remains of the envelope and the car, with its impressive row of twenty oars, plummeted to the ground, where they were immediately torn apart by the enraged crowd, some of whom had invested money in the scheme. Lennox had enough presence of mind to leave the scene before the mob turned its attention to him, and appears to have lost no time in getting out of France. He transferred the company's headquarters to York Road, Kensington, in London, where work on a second airship was begun almost immediately. The craft was completed, but never flew; the company ran into serious debt and it was impounded by the Sheriff of Middlesex. Its eventual fate is not known.

The year 1837 saw the return of Sir George Cayley to the field of aeronautics, with an article 'Practical Remarks on Aerial Navigation' appearing in the *Mechanics' Magazine* for 4 March. This paper, which included several suggestions for directing balloons, was probably inspired by an epic flight made on 7–8 November 1836 by three aeronauts named Charles Green, Monck Mason and Robert Holland, who covered the 480 miles from London to Weilburg in the Duchy of Nassau on board a craft called the *Royal Vauxhall Balloon.*

In this latest article, Cayley referred at some length to his earlier thoughts on the subject of dirigible balloons, stressing once again the need for a streamlined shape. Then, moving on to the question of propulsion, he first of all expanded on the twenty-year-old and totally impracticable inclining plane idea of John Evans, designing a double balloon with one envelope suspended below the other and equipped with a kite-like plane between the two. 'When both balloons operated upon a large oblique inclined plane,' he wrote, 'with a power ascension equal to one-third of the whole weight, it would render the oblique force very efficient in ascending; and when at the highest point the heated air is let off by the valve, and the plane reversed, one-third of the whole gravitation would give it an equally effective oblique descent. A machine on this construction would, on account of its progressive motion, obey a rudder, by which more exact steerage could be effected. It is certainly the most simple and least expensive way of primarily effecting the problem of steering balloons; but there is something unsatisfactory in being obliged thus to resort to such alternating heights and descents, implying such sudden changes of temperature, to say nothing of the devious and prolonged nature of the track, and the consequent waste of power.'

Although Cayley set down the details convincingly enough, it is hard to suppose that the scientist really had any faith in the balloon-and-plane principle; it is far more likely that he saw the notion as a challenge to his ingenuity. His next suggestion, for airscrews driven by a steam engine, was much more plausible in the scientific sense and more characteristic of his inventive mind. 'By oblique vanes, reversing, as it were, the action of the sails of a windmill, the proper fulcrum or resistance for the engine-power to work upon, can be had at a velocity of 25 feet per second, in lieu of $29\frac{1}{2}$; and hence a 47 horse power will be sufficient for our purpose—in round numbers, say a 50 horse power in lieu of the 60 horse power of the former plan. . . . This will enable us to add 5000 lbs more to the cargo, or, by using a 60-horse engine, to go with more speed. . . . More than one [airscrew] may be used on the same axis; and they may be so constructed as readily to apply their power, either to propel or retard, elevate or depress, as occasion may momentarily require.'

It was not Cayley, however, who made the first practical demonstration of the use of propellers. In 1840, Charles Green—who was at that time considering the possibility of a balloon voyage across the Atlantic—built a small model balloon, powered by spring-driven propellers, and exhibited it at the Polytechnic Institution in London. The scientist Charles B. Mansfield described the model's demonstration flight in his book *Aerial Navigation*, published in 1877:

> In 1840 Mr. Green exhibited at the Polytechnic Institution in London a miniature balloon armed with screw-propellers driven by a spring, for the purpose of showing that it was possible to move such a body at a certain slow rate horizontally up or down, for the purpose of seeking appropriate currents. ... The balloon, being filled with coal-gas, was then balanced, that is, a sufficient weight was placed in the car to keep it suspended in the air, without the capacity to rise, or the inclination to sink. Mr. Green then touched a stop in the spring mechanism, which immediately communicated a rapid rotary motion to the fans, whereupon the machine rose steadily to the ceiling, from which it continued to rebound until the clockwork had run out. Deprived of this assistance it immediately fell.

Several model airships were built and flown during the 1840s, with varying degrees of success. One of them was the work of Charles Green's colleague and fellow aeronaut Monck Mason, who in 1843 constructed a model powered by a clockwork motor driving a propeller. The ship was tested, and although its behaviour was somewhat erratic it was reported to have attained a forward speed of five miles an hour. Other inventors persevered with manually-powered designs: Dr Hugh Bell for example, who built a fifty-foot airship fitted with a manually operated propeller in 1848. It was a failure, but it was the first time that a full-scale propeller had been tested in the air in Britain. Two years later, in 1850, a French clockmaker named Pierre Jullien, of Villejuif, built a clockwork-powered airship that might, judging by appearances, have been a scale model of the giant Zeppelins that dominated the skies of Europe over half a century later. It was long and slim, its envelope's cigar-like shape maintained by a framework of light wire. Its gondola, together with elevators and rudder, was mounted well forward under the envelope; the small clockwork motor drove two propellers, mounted one on either side of the centre line. The model was demonstrated at the Paris Hippodrome, where it aroused enormous interest.

Clockwork, however, while adequate for model airships, could never provide sufficient power for a full-scale version. By 1850, several pioneers were considering the steam engine as a possible motive source; the way had already been paved in 1848 by John Stringfellow, who had successfully flown a model aircraft at Chard in Somerset, powered by a steam engine of his own design. This event—the world's first heavier-than-air powered flight—captured the imagination of scientists and inventors in Europe and America, and Stringfellow is often credited with being the first man to test a steam engine in the air; in fact, this credit is due to Dr Le Berrier, who flew a steam-powered model airship in Paris in 1844.

In building the model, Le Berrier had been assisted by a certain Henri Giffard, who had also been involved in the construction of the Comte de Lennox's ill-fated *Eagle* balloon. After the model was tested, Giffard lost interest in aeronautics for several years—until he witnessed the flight of Jullien's clockwork-driven airship in 1850. Giffard afterwards set to work to design a steam-powered dirigible, with an envelope 40 feet in diameter and 144 feet long, tapering to a sharp point at each end. The whole envelope was covered by a net, from which the gondola, attached to a long wooden pole, was slung beneath the craft. The distance between the gondola and the envelope was some forty feet—an insurance against a stray spark from the engine sending the whole ship up in flames. The power-plant of Giffard's craft drove a three-bladed propeller and weighed a total of 350 pounds. As an added precaution against the danger of fire, the door of the furnace was surrounded by a mesh of fine wire and the exhaust chimney was projected downwards from the side of the car away from the envelope. The cumbersome engine, which weighed about 100 pounds for every horse-power it developed, pushed the total weight of the ship up to a ton and a half.

The dirigible's maiden flight took place on 24 September 1852 from the Paris Hippodrome. Its motor hissing and pounding, the ship rose steadily in conditions of almost perfect calm and flew slowly away over the city. The average speed logged during the flight was 5 m.p.h. and the craft made a safe landing at Trappes, seventeen miles from its starting-point.

So ended man's first powered flight. Giffard subsequently went on to make several more in the same craft; on one flight, he demonstrated the effectiveness of the ship's triangular canvas rudder by describing a big circle over the rooftops of Paris. Giffard, however, was the first to admit that he had been exceptionally lucky; he knew that if even a moderate breeze had been blowing the power of his steam engine would not have been great enough to overcome it. His craft was seriously underpowered, but he could see no way of increasing the power without also increasing the weight; the combination of engine and boiler was far too heavy as it was. In an effort to find a solution he built a much bigger ship, with a length of 230 feet and a capacity of 113,000 cubic feet, and incorporated several refinements in its design that resulted in a more streamlined shape. Unfortunately disaster overtook the ship on its maiden flight. As it was on the point of being launched, a sudden leak of gas caused the envelope to become distorted and the ship adopted a nose-up attitude, with the result that a number of the lines attaching the gondola to the envelope tore away and the balloon broke free of its net, bursting a moment later. Giffard and a companion who was in the car with him escaped with nothing more than a few bruises, but the ship was totally destroyed.

Undeterred, Giffard set about designing a third balloon—a monster, 1,970 feet long, 98 feet in diameter and with a capacity of 7,800,000 cubic feet. This vast envelope was designed to lift a steam power plant weighing thirty tons, which Giffard estimated would give the craft a still-air speed of 45 m.p.h.

The project, however, was abandoned through lack of funds, and Giffard lost interest in dirigibles.

Strangely, the successful flight of Giffard's first steam-powered dirigible did not result in a sudden wave of enthusiasm as other scientist-aeronauts tried to emulate it and improve on it, as might have been expected; in fact, for the space of some fifteen years interest in dirigible balloons—the word 'airship' had not yet been coined—actually appeared to wane, and, although a number of successful models were built and flown, the handful of full-scale craft that were tested produced disappointing results, offering no improvement over Giffard's design. The only revolutionary design to make its appearance during these years was for an all-steel dirigible, patented in 1866 by Richard Boyman, but this was never built.

Then came the Franco-Prussian War, and suddenly the whole sphere of aviation took on a new importance. The use of aviation for military purposes was not new; it had been expounded in theory at regular intervals since before the flight of the first Montgolfier balloon, and a Military Aerostatic Company under the command of Captain Coutelle had in fact been formed on 2 April 1794 as part of the French Artillery. The company's first 'operational mission' had taken place on 2 June that year, when Coutelle made an ascent from Maubeuge and reported in detail on the dispositions of the Austrian and Dutch troops who were threatening the town. The balloon was fired on twice—an unknown Austrian artillery crew thus becoming the first 'anti-aircraft' gunners in history. Shortly afterwards the Aerostatic Company moved with the Army to Charleroi and from there to Fleurus, where it played an important part in the French victory over the Austrians during the ensuing battle. For ten hours, Coutelle and General Morlot stayed aloft in the balloon, directing the French tactics by means of written dispatches lowered on a cord.

The campaign of 1795 saw further successes chalked up by the company—notably during the siege of Mainz—and the following year three more balloons were added to the French Army's inventory. Coutelle was promoted General and given overall command of the Balloon Corps, which now had a strength of four companies. Coutelle's hour of glory, however, was almost over. In 1797, the Ist Company accompanied the French Army to Egypt—only to be annihilated by British troops during the battle of Aboukir the following year. When the remnants of the Egyptian Expeditionary Force returned to France, the Balloon Corps was disbanded on the orders of Napoleon.

During the next half-century there were several attempts to re-establish the use of balloons for military purposes, the most ambitious being made by the Austrians during the siege of Venice in 1849. They built two hundred small hot-air balloons, each designed to carry thirty pounds of explosive which was to be released by a time fuse. On 22 June 1849 the armada was launched and the Austrians watched as the balloons drifted towards Venice on the wind, their fuses smouldering steadily. But the wind changed suddenly, causing most of the balloons to drift back the way they had come and to drop their loads on the heads of the Austrians themselves. Only a few reached the target, causing a small amount of damage.

Balloons were used on a fairly extensive scale by the Union forces during the American Civil War, their commitment beginning as a private venture when a group of leading American aeronauts volunteered their services. The first captive observation flight was made in July 1861 from Fort Monroe by John La Mountain, who subsequently made several free reconnaissance flights over Confederate territory. Seven military balloons were built during 1861, each being equipped with five miles of telegraph cable and other signalling apparatus. The Confederates made repeated attempts to destroy the balloons, but with no success; they did however capture one of them, when the steam tug *Teaser*, which was being used to carry the balloon to the battle area, ran aground in the James River and was abandoned after being shelled by the ironclad *Monitor*. The Confederates themselves used at least one balloon, but nothing is known about it.

It was during the siege of Paris in 1870 that the balloon really proved its worth. Between 23 September 1870 and 28 January 1871, one hundred passengers succeeded in leaving the besieged city in sixty-six balloons, which also carried four hundred pigeons and ten tons of mail. The flights were made by both day and night, and not all of them ended successfully: a large number of balloons came down in enemy-occupied territory, and two were lost without trace.

While the balloon flights out of Paris—the first airlift in history—had been something of an epic, it was clear that the venture would have enjoyed infinitely greater success if the balloons had been dirigible. As a direct consequence, a marine engineer named Dupuy de Lôme received a contract to build a dirigible balloon for the French Government. Made of rubberized fabric, the balloon had an interior ballonnet which was fed with air from a pump. The craft was equipped with a big four-bladed propeller, designed to be cranked by a crew of eight men. It made only one flight—with fifteen on board—on 2 February 1872, and succeeded in making a short low-altitude cruise at an average speed of 5 m.p.h. There was practically no directional control, however, and the project was abandoned.

One man who had been inspired by the use of aviation during the Franco-Prussian War was an Austrian named Paul Haenlein, who had been giving serious thought to the problem of powering a dirigible balloon. In 1860 a Frenchman named Étienne Lenoir had patented a gas engine—the forerunner of the internal combustion engine—which worked on the principle of admitting a mixture of gas and air to a cylinder in charges controlled by a valve, each charge then being ignited by an electric spark. The engine was a very primitive affair and in fact did not appear as promising as the latest types of steam engine, but at least it made the use of a boiler unnecessary and Haenlein, who had followed Lenoir's work with keen interest, began to investigate the possibilities of using the gas engine to drive the propeller of a dirigible balloon.

The Franco-Prussian War convinced Haenlein that he ought to lose no time in putting his theories into practice, and he started work on the design of a dirigible in 1872. The craft was 164 feet in length, with a capacity of 85,000 cubic feet. Despite the fire risk there was very little clearance between the

34

envelope and the gondola containing the gas engine. The latter drove a single propeller; unlike the propellers of earlier dirigible designs, Haenlein's was of the tractor type—in other words, it was designed to pull the ship through the air instead of pushing it. Fuel for the motor was to be obtained from the balloon itself, which was filled with coal gas instead of the lighter hydrogen. The balloon was equipped with a ballonnet, into which air would be pumped by the aeronaut to maintain the envelope's shape as gas was progressively drawn off to feed the engine.

The balloon was tested for the first time at Brunn on 13 December 1872. It was a tethered flight, and so was a second that took place the following day. The results were bitterly disappointing: although the balloon attained a speed of between 7 and 9 m.p.h. at the end of its ropes, it was obvious that the engine assembly was too heavy and the balloon too deficient in lift—because of the type of gas used—for a free flight to be attempted. Further development of the project, which might have resulted in considerable advances, for Haenlein was a talented engineer, was abandoned through shortage of funds.

It would be some time yet before the gas engine was sufficiently developed to provide an efficient power source. In the meantime, considerable interest was being aroused by another possibility: the electric motor. In 1881, two brothers, Albert and Gaston Tissandier, created a sensation when they built and demonstrated a model electric-powered airship in Paris. Several influential people were so impressed by the little craft's performance that they immediately offered to provide funds to enable the Tissandiers to build a full-size ship. The full-scale design was completed in 1883 and was 92 feet long, with a diameter of 30 feet and a capacity of 37,500 cubic feet. The power plant used was a Siemens electric motor, driven by 24 batteries each weighing 17 pounds. The ship's propeller—of the pusher type, with two large paddle blades—was situated immediately aft of the open-framework car. The ship, with the two brothers on board, made its first voyage on 8 October 1883, flying from Auteuil to Croissy-sur-Seine in one hour fifteen minutes. A second flight was made on 26 November, this time over a distance of 15½ miles between Auteuil and Mareolles-en-Brie. On both these flights, the motor developed $1\frac{1}{2}$ h.p. at 180 r.p.m. and the ship reached a speed of 3 m.p.h.

Although the performance of the Tissandier airship was better than anything that had preceded it, its success was strictly limited by the poor power–weight ratio of its motor. While the Tissandiers went ahead with their flight tests, however, the craft that was to go down in history as the world's first really successful airship was already under construction. Its designers were two engineer officers in the French Army, Charles Renard and Arthur Krebs, both of whom had been passionately interested in the possibility of dirigible balloon flight for some years. The main obstacle in their path had been shortage of money; the French Government had flatly refused to back the venture, and it was not until the celebrated politician and patriot Leon Gambetta—the man who had virtually recreated the French Army after its defeat by the Prussians in 1870—came to the rescue with an offer of several thousand pounds that the two officers were able to go ahead and get their dirigible off the drawing-board.

Named *La France*, the airship had an envelope 66,000 cubic feet in capacity and nearly 170 feet in length. Renard and Krebs designed their own electric motor to power the craft; this weighed 210 pounds per horse-power, a marked improvement over the 400 pounds of the Tissandiers' power-plant. The power–weight ratio, however, was still appalling, and the Renard–Krebs motor was later replaced by a Gramme motor developing $8\frac{1}{2}$ h.p. The motor and its batteries were housed in a 108-foot gondola that ran three-quarters the length of the envelope. A four-bladed tractor propeller was mounted at the forward end. The ship incorporated almost every notable technical development made so far, including a rudder and elevator, multiple ballonnets, a sliding weight for trimming and a hand-operated mechanism for tilting the propeller to avoid possible damage on landing.

The ship was completed in June 1884 and her maiden flight was made at Chalais-Meudon on 9 August. At four o'clock that afternoon, with the two aeronauts on board, the craft left the ground in a steady ascent. Renard started the electric motor at a height of fifty feet and the ship began to move, cruising slowly towards the south. Gently, Krebs tested the rudder and felt *La France* answer with a perceptible change in direction. The road leading from Choisy to Versailles crept past below and Krebs brought the ship round in a slow turn to starboard, intending to fly west for a time. Then, on an impulse—with the ship still answering her controls like a dream—he changed his mind and continued the turn through 180 degrees until the craft was heading back towards Chalais-Meudon, nosing into a northerly breeze. For the first time, aeronauts were defying the wind; for the first time, an airship was truly dirigible. Twenty-three minutes after take-off the airship was once again directly over Chalais-Meudon and the aeronauts brought her cautiously down for a safe landing. They had covered a total distance of slightly less than five miles.

The second and third 'closed circuit' flights were made on 8 November, the airship reaching an average speed of 14 m.p.h. Four more flights were made early in 1885, but on two of them a stiff wind prevented the ship from returning to her starting-point. The overall outcome of the tests, however, was a successful one: the aeronauts had shown that the ship was fully responsive and controllable in calm or light breeze conditions, even though the electric motor had shown itself to be a far from adequate power source.

The lack of a suitable power plant, however, was not to remain a problem for much longer. In 1885, while Renard and Krebs were still trying to extract the utmost out of their electric motor, a German engineer named Gottlieb Daimler was putting the final touches to a revolutionary development of the earlier four-stroke gas motor: a petrol-driven internal combustion engine. Two years later, in October 1887, Daimler was reading an issue of the *Leipziger Illustrierte Zeitung* when he came across an account of a series of navigable balloon experiments made by a Dr Karl Woelfert, a former Protestant Minister turned professional aeronaut. In 1879, Woelfert and a man named Baumgarten had built an experimental airship fitted with three manually operated propellers, but this had been severely damaged when it crashed at its moorings shortly before it was scheduled

37

to make its first flight. The craft had been repaired with the aid of funds subscribed by the Berlin Aeronautical Society, only to suffer an even worse crash on 5 March 1882, in which Baumgarten was badly injured. He never fully recovered and died in 1883, leaving Woelfert to carry on the work alone and with almost no financial resources. In spite of this major handicap, he built and flew another experimental airship equipped with two manually operated propellers, one mounted below the gondola to provide lift and the other, a pusher type, fitted aft of the car.

As might be expected, this power source was not even partially successful, and this was stated in the *Leipziger Illustrierte* article. Immediately, Gottlieb Daimler began to consider the possibility that his petrol engine might be used to power a dirigible; it had already been tested on a boat, fitted with a propeller, and it had been found to work admirably. Daimler lost no time in writing to Woelfert, outlining his views on the motor's potential as an airborne power source and inviting collaboration.

Woelfert accepted the suggestion readily and arranged for his airship to be taken to the Daimler factory at Seelberg, where it was fitted with a single-cylinder petrol engine developing 2 h.p. After a series of successful ground tests, preparations were made for a trial flight on 12 August 1888. The weather on that historic Sunday morning could hardly have been better, with little or no surface wind. At about 11 o'clock the ship rose from its moorings on a patch of waste land near the factory piloted by a young man named Michael, one of Daimler's employees. Michael had been selected because of his light weight; the airship, with its capacity of only 8,700 cubic feet, had proved incapable of lifting Woelfert's quite substantial bulk.

Keeping the engine running in flight presented something of a problem: the little motor's burner kept going out in the rush of air from the propeller, and each time it had to be re-lit by Michael. To do the job he used a lighted candle; the risk he ran in the process was enormous, for the ship's gondola was fitted flush with the envelope, and if the naked flame had come into contact with any leaking hydrogen the entire craft would have gone up in a gush of fire. By some miracle, however, Michael and the ship came down without incident at Kornwestheim, a little under three miles from Seelberg. Michael reported that apart from the trouble with the burner, the engine had functioned well and the ship had responded easily to her controls. Daimler was justifiably pleased, but he realized that the power–weight ratio of his engine would have to be improved considerably if it was to be employed with real success. While he was working on this problem, Woelfert's airship made two more short flights with the original engine, the second taking place in November.

It appears that after the initial series of flights, Daimler turned the whole of his attention to perfecting the internal combustion engine for use in the 'horseless carriage' and lost interest in the airship project to a great extent. This was a severe blow for Woelfert, who had depended almost entirely on Daimler for his financial support; nevertheless, he managed to scrape together enough money to build an improved version of his airship, fitted with a two-cylinder Daimler engine developing 6 h.p. This craft was put on static display at the Berlin Trade Fair of August 1896 and aroused considerable interest. A group of businessmen offered to back the development of further airships for possible commercial use, and soon afterwards there came a real windfall when, as a result of a close inspection of the ship, Kaiser Wilhelm II became enthusiastic about the idea and extended facilities for the further development of Woelfert's craft at Tempelhof near Berlin, the headquarters of the Prussian Balloon Corps.

After some modifications, the ship—100 feet long and 36 feet in diameter—was ready for flight testing on 12 June 1897. One of the major modifications was to the propeller, which instead of wood was now made of aluminium. The use of this metal in an airship was new; in fact, it was only ten years since the commercial production of aluminium had been made possible by the invention of the electrolytic process.

The ship was launched from Tempelhof in the early evening of 12 June, watched by a crowd that included the representatives of several foreign governments. Some of the spectators were horrified when they saw the jet of flame that shot from the open burner of the ignition system when the engine was started, but Woelfert assured them that this was normal and ordered the ground crew to cast off. With him, in the car, was Robert Knabe, his engineer.

It was a few minutes after seven o'clock. The ship climbed rapidly towards the boundary of the field, heading in the direction of Tempelhof Station. The crew seemed to be having difficulty in keeping the craft on a straight course; alarmed, one or two of the spectators said that they thought they could see a streamer of torn fabric trailing from the rudder. The ship levelled at 3,000 feet, still flying erratically towards the station, watched by hundreds of people standing in the streets and gardens below. Suddenly, a cry of horror went up as two vivid ribbons of flame were seen to spurt out from the engine. They spread with terrifying speed, licking up the side of the envelope like malignant tentacles. Less than a second later, with a wicked thud, the petrol tank exploded. Almost instantly, the ship became a great balloon of flame. From out of the heart of that burning mass there came one tortured scream of anguish and terror: nothing more. The blazing wreckage plummeted earthwards, staining the sky with a mushroom of smoke, and slammed tó the ground in a timber yard, narrowly missing some houses and a school. The charred remains of both aeronauts were found later among the smouldering piles of wood.

Although the tragedy gave rise to serious doubts over the use of petrol engines in dirigibles, it was clear that if Woelfert had taken a few elementary safety precautions the accident would probably never have happened. Although well aware of the serious fire risk, he had not considered it necessary to suspend the car at a safer distance below the airship's envelope; in addition to that, he had persisted in using the earlier type of Daimler engine with the exposed burner, even though by the middle of 1897 an improved ignition system which eliminated this hazard had been developed.

The accident, however, did not prevent the trials of a second petrol-engined airship from taking place at Tempelhof some five months later. These, too, ended in disaster—but not a fatal one, and for a different reason.

The ship was the first in the world to employ rigid aluminium construction. The brainchild of an Austrian engineer named David Schwartz, the craft had been laid down in 1895, but construction had been held up for a short time following Schwartz's death early in 1897 and had been subsequently completed under the direction of his widow. The ship was 156 feet long, with a width of 39 feet and a depth of 46 feet. Capacity was 130,000 cubic feet, and the craft's tubular aluminium framework was covered with a very thin skin of the same material. The engine was a 12-h.p. twin-cylinder Daimler, belt-driving three aluminium tractor propellers, two mounted on either side of the car and the third above the stern. The latter, of the pusher type, could be moved on its axis to provide directional control.

The ship was inflated at Tempelhof on 2 November 1897, and the following morning everything was ready for the maiden flight. On this first trip, the ship was to be crewed by one man, and there is a good deal of doubt as to his identity. The most likely theory is that he was Schwartz's chief engineer, although some accounts state that he was an officer of the Prussian Balloon Corps. Whoever he was, he must have been confronted with a formidable task: controlling the airship single-handed would have been virtually impossible in anything but the most ideal conditions, and on this occasion the surface wind was blowing at 15 m.p.h.

As soon as the ship was released, it rose to a height of 80 feet. Within seconds, it was obvious to the spectators that the craft was out of control. Suddenly, with a loud thump that must have made the pilot think his last moment had come, the belt that drove the propellers flew off its pulley and the ship wallowed helplessly, deprived of both power and the means of control. Hastily, the pilot opened the release valve, intent only on getting down in one piece. It was a rash thing to do: the ship literally fell from the sky and landed heavily in a field, crumpling like tissue paper. The pilot jumped out of the car at the last moment before the mass of twisted aluminium fell on top of him and escaped with only a few bruises, but £10,000-worth of ship—the product of the late Schwartz's dream and of three years' work—

was totally beyond repair. Nevertheless, it had been proved that an airship built entirely of aluminium could fly; there were those who had said that it would never rise off the ground, just as—a century earlier—their ancestors had said with conviction that an iron-hulled ship would never sail.

While these experiments were being carried out in Germany, the development of airships in France—whose pioneer aeronauts had played a leading role in aeronautics since the Montgolfier brothers made their first ascent—remained at a standstill. In fact, nothing at all had been achieved since 1885, when Renard and Krebs made their series of flights in *La France*. The lack of suitable power was still regarded by French aeronauts as a serious drawback; the cumbersome electric motor, although developed as far as possible, was still too inefficient—and the fearful death of Woelfert and Knabe had turned many promising designers against the idea of using petrol engines.

It was at this point, in 1897, that Alberto Santos-Dumont arrived on the Parisian scene. Born in Brazil in 1873, Alberto possessed two attributes that were absolutely vital to any would-be aeronaut of the late nineteenth century: excellent mechanical ability and considerable wealth. Thanks to his wealth—his father owned one of the biggest coffee plantations in Brazil—Alberto had experienced no difficulty in being accepted by Parisian high society, nor had he been slow to savour the pleasures of the French capital. However, his main interest in life was quickly established when the French aeronaut Alexis Macheron took him for a flight in a balloon. From that moment on—while still participating to the full in the social life of Paris—aeronautics became his passion; he went on to become a competent aeronaut in his own right, making numerous ascents. His other major interest was in the embryo sport of motoring, and he owned a De Dion tricycle. This machine was fitted with one of the most compact and advanced petrol engines produced at that time, and it was not long before Santos-Dumont began to consider the possibility of using it to power an airship. The motor used an electrical ignition system, considerably reducing the fire hazard.

The design of Santos-Dumont's first airship was inspired to a great extent by the earlier work of Giffard and the Tissandier brothers. Thanks to his financial status, the Brazilian had no difficulty in recruiting a team of skilled mechanics to aid him in the construction of his first craft, known simply as *Dirigible No. 1*. On 18 September 1898 the ship was taken to the Jardin d'Acclimatation, Paris, and made ready for its maiden flight. Watched by a large crowd, Santos-Dumont—a dapper figure in top hat and stiff collar—climbed into the car and prepared for take-off. A few minutes earlier, he had been involved in a heated argument with a number of veteran aeronauts who had turned up to watch the flight; they had seen that Santos-Dumont planned to take off into wind with the engine running, a technique that had not been used before and one they considered to be foolhardy in the extreme. Every aeronaut, they told Alberto, knew that a balloon must take off downwind. Somewhat reluctantly, Santos-Dumont had given in to what he believed to be the voice of experience and had turned his dirigible downwind. The result was unfortunate: seconds after the ship was released it became hopelessly entangled in the branches of a tree and had to be hauled down by the ground crew, luckily without damage.

A second attempt was made from the same spot two days later, and this time Alberto took off into wind with his engine chugging away loudly. The ship cleared the treetops easily and went on climbing steadily, nosing into the breeze. When he had reached what he considered to be a safe height, Alberto turned downwind and brought *No. 1* back over the heads of the crowd, now waving and cheering wildly. Santos-Dumont was now getting the feel of the ship's controls; she was answering well and he brought her round in a slow turn to starboard, heading into the wind once more until she was back over the starting-point. Then another turn, to port this time, completing a broad figure of eight in the sky until the ship's nose was pointing towards the suburbs of Paris. The pilot now held the ship on a steady course, cruising towards the capital and climbing slowly to 1,300 feet.

After holding this altitude for a minute, he began to descend again—and it was then that things began to go wrong. The ship had valved off a considerable amount of gas at its peak altitude, and now, as it descended, the gas that remained started to contract rapidly—so rapidly, in fact, that the air-pump feeding the ballonnet was unable to compensate for the loss. The result was that to Santos-Dumont's horror the airship began to fold up in the middle, dropping with ever-increasing speed towards the fields below as its lift was gradually destroyed. Fortunately, Santos-Dumont was not the kind of man to lose his head easily. Looking down, he saw that the ship was falling towards a field where a number of boys were playing. Throwing out the trail rope, he shouted to them to catch hold of it and run as fast as they could into wind. The boys quickly grasped the situation and did as they were asked, dragging the airship round into wind a matter of seconds before it hit the ground. Thanks to the resulting lift, the ship, although she landed heavily, came to rest without serious damage and the pilot climbed from the car shaken but unhurt.

During the next two years Santos-Dumont built three more dirigibles, each a slight improvement over its predecessor. *No. 2* made its first flight on 11 May 1899, and on 13 November of that same year the little Brazilian reached a speed of 15½ m.p.h., his highest so far, in *Dirigible No. 3*.

In 1900, Henri Deutsch de la Meurthe—one of the leading members of the Paris Aero Club, and an industrialist possessing a substantial fortune—offered a prize of £30,000 to the first aeronaut who successfully flew from Saint-Cloud, the site of the Aero Club, and returned to the starting point after making a circuit of the Eiffel Tower. The distance involved was seven miles, and the course had to be completed within thirty minutes.

The offer immediately aroused Alberto's interest—not because of the money, which meant little to him, but because he enjoyed a challenge. He was confident that he could win; taking wind conditions into account, he worked out that he would need an average speed of 15½ m.p.h. to complete the distance within the stipulated time—and his latest dirigible, *No. 4*, was capable of more than that. To make absolutely certain that he would have a good margin of speed, however, he started on the design of a fifth airship—the most advanced so far. The main feature of *Dirigible No. 5* was a wooden keel, triangular in cross-section and sixty feet long, slung under the envelope and supporting the 12-h.p. engine and the car.

After taking the ship on a successful test flight on 12 July 1901, Santos-Dumont announced that he would attempt to complete the course the following day. He started early, casting off at 6.41 a.m., watched by a crowd of spectators and official Aero Club timekeepers who had assembled at Saint-Cloud. The first half of the flight went well and the airship cruised towards the Eiffel Tower, assisted by a tailwind of over 13 m.p.h. Ten minutes after take-off, Santos-Dumont rounded the tower and turned the ship back towards Saint-Cloud—heading right into trouble. The stiff wind, which had helped his progress so much on the outward flight, now became his enemy. Even with the engine flat out, the ship hardly seemed to be moving; the ground crept past with painful slowness. Keeping the dirigible trimmed and heading directly into wind was tiring work, and it seemed an age before Saint-Cloud appeared under the nose. Just a few more minutes, and the struggle would be over.

It was then that the unexpected happened: the engine stopped. Despite repeated efforts by the pilot, it stubbornly refused to start again and the wind began to drive the airship relentlessly back towards Paris. There was nothing for it but to land. Santos-Dumont vented gas and the dirigible slid earthwards, finally coming to rest in the branches of a tree on an estate owned by the Rothschild family. The flight had lasted forty minutes.

Santos-Dumont lost no time in repairing the airship, which had been slightly damaged in the landing, and getting ready for a second attempt. Once again, he was dogged by bad luck. He took off from Saint-Cloud on 8 August and, as before, all went well until he rounded the Eiffel Tower and found himself battling against a headwind. This time, however, the trouble did not end there. While *Dirigible No. 5* was still over the rooftops of Paris, there was a sudden loud explosion as the envelope burst. There was nothing the pilot could do but hold on tightly as the ship lost height fast, with gas rushing out of the torn envelope. Fortunately, the dirigible had been flying at low level—about

45

150 feet—and before the rate of descent could become dangerously high the craft draped itself over the roof of a six-storey house in the rue Henri Martin. Santos-Dumont climbed from the car and perched on the roof, waving cheerily to the crowd that had quickly gathered in the street below, until he was rescued by the fire brigade a few minutes later.

The Brazilian, still as determined as ever to win the prize, at once began work on a sixth airship, similar in design to *No. 5*. The craft was completed within a month, but the third attempt on the prize was delayed when the ship suffered some damage on landing after its maiden flight on 6 September. Because of this, and with adverse weather conditions, the attempt was delayed until 19 October 1901. Quite a strong wind was blowing that afternoon, and several of Alberto's friends advised him to postpone the flight still further. The little Brazilian's mind was made up, however, and at 2.42 p.m. *Dirigible No. 6* rose from the Aero Club park on the first leg of its flight. The Eiffel Tower was rounded at 2.51 and the ship turned on the homeward run, nosing into the wind. This time, everything seemed to be going well: the ship was making slow but steady progress, and Santos-Dumont calculated that he would reach Saint-Cloud with more than a minute to spare. He was just beginning to congratulate himself when the engine spluttered and died. Frantically, the pilot climbed out of the wickerwork car and scrambled back along the keel to the engine. Fortunately, the motor started again almost immediately and the ship was able to continue, but precious time had been lost. At 3.11, Santos-Dumont brought the dirigible low over the heads of the Aero Club judges clustered around the spot from which he had started twenty-nine minutes earlier. Then he circled and came in for a landing, touching down at 3.12 and forty seconds.

A heated argument followed among the judges, some of whom maintained that Santos-Dumont had failed to qualify for the prize because his time from take-off to touchdown had been forty seconds over the stipulated half-hour. Others claimed that it was the time overhead that counted. The matter was put to the vote, and Alberto's supporters carried the day. The official time was set at 29½ minutes, gaining the prize for Santos

Dumont by a very narrow margin. Characteristically, the Brazilian kept none of the money for himself: some he divided among his faithful mechanics, and the rest he gave to various charities for distribution among the poor of Paris.

Alberto Santos-Dumont went on to build and fly no fewer than nine more dirigibles, bringing the total to fifteen. Some of the flights he made were adventurous: on 14 February 1902, for example, he was fished out of Monaco Bay after becoming the first pilot ever to 'ditch' a dirigible. On 27 June 1903 he achieved another 'first'—albeit a more pleasant one—when he took a lady named Melle d'Acosta for a short flight in his *Dirigible No. 8*; she was the first woman ever to fly·in an airship. The most famous of all Santos-Dumont's airships was also the smallest: *Dirigible No. 9*, with a capacity of only 7,770 cubic feet. Alberto used the little craft in exactly the same way that other people used carriages and automobiles; he would quite literally drop in at his favourite café, tethering the ship to a lamp-post or some convenient railings while he went and enjoyed a leisurely drink. On another occasion—on 14 July 1903, Bastille Day—he caused a mild sensation by flying the full length of a military parade at Longchamp, just a few feet above the heads of the troops.

The exploits of Santos-Dumont—'the little man that Paris loved'—were a source of inspiration to many other aeronauts at the turn of the century. One of them was a skilled balloonist named Augusto Severo, who built a dirigible which he called *Pax* and took the ship up on her maiden flight on 12 May 1902, together with his mechanic Sachet. The craft climbed rapidly, so rapidly that the aeronauts panicked and threw out more ballast instead of venting gas. The result was that the airship climbed still faster and its envelope burst, exploding in flames. It crashed in Paris's Avenue de Maine, killing both men. An investigation of the wreckage later revealed that Severo had filled one of the envelope's two safety valves with wax, believing that only one would be sufficient. The remaining valve had not been able to cope with the build-up of pressure during the climb, and the result was a sudden explosion. A spark from the ship's engine had done the rest.

A second disaster followed quickly. On 13 October 1902

Ottokar de Bradsky and his assistant, Paul Morin, ascended from Vaugirard in an airship of Bradsky's design and headed towards Issy-les-Moulineaux. They ran into a strong headwind and the ship went out of control, drifting back across Paris and turning slowly around its own axis. Finally, near Globe de Stains, the ship adopted a sudden nose-up attitude and the car tore away. Eye-witnesses in the village saw it plunge to earth like a stone. The mangled remains of the two aeronauts were found trapped in the wreckage.

Exactly a month later, on 13 November 1902, another airship appeared in the sky over Paris. Its design dated back to 1899, when Paul and Pierre Lebaudy, the owners of a big sugar refinery, had commissioned their chief engineer, Henri Julliot, to construct a dirigible. The craft, known as the *Lebaudy No. 1*, was completed early in November 1902. It was 187 feet long, with a diameter of 32 feet and a capacity of 90,000 cubic feet. The envelope of the ship was fixed to a floor made from steel tubing, running along slightly less than half the ship's length, to which the gondola was attached. The ship's twin propellers were mounted one on either side of the gondola and were powered by a Daimler engine developing 35 h.p. The whole craft weighed $2\frac{1}{2}$ tons, including fuel, ballast and water. Because of the yellowish colour of its envelope, the dirigible was nicknamed *Le Jaune*, although *Lebaudy No. 1* remained its official designation. During its first flight on 13 November, made after a series of captive ascents, it reached a speed of 25 m.p.h. and was found to manœuvre well, returning to its starting-point without difficulty. Thanks to its ballonnet, which was divided into three compartments, the craft could climb to 5,000 feet without valving gas.

Between its maiden flight and July 1903, the airship made a total of twenty-nine flights from Moisson near Nantes. On 8 May it set up a distance record for dirigibles when it covered 23 miles in 1 hour 36 minutes, beating this on 24 June by making a flight of 61 miles in 2 hours 46 minutes. On 12 November that same year, it covered the 39 miles from Moisson to Paris in 1 hour 41 minutes, landing in the Champ de Mars. After being placed on display for a week in the nearby *Galerie des Machines*, it was taken out to make another flight on 19 November, only to be severely damaged when its pilot, Juchmès, had to make a forced landing near Chalais-Meudon. The envelope became entangled in a tree, and the airship had to be dismantled. It was later rebuilt completely and, renamed *Lebaudy II*, went on to make many more successful flights. During one of these, made on 3 July 1905, crewed by pilot Juchmès and mechanic Rey and carrying a passenger named Voyer, it smashed its own endurance record by remaining airborne for 3 hours 21 minutes. This was achieved on the last leg of a flight from Moisson to Cap de Chalons; in all, the ship was in the air for 6 hours 38 minutes that day, covering a total distance of 126 miles.

Lebaudy II was subsequently acquired by the French Army, in which she served until the middle of 1909. She was the first of a line of Lebaudy airships—highly successful craft which served in several countries.

At the dawn of the twentieth century, however, it was not the French who dominated the airship scene in Europe. Like a comet, the name of one man was climbing rapidly over the horizon to eclipse all others; a name that was to become inseparable from the word airship.

Count Ferdinand von Zeppelin.

3 Zeppelin—the Name that made History

Ferdinand von Zeppelin was born in Konstanz on 8 July 1838, the son of Count Frederick Zeppelin and his French-born wife Amalie. In 1857, at the age of nineteen, Ferdinand was commissioned as a Lieutenant in the German Army, following the tradition of most young German aristocrats. After further training in a military academy, he was transferred to the Engineer Corps and, in 1863, became a member of a German military mission which went to the United States to observe the American Civil War at close quarters. It was there that he entered into his first flirtation with aeronautics, making a balloon ascent from St Paul in Minnesota. Returning to Germany, he fought with distinction in the war between Prussia and Austria in 1866, being decorated for gallantry. Four years later he was in action yet again, this time in the Franco-Prussian War. On one occasion during this conflict he was accused of having deserted the patrol he was leading, leaving his men to be killed or captured by the French. It was only partly true: Zeppelin had in fact gathered certain vital information during the course of the patrol, which had then run into a heavy concentration of French troops. Zeppelin had realized that the best chance of getting his information back was to order the patrol to split up, which he did. It was sheer fate that he alone managed to slip back to the Prussian lines.

Zeppelin's serious involvement with airship development really began in 1874, when he read a lecture on 'World Mail and Airship Travel' by the German Postmaster-General. Ten years later, when Renard and Krebs made their first flight in *La France*, Zeppelin began to feel a sense of urgency: he was not slow to realize the potentialities of the airship as a weapon, and his main fear was that Germany would be left behind in the race to develop an 'air cruiser'.

By this time, Zeppelin had reached the rank of Lieutenant-General. He was a man of considerable influence, with the reputation of being one of the best engineers in Germany, and his proposals to put Germany on a sound aeronautical footing were being viewed favourably in high quarters. However, the Army was still his career, and his aeronautical work still had to take second place to military duty. It was a situation which, had it endured, might have forced the name of Zeppelin into the ranks of forgotten pioneers; men whose ideas on aeronautical design were revolutionary, but who were prevented from turning those ideas into practical reality through lack of time or money.

In Zeppelin's case, however, the picture was to change dramatically—and it was Ferdinand's own rashness that brought it about. In the latter part of the nineteenth century, Germany was still composed of semi-independent states, each with its own government and locally levied army. Zeppelin believed passionately in the continued autonomy of his own state, Württemberg, and in 1889 he wrote a strongly worded letter to the German War Ministry protesting that the state's army was being progressively brought under complete Prussian control. The letter came into the hands of the Kaiser, who, infuriated by its tone, ordered Zeppelin to retract his statements. Zeppelin, however, remained unrepentant, and the result was predictable: in 1890, the Kaiser asked for his resignation on the grounds that he was no longer fit for high command.

With his military career now at an end, Zeppelin—at the age of fifty-two—turned his whole attention to airship design. In 1893, in collaboration with an engineer named Theodore Kober, he submitted a design for a rigid airship to the War Ministry, having already carried out a series of ground tests with engines and propellers at Cannstadt and Konstanz the previous year. Despite his previous grudge against Zeppelin, the Kaiser was sufficiently impressed to appoint a scientific commission to examine the Count's proposal, which involved an airship 384 feet long and 36 feet in diameter, powered by two 11-h.p. Daimler engines. Zeppelin envisaged a kind of aerial train, the main airship towing a series of unpowered rigid craft linked together like railway coaches; these would carry the passengers and freight.

The scientific commission, however, pointed out many serious flaws in the design and in Zeppelin's performance estimates; its final recommendation was that no public money should be risked on the venture. Not all the members of the commission were convinced that Zeppelin's theories were foredoomed to failure; one of them, Professor Müller-Breslau, subsequently proved to be of invaluable assistance to Zeppelin, suggesting many improvements on the existing airship design. It was at Müller-Breslau's suggestion that Zeppelin adopted the cigar-shaped hull that was to characterize all his airships, and also the 'Schwedler cupola', a structure of braced transverse rings that resulted in a light but strong framework.

Undaunted by the commission's report, Zeppelin immediately embarked on the design of a second airship. In May 1898, he formed the 'Joint Stock Company for Promotion of Airship Flight', sinking almost the whole of his personal fortune into the venture and providing over half the total capital of £40,000. The rest was raised by the Union of German Engineers. Construction of his first airship, the *LZ.1* (*Luftschiff Zeppelin No. 1*) was begun in under a year from the date when the company was first formed, the structure gradually taking place in a huge floating shed which Zeppelin had built at Manzell, near Friedrichshafen on Lake Constance. The airship was a monster, 420 feet long and 38 feet in diameter. Zeppelin's decision to build such a large craft had been influenced by the work of a German inventor named Hermann Ganswindt, who in 1884 had published a book in which he outlined a design for a dirigible 500 feet long, pointing out that the air resistance of an elongated airship did not increase in proportion to the craft's volume, and that consequently a very large airship would enjoy an enormous advantage in terms of lifting power.

The framework of Zeppelin's first airship was made of aluminium, covered in fabric and divided into seventeen compartments. Altogether, these compartments held 400,000 cubic feet of hydrogen. The ship carried two gondolas, or cars, mounted one behind the other beneath the hull, and each containing a

Daimler engine weighing 850 pounds and developing 15 h.p. The ship's total weight was 25,350 pounds, and it must have been apparent to Zeppelin that she was very badly underpowered. Nevertheless, construction went ahead without any attempt being made to equip the *LZ.1* with more powerful engines.

Construction of the *LZ.1* was completed in 1900, and the airship's maiden flight was made on 2 July that same year. On this occasion, the *LZ.1* carried a crew of five: Count Zeppelin, Eugen Wolf, Baron Bassus, Ludwig Dürr and a mechanic named Gross. The airship was towed out of its hangar by a steam launch; the engines were started, the tow cast off, and the *LZ.1* climbed somewhat unsteadily to a height of about 1,000 feet. She remained in the air for an hour and a quarter, cruising around erratically over Lake Constance. The ship was found to be horribly unstable; her two tiny rudders were almost useless, making directional control practically non-existent, and some trouble was experienced with the 550-pound sliding weight that governed vertical control. Despite the fact that the ship could not be trimmed properly, her crew managed to bring her down for a safe landing on the surface of the lake.

The LZ.1 was towed back to her hangar, where she stayed for three months while parts of her structure were strengthened. There were very few spectators to witness her second flight, which took place on 17 October 1900; the local newspapers had been so unimpressed by her performance in July that they had not even considered it necessary to send a reporter to cover this latest attempt. The *Frankfurter Zeitung*, however, commissioned a young economist named Hugo Eckener—who had already contributed a number of short articles to the paper—to be present at the *LZ.1*'s second flight and to make a report on it. The resulting article was fairly lukewarm, being neither for nor against Zeppelin's airship; however, Eckener made a number of useful suggestions and criticisms. A sailor of considerable experience, he pointed out that the maximum speed of 16 m.p.h. attained by the airship was too slow for her to make progress against even a moderate headwind.

53

Zeppelin himself later contested this statement, but subsequent events were to prove that Eckener was right. Zeppelin was angered that a man who appeared to be nothing more than a disinterested onlooker should have so much criticism to offer; he never dreamed that Hugo Eckener would, in the future, play such a vital part in the story of the Zeppelin airships.

The *LZ.1* made a very short flight on 21 October 1900, bringing her total flying time to 2 hours 1 minute. By this time, there was no longer any doubt that the airship was a failure, and—with the company's funds almost exhausted—she was broken up soon afterwards. Lack of funds delayed further progress for some time, until Zeppelin obtained permission from the State of Württemberg to run a lottery in order to raise more money. This in itself would still not have been enough, but a substantial grant towards the building of a second airship was made by an aluminium manufacturer called Berg, who saw enormous commercial possibilities for his product if Zeppelin's rigid airship designs met with success.

Construction of the *LZ.2* was begun in 1905. She was almost identical with her predecessor, having a length of 413 feet, a diameter of 38 feet 6 inches, and a capacity of 367,500 cubic feet. Her two engines, however, represented an enormous improvement, developing 85 h.p. each, compared with the 16 h.p. of the *LZ.1*'s motors. The *LZ.2*, with her strengthened structure and vastly improved power-weight ratio, should have been an unqualified success. It seemed, however, as though the ship was dogged by ill-luck right from the start. Seconds after being launched on her first flight on 30 November 1905, her forward engine cut out abruptly and her stern dropped into the water, shattering her rudder. She bounced back into the air again and, with no means of control, drifted helplessly towards high ground on the Swiss shore of the lake. Fortunately, a fast launch was standing by and it now raced after her, its crew catching the airship's trail rope and averting what might have been a disaster in good time.

Hugo Eckener had witnessed the fiasco, and he was present again when the *LZ.2* was towed out of her hangar on 17 January

1906 for a second attempt. It was bitterly cold, and the airship's engines stubbornly refused to start. It was an hour before the crew managed to coax them into life, and Eckener noticed that during this time the ground crew was having increasing difficulty in holding the ship steady against a wind that was growing more fierce with every passing minute. When both engines were running to the crew's satisfaction, the *LZ.2* was launched and climbed rapidly to a height of over 1,500 feet, manœuvring with apparent ease over the lake and reaching speeds of up to 33 m.p.h. Everything appeared to be going well —and then, without warning, the forward engine spluttered and died. As the crew tried desperately to restart it, the ship drifted away towards the north, finally disappearing in the mist that hung over the horizon. With the engine still out of action, the crew was forced to crash-land the *LZ.2* at Kisslegg, twenty miles away. During the landing the airship's stern became entangled in the branches of a tree, causing some damage, and since it would soon be too dark to enable repairs to be carried out it was decided to moor the craft and leave her where she was until the following day.

Fate, however, had not finished with the *LZ.2*. During the night, a violent storm broke over the area; gale-force winds and sleet lashed the airship, and under the continual onslaught her framework gradually began to break up. By first light, she was little more than a battered wreck, damaged beyond repair. Count Zeppelin stood by helplessly, with tears in his eyes, as his men broke up the remains with axes for transportation back to Friedrichshafen.

Neither the State nor the public was willing to contribute any more money to what by this time was regarded as Count Zeppelin's crazy schemes. Nevertheless, by scraping together the last reserves of his fortune and by borrowing from a group of faithful friends, Zeppelin was able to begin construction of a third airship with the minimum delay. The dimensions of the *LZ.3* were similar to those of her two predecessors, and, like the *LZ.2*, she was equipped with two 85-h.p. engines. She was completed remarkably quickly, making her maiden flight on 9 October 1906. This time, good fortune favoured the Count;

55

on her maiden flight, the *LZ.3* flew sixty miles in two hours, returning to her base without difficulty. This exploit was repeated during a second flight, made the following day.

The *LZ.3* went on to make several more successful flights during the months that followed, and, in September 1907, she set up a new endurance record for airships by remaining airborne for eight hours. Now that Zeppelin's airship designs were beginning to vindicate themselves, the authorities began to take considerable interest in his work. In 1907, the Airship Commission awarded him half a million marks—about £25,000 —to enable him to carry out further development work. Part of this sum was used to build a larger and better-equipped floating hangar. The German Army also placed a tentative order for a Zeppelin airship, on the condition that such a ship must be able to remain airborne for twenty-four hours, cover a distance of 435 miles non-stop, be able to fly to any selected point, return to base after each flight, and operate from a land base. The *LZ.3* did not have sufficient endurance to meet this requirement, and Zeppelin immediately embarked on the construction of a fourth airship, the *LZ.4*. She was of the same diameter as the *LZ.3*, but longer, measuring 446 feet from stem to stern. Her capacity was also increased to 530,000 cubic feet. She carried a small passenger cabin amidships and was fitted with two engines, each of 105 h.p. Her maiden flight, made on 20 June 1908, was an enormous success. Her crew reported some trouble with the steering mechanism, but this was quickly rectified and three days later she made a second flight, lasting two hours. During a third flight, on 1 July, she made a twelve-hour flight over Switzerland, covering a distance of nearly two hundred miles.

Then, on 3 July, came a flight that raised Zeppelin's prestige enormously. The King and Queen of Württemberg made a short flight in the *LZ.4*, becoming the first royalty to fly in an airship. Zeppelin had gradually been working the *LZ.4* up towards a full twenty-four-hour flight, and this was scheduled to take place on 4 August 1908. At seven o'clock that morning, the airship, with eleven people on board, lifted majestically away from the waters of Lake Constance and turned westward to follow the course of the Rhine. The authorities in towns along the route had been warned in advance that she would be flying over, and the townspeople of Basel, Strasbourg, Speyer and Worms turned out in their thousands to watch her as she droned serenely across the sky. Count Zeppelin's plan was that the *LZ.4* should fly as far as Mainz, circle the city, and then return to Friedrichshafen by the same route.

For eleven hours she cruised steadily on, her crew watching the picturesque landscape around the Rhine unfolding beneath them. Then, with only ten miles to go to Mainz, the forward engine began to give trouble. The mechanics tried to rectify the trouble, but it was no use. A couple of minutes later, the engine cut out altogether and there was nothing for it but to make an emergency landing in a field near Oppenheim, some eight miles south of Mainz. Fortunately, the trouble did not appear to be serious and the mechanics were able to get the motor started again, enabling the *LZ.4* to continue her flight to Mainz ninety minutes later.

She flew in a slow arc over the city while people waved and cheered in the streets below; then she set course southwards once more. For a time, both engines continued to run smoothly and it began to look as though the airship would arrive back at Friedrichshafen without further mishap. Then, over Karlsruhe, the forward motor broke down again without warning. The wind was rising steadily, and Zeppelin had no wish to attempt another emergency landing. Instead, he decided to divert to the Daimler factory at Stuttgart, where he hoped that permanent repairs could be made to the faulty motor. With only one engine in action, progress was painfully slow, and it was almost dark by the time the ship landed at Echterdingen, not far from the Daimler works. A number of soldiers from a nearby barracks volunteered to act as ground crew, holding the ship down while Daimler mechanics took the forward engine apart. They were still working on it when, an hour later, a sudden thunderstorm burst over the field. The soldiers and mechanics moored the ship hastily, then ran for cover as the rain came down in sheets. Violent gusts of wind buffeted the ship, and before long some of the mooring-ropes began to work loose. Seeing the

57

danger, the ground crew rushed forward and clung on grimly, but the wind was too strong. The airship seemed to have become a vicious thing, with a will of its own, and the ropes were torn brutally from their grasp as she bounded suddenly into the rain-filled air. For a moment, it seemed that the wind was going to carry her away; and then, with a violent thud, she erupted in flames and sank slowly back to earth, blazing fiercely. Within a matter of minutes, all that remained of the *LZ.4* was a heap of charred and twisted wreckage. It was a miracle that no one had been injured.

Most of Zeppelin's friends were convinced that the disaster would mark the end of the seventy-year-old airship designer's aspirations; they believed that the loss of the *LZ.4* would break his heart. In fact, the reverse was true. Almost before the glow of the flames had died away, Zeppelin had expressed his determination to build another airship. However, the stubborn will of the old man would not have been enough in itself, had it not been backed up by the efforts of Hugo Eckener, who had assumed the role of part-time publicity officer for Zeppelin's company. As soon as the news reached him, Eckener telegraphed every major newspaper in Germany and gave them the story, trading on Zeppelin's considerable popularity and stressing that the loss of the *LZ.4* was a severe blow to the Fatherland.

The result was dramatic. Within hours of the story breaking, Zeppelin received telegrams from people all over the country, offering various sums of money to help finance the building of another airship. Voluntary contributions poured in from people in all walks of life, both rich and poor, and within three months a sum amounting to six million marks—some £300,000—had been assembled. With this capital Zeppelin formed another company; the Zeppelin Foundation for the Promotion of Aerial Navigation, whose task was really to hold the purse-strings and counter any attempt to bring Zeppelin's work under the control of a board of trustees, which the Kaiser wanted to appoint in order to bring the concern under more close control. With the Foundation handling this aspect, the Zeppelin Airship Company was free to concentrate on technical development. It was at this stage that Hugo Eckener became a full-time employee of the company, handling what would now be called public relations and some aspect of sales promotion.

Fortunately, the loss of the *LZ.4* had not caused the Army's interest to wane, and the High Command immediately ordered a replacement. Meanwhile, Zeppelin concentrated on the completion of his one remaining airship, the *LZ.3*, which was being virtually rebuilt. It was completed in October 1908, and on 7 November it flew to Donaueschingen to make a demonstration flight before the Kaiser. On this occasion, one of its passengers was the Crown Prince.

Zeppelin had planned to subject the *LZ.3* to an intensive series of operational trials, but before these got under way the German Army took over the airship and pressed it into service under the designation *Z.1*. The craft was formally delivered to its new owners at Metz on 3 July 1909, after an eventful flight during which it was forced down by heavy rain and a gas leak. For most of her military service, the *LZ.3* was used as a training ship. A month before her delivery, at the end of a flight to Munich, she had become the first Zeppelin to make a touchdown on dry land.

On 26 May 1909, while the *LZ.3* was still undergoing her military trials, Zeppelin's latest airship—the *LZ.5*—flew for the first time. She was larger than the *LZ.4*, with a capacity of 501,000 cubic feet, and her two engines developed a total output of 220 h.p. A matter of hours after her maiden flight, German newspapers carried the announcement that the new airship would visit Berlin in three days' time and circle the Imperial residence in Potsdam before flying back to Friedrichshafen non-stop. The airship took off from her base at 9.40 p.m. on 29 May 1909, and set course north-eastwards in the gathering darkness. There was a strong headwind, and progress was slow; it was 8.30 the following morning before she passed over Nuremberg, a distance of 168 miles from her starting-point. The hours wore on, and by 7.20 p.m. the *LZ.5* had put 348 miles behind her. Berlin was now only 100 miles away, but the weather was deteriorating rapidly and fuel was running low; the *LZ.5* had taken off with two tons of petrol on board—adequate for a flight to Berlin with eight

59

people on board in still-air conditions, but making no allowance for a stiff headwind all the way.

Reluctántly, knowing that the ship would be hard put to reach her destination, Zeppelin ordered the pilot to turn back and head for home. Assisted now by a tailwind, the *LZ.5* made good time as she headed south—but even so, her fuel ran out when she was still 95 miles from base and the crew had to bring her down for an emergency landing in a field near Göppingen. During the landing, a strong gust of wind swung the *LZ.5*'s nose round and it struck the one and only tree in the field, sustaining slight damage. It was a sad end to a record-breaking endurance flight that had lasted 37 hours 40 minutes, covering a total distance of 603 miles. Fortunately, the damage was repairable on the spot, and the *LZ.5* was able to continue on the last leg of her flight, which she covered in 14 hours after making a second forced landing.

After a thorough overhaul, the *LZ.5* was turned over to the Army and re-designated *Z.2*. Her operational career was destined to be short: on 25 April 1910 her framework crumpled after a heavy landing at the hands of an Army crew at Weilburg, and a gale completed the work of destruction some hours later.

The next ship in line, the *LZ.6*, was built in anticipation of further Army orders and made her first flight on 25 August 1909. Two days later, she set off on a demonstration flight to Berlin, only to be delayed *en route* by technical troubles. She eventually arrived over the German capital on 29 August, landing at Tegel before a vast audience that included the Kaiser. The ship flew home a week later, having experienced more technical troubles on the voyage, and subsequently made a series of demonstration flights carrying passengers, one of whom was Orville Wright. The *LZ.6* was not, however, purchased by the Army, as Zeppelin had hoped. Her career ended on 14 September 1910, when she was destroyed in an accidental hangar fire at Baden-Baden.

The German Army's sudden cold attitude to Zeppelin's airships was largely the result of a good deal of hostile behind-the-scenes manœuvring on the part of the Prussian Airship Battalion, which was at that time building a non-rigid airship of its own design. Public interest in Zeppelin and his work, however, was still as great as ever, and it was becoming increasingly obvious that if the company was to survive, this interest would have to be exploited in some way.

It was the company's recently appointed business manager, Herr Colsman—nephew of Herr Berg the aluminium tycoon and a brilliant businessman in his own right—who came up with a possible answer. He pointed out that since the military authorities no longer appeared to be interested in Zeppelin's rigid airships, the logical step would be to concentrate on the development of the ships as civilian passenger and freight carriers. Before taking the proposal to Count Zeppelin, Colsman talked it over with Hugo Eckener, who was dubious at first; he believed that the poor safety record of the ships—three out of four having been destroyed accidentally—would deter the public from risking life or money in such a venture. Nevertheless, Colsman managed to convince him that it was the only course left open to the company, and together the two men submitted the proposal to Zeppelin. The Count was not impressed, being still convinced that the true role of his airships lay in the military field, but in the end he gave his grudging approval for the plan to go ahead.

On 16 November 1909 the German Airship Transport Company Ltd—*Deutsche Luftschiffahrts-Aktien-Gesellschaft*, or DELAG—was formed at Frankfurt. The response was fantastic. The mayors of Frankfurt, Cologne, Düsseldorf, Baden-Baden, Munich, Leipzig, Dresden and Hamburg all contributed capital and joined the Board of Directors, and construction of airship hangars was begun immediately in several of these major German cities.

Ten days after the world's first airline was created, the first passenger-carrying airship—the *LZ.7*—was ordered. She was completed in May 1910, by which time the first crews had been trained. On 22 June the new airship—named the *Deutschland*—made a successful flight lasting 2 hours 30 minutes to Düsseldorf, with thirty-two people on board. It was a good beginning to what the DELAG directors hoped would turn out to be a highly successful and lucrative regular airship service between

61

Frankfurt, Düsseldorf and Baden-Baden, and their hopes were strengthened when the *Deutschland* made five more flights during the week that followed. Then, during the sixth flight on 28 June, Zeppelin's jinx struck again. One of the *Deutschland*'s engines failed, and, unable to hold her own against a strong westerly headwind, she came down in the Teutoberg Forest and was totally wrecked, fortunately without loss of life. The airship's commander—perhaps unjustifiably—was held responsible for the accident and was dismissed.

Hugo Eckener was invited to assume the post of Director of Flight Operations, a job which—because of his championship of the Zeppelin cause—he could not very well refuse, as he later admitted. Once he had made his decision, he tackled the job with his usual enthusiasm and set about finding a solution to three major problems: the difficulty of manoeuvring airships into and out of their hangars in a crosswind, the training of high-quality crews, and the creation of an efficient meteorological service along the airships' routes.

Eckener received his airship captain's ticket on 6 February 1911 and immediately took command of the latest Zeppelin airship—the *LZ.8*, named *Deutschland II* (*Ersatz Deutschland*). She made her first passenger flight from Baden in March 1911 and operated with considerable success until 16 May—the day when Eckener made one of the biggest errors of his career. That morning, the ship was scheduled to take off on one of her regular runs with a large number of VIPs on board, and in order not to disappoint them Eckener decided to take a risk and bring the *LZ.8* out of her hangar while a strong crosswind was blowing. As she was being walked out, the wind caught her and slammed her brutally against the hangar doors, damaging her so badly that she had to be almost completely rebuilt. From that moment on, Eckener had no hesitation in cancelling a flight if conditions were in the slightest unfavourable. The accident had one immediate result: Eckener's plan to set up a weather forecasting service was given priority. From now on, advance warning of adverse weather conditions would enable DELAG to give passengers several hours' notice of cancelled flights.

The meteorological service was already partly operational by the time the next Zeppelin airship, the *Schwaben*, was completed on 15 July 1911. She made her maiden flight five days later, flying from Friedrichshafen to Lucerne, with Eckener in command. In eleven months, she made a total of 218 flights and carried 1,553 passengers. She finally came to grief on 28 June 1912, when, after reaching Düsseldorf minutes ahead of a violent storm and unloading her passengers safely, she began to break up under the repeated blows of a gale-force wind and caught fire. The ship was a total loss, but no one was hurt.

Meanwhile, another airship had entered DELAG service. She was the *Viktoria Luise* (*LZ.11*) and she made her maiden flight on 14 February 1912. Between that date and 31 October 1913, she made 384 flights, logging 838 hours' flying time, and carried 8,135 passengers. During this period, DELAG's network of routes continued to expand steadily, with services inaugurated to Hamburg, Fuhlsbüttel and Potsdam. Two more airships, the *Sachsen* and the *Hansa*, were added to the fleet, and in June 1913 Eckener captained the former on a flight to Vienna and back. In four years of service, up to August 1914, DELAG's ships had covered a total of 107,231 miles on 1,588 flights, carrying 10,197 passengers. Much of this passenger traffic was accounted for by pleasure flights, made during the summer months. Twenty passengers were usually carried in comfort, being treated to a sumptuous meal during the two-hour trip.

During these pioneer years, Zeppelin had been able to continue his work in the rigid airship field with the knowledge that he had no rival. A number of airships had been built by other concerns, but these were of the non-rigid or semi-rigid type. The smallest of these concerns was the government-controlled balloon factory in Berlin, directed by a Major von Gross, which between 1908 and 1914 produced four semi-rigid airships designed by an engineer named Nikolas Basenach. The first of these, the *Gross-Basenach No. 1*, was destroyed accidentally on 1 July 1908, but the second proved to be highly successful. On 12 September 1908 it made a flight lasting thirteen hours, most of it in darkness, and on 23 January the following year it carried Prince Heinrich of Prussia on a three-hour flight over Berlin. The last Gross-Basenach ship, the *M.4*, reached a speed of over 50 m.p.h. She was powered by three 180-h.p. Maybach engines, and served on patrol duties during the First World War.

The leading designer of non-rigid airships in Germany in the years before the First World War was Major von Parseval, who began work in 1906. The first of his ships reached a speed of 25 m.p.h. under the power of a single 50-h.p. Mercedes engine, and had a capacity of 88,000 cubic feet. On 30 October 1909 *Parseval I*—together with *Gross-Basenach II* and the German Army Zeppelin *Z.2* (*LZ.5*)—carried out a simulated air attack on a fort near Koblenz during a military manœuvre, and a month later *Parseval I* and *Gross-Basenach II* flew from Cologne to Metz in formation. Altogether, twenty-seven Parseval airships were built. The later ones, produced in 1913–14, had a capacity of 300,000 cubic feet and a maximum speed of 45 m.p.h. The Parseval was the first airship to be successfully exported, several being supplied to foreign countries—including one to the Royal Navy.

It was not until 1911 that a serious competitor to Count Zeppelin in the design of rigid airships entered the field: the *Luftschiffbau Schütte-Lanz* of Mannheim–Rheinau. The firm had been created in 1909 by Dr Johann Schütte, Professor of Naval Architecture at Danzig University, with the backing of a number of wealthy industrialists, and had been actively encouraged by the War Ministry. Nevertheless, it was not until 17 October 1911 that the first ship—the *SL.1*—made her first flight. Instead of aluminium, the ship's hull was constructed of laminated plywood girders, crossing each other in a diamond-shaped pattern. She was 420 feet long and 59 feet in diameter, with a capacity of 750,000 cubic feet. Her two engines, developing a total of 540 h.p., gave her a top speed of 38 m.p.h. Later Schütte-Lanz ships, beginning with the *SL.2*—which was completed on 24 February 1914—were powered by four Maybach engines. They were extremely advanced for their day, being beautifully streamlined and fitted with a simple, cruciform tail unit. The forward control car was completely enclosed, in contrast to the draughty, open gondolas of the Zeppelin airships. (It was a long time before Count Zeppelin renounced his pet theory that an airship could only be landed properly if its pilot was able to feel the wind in his face!) Only a few Schütte-Lanz ships were built. In August 1914, the firm was taken over by the German Government and absorbed into the Zeppelin organization, although the handful of ships built during the war years retained the *SL* designation.

Meanwhile, in 1911, the German Navy had begun to show an increasing interest in Zeppelin's rigid airships. Prior to that, the Navy had remained a lukewarm and neutral onlooker, content to observe how the Army fared with its early airships. This original lack of interest was largely due to the Navy Minister, Grossadmiral Alfred von Tirpitz, who since 1897 had directed all his efforts towards one goal: the creation of a large and powerful offensive naval force of modern battleships and destroyers. Tirpitz had in fact considered the use of airships for reconnaissance purposes as far back as 1906, and in September the following year he assigned a naval officer, Fregattenkapitän Mischke, to fly as a passenger on board the *LZ.3* when she made her eight-hour flight over Lake Constance. Mischke's subsequent report was extremely favourable, but Tirpitz remained unimpressed. While admitting that the use of airships could be of value, he pointed out that to fulfil its task adequately a naval airship must be a large, long-range craft, and this view was substantiated by the head of the Naval Dockyard department, who drew up a specification for a craft with a range of 1,000 nautical miles and a speed sufficient to overcome a headwind of 47 m.p.h.

Tirpitz, however, was not a man to eliminate what might be a promising development without being in possession of all the facts, and in 1910 he sent one of Germany's leading naval architects, Felix Pietzker, to Friedrichshafen to make a close study of the progress being made by Zeppelin and to submit a comprehensive report. Pietzker surveyed Zeppelin's work with a more scientific and critical mind than Mischke, and he did not hesitate to inform Tirpitz of the shortcomings of the airships then being produced. He stated that they were much too slow to cope with the high winds experienced over the North Sea, that they could only be operated in good weather conditions and that they did not possess sufficient range. However, he informed the

Minister that, in his opinion, a large and streamlined Zeppelin with a speed of 45 m.p.h. could be built, and submitted his own rough design for such a craft. The airship he envisaged would be powered by six 140-h.p. engines, and would have a capacity of 1,223,100 cubic feet.

Cost was the main drawback: it would take £150,000 to build an airship of these proportions and to set up the necessary handling equipment, and the Navy's funds—already the subject of bitter arguments between Tirpitz and the Government—were fully committed to the construction of new surface vessels. Moreover, Count Zeppelin insisted that it would take several more years of development work before he would be in a position to build a ship to meet the Navy's requirements.

Then, early in 1911, the Kaiser started to bring pressure to bear on the Admiral, mainly as a result of intelligence reports on the progress that was being made in airship development in other countries. In the end, Tirpitz reluctantly agreed to order an airship without delay, but even so it was not until 24 April 1912 that the Navy's *Luftschiff 1* (*L.1*) was finally ordered after protracted discussions between the Navy Ministry and the Zeppelin Company. The *L.1* (company designation *LZ.14*) was a compromise between the Zeppelin airship models then being produced, with a capacity of 706,200 cubic feet, and the Navy's requirement for a big four-engined ship of 882,750 cubic feet capacity.

While the ship was under construction, the Navy began developing Nordholz, near Cuxhaven, as an airship base at a cost of £83,400. Work began in conditions amounting to strict secrecy, and the belief was carefully fostered throughout the area that the site was being developed for use as a firing range. Meanwhile, the Navy rented the DELAG hangar at Fuhlsbüttel to accommodate their ship until the base at Nordholz was completed.

The next step was to recruit suitable crews for the newly formed Naval Airship Division, which was placed under the command of Korvettenkapitän Friedrich Metzig. There was no shortage of volunteers, and by 1 July 1912 the first complete crew had begun training at Fuhlsbüttel aboard the DELAG

66

passenger ship *Viktoria Luise*. As the crew—under the command of Kapitänleutnant Carl-Ernst Hanne—grew more experienced, they were permitted to handle the *Viktoria Luise* and her sister ship, the *Hansa*, on pleasure flights.

The Naval Zeppelin *L.1* was completed on 25 September 1912. To all appearances, she was indistinguishable from the passenger airships. She was 518 feet 2 inches in length, with a diameter of 48 feet 6 inches and a capacity of 793,600 cubic feet. Her maiden flight was made on 7 October, and a week later, on the 13th, she took off from Friedrichshafen on an endurance flight to the north coast of Germany. She returned safely the following day having covered 900 miles on a flight lasting thirty hours and flown for part of the way at 5,000 feet. On 17 October she was transferred to Johannisthal, not far from Berlin, where a temporary training school had been set up, and several more officers were trained during the course of the autumn and winter months. The failure rate was high: some men proved incapable of adapting themselves to the new element, and had to be returned to their units. Airship handling was, to a great extent, 'seat of the pants' flying, involving an ability to judge the lightness and general behaviour of the ship by 'feel' alone. Some applicants, through no fault of their own, did not possess this ability, and it was something that did not always come with practice.

On 18 January 1913, Tirpitz—now committed to an airship procurement programme—submitted a proposal to the Kaiser calling for a five-year expansion programme. The proposal, to which the Kaiser gave his immediate approval, outlined three requirements: the purchase of ten Zeppelins to equip two airship squadrons, the establishment of Nordholz as a permanent central airship base, and the construction of Government-subsidized private airship hangars throughout the country for use in time of war.

The first of the new ships ordered under the expansion scheme, the *L.2*, was laid down in May 1913 with the factory designation of *LZ.18*. She was designed by Felix Pietzker, and was the largest airship built up to that time. Although she had the same length as the *L.1*, to enable her to fit inside the existing airship hangar at Fuhlsbüttel, her hull diameter was increased by six feet and her capacity was 953,000 cubic feet. The *L.2* was powered by four 165-h.p. Maybach engines mounted in two gondolas; her control car, which was fully enclosed, was fitted flush underneath the hull some 25 feet ahead of the forward engine gondola. The airship's design incorporated a number of innovations: the engine gondolas, for example, were fitted much closer to the hull than on previous Zeppelins, and had windscreens attached to their bows, forming a link between the gondola and the hull itself. Zeppelin's engineers had voiced some misgivings about this arrangement, justifiably believing that the space between the gondolas and the hydrogen-filled hull was too small. But Pietzker's argument won the day: a tragic mistake, as later events were to prove.

While the *L.2* was building during the summer of 1913, the *LZ.1* continued with her trials and crew-training at Johannisthal. On 15 August, on the orders of Tirpitz, she was transferred to Fuhlsbüttel to take part in the autumn manoeuvres of the High Seas Fleet. Adverse weather held up her participation until 8 September, when she earned the praise of the Commander-in-Chief by locating the 'enemy' naval forces and shadowing them, reporting their progress to the 'friendly' warships that were racing to intercept.

The following morning, the *L.1*'s crew—twenty officers and men in all—were briefed for another reconnaissance mission. The airship took off at 1.25 p.m. and climbed steadily to 1,650 feet over the Elbe Estuary, heading out into the German Bight in calm, clear weather. At 3 p.m. she was over Heligoland. A few minutes later, her wireless operator picked up a signal which indicated that bad weather was approaching from the north-north-west, and her captain, Korvettenkapitän Metzig, decided to turn back and head for home. But the storm was faster than the ship, and when she was still only 16 miles east-south-east of Heligoland the wind and rain struck with all its fury. The ship ploughed on, battered by torrential rain and severe turbulence. Suddenly, she was caught by a vicious downcurrent and plummeted towards the sea, only to be arrested

within seconds of hitting the water and flung brutally up to a
height of 5,200 feet. Then she began to drop again, and this time
there was no stopping her. Out of control, her engines running
flat out, she slammed into the sea and broke in half, her bow
rearing a hundred feet into the air like a great accusing finger.
A trawler and the battleship *Hannover* arrived on the scene very
quickly and began to search for survivors, but there was little
they could do. Most of the airship's crew had been trapped in
the gondolas by the tangled mass of aluminium when the airship broke up, and were dragged down with her. Only six
survivors were picked up, and Korvettenkapitän Metzig was not
among them.

It was the first time that lives had been lost in a Zeppelin
crash, and the incident caused a public outcry against the Navy,
which was subsequently accused of incompetence by several
leading German newspapers. These accusations were strongly
denied by the Navy Ministry, as was an allegation by Hugo
Eckener that the *L.1* had been overloaded. In fact, Eckener
was right. The airship had been overloaded for the weather
conditions that prevailed at the time of the crash, but the savage
line-squall had been totally unexpected and no one, least of all
the crew, could be held responsible for the disaster that followed. The ship had lost so much gas during her last terrifying
climb to over 5,000 feet that she had simply become too heavy
to remain airborne, despite the frantic efforts of the crew, who
had jettisoned all the ballast in an attempt to bring the ship
under control just before she struck.

Ironically, the Navy's new airship—the *L.2*—had made her
successful maiden flight at Friedrichshafen only a matter of
hours before the *L.1* was destroyed. On 20 September she flew
to Johannisthal to carry out a series of height, speed and endurance tests. On the morning of 17 October she was made
ready for her tenth flight, which was to be an altitude test. On
this occasion, in addition to the fifteen Navy men who formed
her crew, she carried a number of Zeppelin engineers and
Admiralty representatives—including Felix Pietzker. Altogether, there were twenty-eight people on board when she
finally took off at ten o'clock in the morning, after a delay of

69

two hours caused by a fault in the ignition system of one of her engines.

She was very light on take-off, the hydrogen in her tanks having expanded under the warm rays of the morning sun, and she climbed rapidly towards the west after making one circuit of the field. Suddenly, a shout of horror went up from the spectators on the ground as a lurid ribbon of flame was seen to shoot from the forward engine gondola, licking hungrily along the hull. An instant later, a dull glow flickered inside the hull from stem to stern. By the time the noise of the explosion reached the spectators, flames had burst through the *L.2*'s hull and she had begun to fall, the fire spreading with horrifying speed until the ship was a glowing torch. Faster and faster she fell, her nose dropping with terrible finality. Another explosion shook her as the after gas cells erupted. She was little more than a skeleton now, her outer covering consumed by the flames, her aluminium framework crumpling as she fell. She struck the ground and disintegrated in a sheet of burning fuel as her petrol tanks exploded, sending a mushroom of oily smoke climbing into the morning sky.

A group of soldiers—engineers—were the first to reach the scene. They did what they could, trying to form a road into the incandescent heart of the wreckage by throwing earth on the flames, but it was no use; the heat was too intense. It was thirty minutes before the soldiers managed to hack their way into the tangle of red-hot girders. Miraculously, three men were still alive, but they were burned beyond recognition and died soon afterwards, mercifully without regaining consciousness.

An inquiry into the cause of the crash revealed that the windshields on the bows of the *L.2*'s engine cupolas had been the main factor. During the climb, hydrogen had spilled through the valves in the underside of the full gas cells and had mixed with air in the internal gangway running along the ship's keel; the large windscreens at the front of the engine gondolas had formed a partial vacuum and the highly explosive mixture had been sucked down into the forward gondola, where it had ignited. What followed then was a chain reaction that ended in the destruction of the entire ship.

Almost every experienced crewman in the Naval Airship Division had been killed in either the *L.1* or the *L.2* disaster, and the Navy was left without another airship to train any more. For a time, the whole future of the Airship Division was in jeopardy: Tirpitz was reluctant to order more ships unless the Zeppelin Company agreed to build them bigger, and the only excuse for not disbanding the Division appeared to be one of national prestige.

Nevertheless, a new commander had been appointed to the Airship Division a fortnight or so after Metzig's death, and he had the unenviable task of turning the Division into an efficient force with practically nothing at his disposal in the way of men or material. However, the new man possessed one asset: boundless enthusiasm coupled with great determination. His name was Korvettenkapitän Peter Strasser, and he was a gunnery expert who had been serving in the Admiralty's ordnance department. When the *L.2* crashed, Strasser was in Leipzig, undergoing training in airship handling from Captain Ernst Lehmann, commander of the passenger airship *Sachsen*. He immediately travelled to Johannisthal, where an inspection of the three naval airship crews who were waiting to begin training convinced him that something had to be done quickly to boost their flagging morale. What they needed was a ship— and, since the Navy did not have one, he persuaded the Admiralty to hire the *Sachsen* on a temporary basis. Then, on his own initiative, he enlisted the services of Hugo Eckener and Captain Lehmann to carry out training until he himself was qualified to command an airship. By the end of October, the three trainee naval crews had begun flying. By the beginning of December all three had acquired a certain amount of experience, and on the 7th of that month the *Sachsen* was transferred to Fuhlsbüttel, from where the crews began navigational training flights over the sea.

Strasser's enthusiasm did not go unrecognized by Tirpitz, who realized that no time should be lost in ordering another naval airship, and on 21 March 1914 an order was placed with the Zeppelin Company for the construction of the *L.3*—a craft virtually identical to the *L.1*, and falling far short of the Admiralty specification in terms of size. Inferior to the Navy's requirement though it was, the Zeppelin design was accepted in preference to one submitted by Professor Schütte in October 1913; this involved an airship with a capacity of 1,112,265 cubic feet, powered by four engines giving it an estimated speed of 47 m.p.h. This design would have fitted the naval specification much more closely than the *L.3*, and the main reason why it was not accepted was one of personality: Schütte was an extremely difficult man to deal with, and he was prone to write rude letters to people in authority, including Admirals—with the result that Tirpitz expressed a desire to have as little as possible to do with him.

The *L.3* (*LZ.24*) made her first flight on 11 May 1914. On 16 May, in the course of a thirty-five-hour endurance flight, she reached an altitude of 10,200 feet, the highest so far achieved by an airship. On 28 May she arrived at Fuhlsbüttel and training began in earnest, continuing throughout the splendid weather of that summer of 1914. On 18 July she took off from Fuhlsbüttel and flew westwards along the full length of the Frisian Islands as far as the Dutch coast, returning to base in the early hours of the following morning after a flight lasting twenty-two hours. It was the prototype of the kind of reconnaissance mission which Strasser saw as the primary role of the Navy's airships in time of war.

There was to be no further opportunity for the Airship Division to make any more long training flights in peacetime. On 28 July the German High Seas Fleet assembled in Kiel and Wilhelmshaven and mobilized its reserves. It was exactly one month since the bullet of an assassin had cut down Archduke Franz Ferdinand, heir to the Austrian empire, in Sarajevo.

4 The Airship Scene in Britain
and Other Countries

Despite the fact that balloons had been proving their worth as military observation vehicles for the best part of a century, it was not until 1878 that Britain entered the field of military aeronautics with the establishment of an Army Balloon Equipment Store at Woolwich. In 1890 the Balloon Store was transferred to Aldershot, where it became part of the Royal Engineers, and captive observation balloons were subsequently used in Egypt, Bechuanaland and during the early phase of the Boer War.

Right from the start, the development of military aviation in Britain was frustrated by almost complete apathy on the part of the War Office, and repeated requests by the Director of Military Balloons—Colonel J. Templer, RE, one of the founder-members of the Aero Club—for funds to continue development work were continually turned down. Finally, in 1902, the War Office, no longer able to ignore the progress that was being made in France and Germany, grudgingly allocated a small fund which enabled Templer and his colleagues to initiate the design of a British military airship at Farnborough. Work on the ship's envelope was begun almost immediately. It was made from goldbeater's skin—membranes from the caecum of the ox, a material superior in strength to the more conventional doped fabric but considerably more expensive. Five layers were used, the envelope being built up from sections measuring eight inches by thirty, hand-stitched together with silk thread. The finished envelope was inflated satisfactorily, but proved to be too heavy to lift itself off the ground. A second envelope was made, using only three layers of goldbeater's skin, and initial tests on this were more encouraging. Soon afterwards, however, the project ran out of funds and had to be shelved, the War Office flatly refusing to subscribe any more.

The honour of becoming the first Englishman to build and fly a dirigible, meanwhile, had gone to a well-known aeronaut named Stanley Spencer, who in 1902 constructed a non-rigid airship 75 feet long and 20 feet in diameter, with a capacity of 20,000 cubic feet. The craft was powered by a water-cooled Simms engine developing $3\frac{1}{2}$ h.p., which drove a wooden propeller ten feet in diameter at 250 r.p.m. through reduction gearing. The craft's fuel tank carried two gallons of petrol, giving it an endurance of two hours. The little airship was designed to carry only one man, having a basket four feet square suspended from a bamboo framework under the envelope.

At 4.15 p.m. on 22 September 1902 Spencer took off from the Crystal Palace and flew an erratic course over the rooftops of London, crossing East Dulwich, Battersea, Victoria Bridge, Earls Court, Gunnersbury, Ealing, Acton and Greenford before making a safe landing at Eastcote at 5.55 p.m. Control throughout the flight had been only partial, the ship's engine developing insufficient power to overcome the resistance of a light southerly wind. Spencer subsequently made several more flights in his ship for advertising purposes, sponsored by various firms. He later went on to build a larger ship, but this was less successful than the first: its envelope folded up on take-off during a public demonstration at Ranelagh Gardens, and it was afterwards flown only as a free balloon without its engine.

Early in 1903, work was begun on two more British airship designs—in both cases as a private venture. The first was the creation of a medical practitioner named F. A. Barton, who took out a patent for an airship and built a small clockwork-powered model, which he demonstrated to the War Office. Surprisingly, in view of its attitude towards Colonel Templer's army airship, the War Office showed an interest in purchasing a full-size craft for £4,000, on condition that the ship would be able to remain airborne for three days with a crew of three and reach a speed of 16 m.p.h. Barton—an experienced aeronaut—must have known that it was virtually impossible to meet this requirement with the techniques that existed at that time, but he went ahead with the construction of a full-size ship in a shed at Alexandra Palace, in north London. A spate of technical snags and accidents held up the work, but the airship—180 feet long, with a capacity of 230,000 cubic feet and powered by two 50-h.p. engines—was finally ready to make its maiden flight on 22 July 1905. The craft took off safely with Barton and four others on board, but its engines were unable to develop sufficient power and it was swept several miles downwind. Finally, as the crew prepared to make an emergency landing, the ship started to fold up a few feet above the ground and collapsed in a heap of fabric. No one was hurt, but the ship was a total loss.

The other private-enterprise airship manufacturer, the firm of E. T. Willows, enjoyed far greater success. The firm had been producing balloon envelopes for a number of years, and the design of the first Willows non-rigid airship—begun in 1904— was a logical progressive step based on sound technical experience. The craft—74 feet long and 18 feet in diameter, with a capacity of 12,000 cubic feet—flew for the first time in 1905, powered by a 7-h.p. Peugeot engine. *Airship No. 2* was four times as powerful and had over twice the capacity, and on 8 August 1910, after substantial modifications, it flew from Cardiff to London in nine hours. This was followed by an even greater success on 4 November of that same year, when the airship— now named *City of Cardiff*—took off from London at 3.30 p.m. and landed at Douai in France at two o'clock the following morning after crossing the Channel in fog. It was the first time that an airship had made the Channel crossing from England to the Continent. Two more Willows airships were built before 1912, the fourth being handed over to the Royal Navy shortly before the outbreak of war in 1914. This ship—*Willows IV*— was the forerunner of a line of naval airships whose wartime exploits will be described in a later chapter.

Meanwhile, in 1907, the new Commandant of the Balloon Factory at Farnborough, Colonel John Capper, RE—who had taken over from Colonel Templer on the latter's retirement— had managed to squeeze a further £2,000 out of the War Office to continue work on the army airship project. (This at a time when Germany was spending more than £50,000 on airship development!) The flamboyant 'Colonel' Samuel F. Cody—the first man to make a powered flight in Britain, who had been attached to the Balloon Factory for three years as Chief Kiting Instructor to the Army—was commissioned to install the ship's engine and to design the gondola and steering gear.

Capper and his staff decided to use the second of the two airship envelopes designed by Colonel Templer, which had a length of 122 feet, a diameter of 26 feet, and a capacity of 55,000 cubic feet. A net slung over the envelope supported the gondola, which was little more than an open platform. The ship was fitted with a small elevator forward, and a large rudder aft—the latter based on one of Cody's kite designs. The engine selected to power the airship was French, a 50-h.p. Antoinette which cost £500 and drove two contra-rotating metal-bladed propellers.

On 10 September 1907 *British Army Dirigible No. 1*—christened *Nulli Secundus* ('Second to None')—was taken out of its 160-foot airship shed and manhandled as far as Farnborough golf course, where it made a short captive ascent followed by a flight of 1,000 yards. On this first short hop, the ship carried a crew of three: Capper, Cody, and Captain W. A. de C. King, the Balloon Factory's adjutant. More flights were made on 30 September and 3 October, when the ship stayed in the air for an hour.

These initial flights were made under conditions of strict secrecy, and the 'cloak and dagger' atmosphere that hung over Farnborough was carefully fostered by Capper—not because he wanted to prevent curious spectators from examining the ship too closely, but because he knew that it was a sure method of arousing the interest of the Press and the general public. The Press fell for the bait: before long, hotels around Farnborough were crowded with reporters, and the Balloon Factory's guards derived considerable enjoyment from winkling photographers out from behind the bushes of Laffan's Plain and sending them on their way. By this time, the Press was convinced that something new and revolutionary was under development at Farnborough, and Capper—a born publicity man—allowed the excitement to reach fever pitch before leaking the news that the

Nulli Secundus would provide the newspapers with a spectacular story in the very near future.

At 10.40 in the morning of 5 October, Capper and Cody climbed into the airship's gondola and prepared to take the *Nulli Secundus* on a flight they had been secretly discussing for some time now: a voyage across the heart of London. The timing of such a flight could hardly have been better; the Kaiser was staying in Britain as a guest of Edward VII, and the national papers carried the news that Count Zeppelin's latest airship was about to make a flight of twenty-four hours prior to being accepted by the German Army. It was high time for a British airship to make a public appearance.

The Press had not been given advance warning of the flight over London, and the reporters in the Farnborough area were taken completely by surprise when they learned that the airship had slipped quietly away from her moorings and was heading along the Aldershot–London road at a height of 800 feet. Along the route, people in fields and villages stared skywards in amazement as the sausage-shaped craft sailed overhead, its plum-coloured envelope resplendent in the sunlight. From their vantage-point in the gondola, Capper and Cody watched the broad ribbon of the Thames creep past as they reached Staines. Behind them, the ship's ground crew—seven sappers—were following at top speed in Cody's car, and over Brentford Cody reduced speed to allow a message to be dropped, informing the soldiers that he and Capper intended to circle St Paul's.

The Nulli Secundus cruised on at a steady 16 m.p.h. At noon the ship was approaching Shepherd's Bush, where thousands of Londoners, on their way home from work at the close of that Saturday morning, jostled and trampled one another in an effort to get a good view of her as she droned across the sky. It was getting steadily warmer; the gas inside the ship's envelope was expanding rapidly, and she climbed to 1,400 feet as Capper steered towards Hyde Park before turning southwards and heading for Buckingham Palace. Both he and Cody had hoped that the Royal Family and their German guests would turn out to see the airship, but they were disappointed; although they manœuvred the ship in front of the palace for several minutes, the balcony remained empty. At 12.25 p.m. the ship cruised over Trafalgar Square, and the two occupants had the satisfaction of seeing a group of officials on the roof of the War Office waving enthusiastically. A few minutes later, Capper brought the *Nulli Secundus* round the dome of St Paul's in a tight circle, heading back the way she had come at a height of 600 feet.

It was then, for the first time, that the *Nulli Secundus* ran into serious difficulty. Against the headwind, she was making almost no progress at all—and, to add to the difficulty, she was growing more sluggish as the temperature dropped and the gas inside her contracted steadily. With the strength of the wind increasing, both Capper and Cody knew that there was no chance of bringing the airship safely back to Farnborough. Instead, they decided to make for Clapham Common. It was only four miles from St Paul's, and with luck they should be able to reach it before the wind—already subjecting the airship to a severe buffeting—grew too strong.

It took the *Nulli Secundus* eighty-five minutes to cover those four miles, her engine running at full throttle. When the ship finally arrived over the Common, Capper and Cody were alarmed to find that the ground crew was not yet there; the sappers had been held up somewhere along the route among the vast crowd that streamed in the airship's wake. There was nothing for it but to try to enlist the help of the people assembled on the Common. While Cody did his utmost to hold the ship steady, Capper released gas and threw out the trail ropes, shouting instructions to the crowd below—who waved back furiously and cheered, but did nothing more. After a hurried conference, the two men decided that their best course of action would be to make for the Crystal Palace, south of the Common, and to attempt a landing on the football ground. When they arrived overhead, however, they found that a match was in progress; both players and spectators seemed frozen with amazement at the airship's sudden appearance, and the game came to a temporary halt. One enterprising player, taking advantage of the distraction, slipped through the other side's defence and scored a goal—which was subsequently disallowed by the referee!

The airship circled the Palace's North Tower, its crew looking for an alternative place to land and noting with considerable relief that the sappers had turned up at last. A few minutes later, at the invitation of the Crystal Palace's manager—who hailed them through a megaphone—Cody and Capper brought the ship down for a landing on the cycling stadium. The sappers and a host of willing helpers grabbed the trail ropes and the *Nulli Secundus* touched down with a light bump. She had been airborne for three hours and twenty-five minutes, and had covered a distance of fifty miles.

Capper and Cody hoped fervently that the weather would improve enough to allow them to fly the airship back to Farnborough, but they were disappointed. The weather grew steadily worse and the ship was marooned at the Crystal Palace for five days, her envelope reduced to a sorry state by the torrents of rain that poured down. In the end, the sodden mass had to be deflated and taken back to Farnborough by road.

The airship never flew again in its original form. It was completely redesigned as a semi-rigid, its capacity increased to 56,000 cubic feet. The *Nulli Secundus II* made its first flight in July 1908, when it reached a speed of 22 m.p.h. Several more flights were made in the Farnborough area until the middle of August, when the airship was finally dismantled.

Meanwhile, work had begun on the construction of a new army airship at Farnborough. Named *Beta*, she was 84 feet long, with a diameter of 24 feet 8 inches and a capacity of 22,000 cubic feet. She was fitted with two 8-h.p. Buchet engines, but these were found to develop only a fraction of their stated power and they were subsequently replaced by a single 25-h.p. air-cooled engine driving two contra-rotating propellers. The project ran into more trouble when the airship was found to be too short in relation to her diameter. She had to be redesigned and rebuilt, her length being extended by twenty feet and her capacity increased to 33,000 cubic feet. She was also fitted with a new power plant for the second time in her career, the 25-h.p. motor being replaced by a 35-h.p. Green engine. Reconstruction was completed in May 1910 and *Beta* made the first flight in her new form on 3 June, flying from Farnborough to London and back in four hours and four minutes. During the weeks that followed she took part in army manœuvres in the west country, covering over one thousand miles and making several night flights.

Several months earlier, in October 1909, the Balloon Factory at Farnborough had come under civilian control and a consultant engineer named Mervyn O'Gorman appointed as its Superintendent. Colonel Capper remained in control of the military side, and it was under his direction—while *Beta* was still being rebuilt—that a new army airship began to take shape. Named *Gamma*, the new craft had a capacity of 72,000 cubic feet and was powered by a Green engine developing 80 h.p. Her twin propellers were mounted on swivelling axes to provide additional control over climb and descent. Apart from her size, *Gamma* differed from *Nulli Secundus* and *Beta* in that her envelope was made of French cotton, coated with a rubberized solution, instead of goldbeater's skin. She made her maiden flight on 12 February 1910, and trials continued until August, when she was withdrawn for modifications. During this series of flights, she reached a speed of 35 m.p.h. and carried a crew of five.

Although *Beta* and *Gamma* suffered from a long succession of technical troubles during the early part of their careers—particularly with their engines, which broke down frequently—they provided the Army with invaluable experience in airship handling, both in flight and on the ground. The crews became adept in carrying out repairs in flight, and developed techniques for carrying out emergency landings without the aid of a ground crew. Several officers who were later to form the nucleus of the Army and Navy units got their first taste of flying in one or other of these craft.

The interest of the War Office in lighter-than-air craft was now rapidly awakening, although in 1910 it was overshadowed to a great extent by work in the heavier-than-air field and funds were still hard to obtain from official sources. In the summer of 1910, however, two more airships were ordered for use by the Army; both were French, one being a semi-rigid Lebaudy type and the other a non-rigid Clément-Bayard. Both ships were ordered on the recommendation of the newly formed Parliamentary Aerial Defence Committee, and considerable pressure was needed to persuade the War Office to accept the Clément-Bayard despite the fact that a large proportion of the cost was covered by a public subscription raised by the *Morning Post*. The War Office gave its provisional consent in the long run, but only on the understanding that the ship would be able to fly for three hours at a speed of 32 m.p.h. and an altitude of 6,000 feet with a crew of six and full radio equipment, that it could cover a 300-mile closed circuit course in 14 hours, and that its envelope would be strong enough to withstand prolonged exposure to a 20-m.p.h. wind while the ship was at its moorings.

While negotiations for the purchase of the Clément-Bayard were going on, another publicity campaign—launched this time by the *Daily Mail*—raised £6,000 to cover the construction of a shed for the airship. The shed, 365 feet long and 75 feet wide, with a height of 100 feet, was built in less than two months by R. Moreland and Sons Ltd. Its construction was almost entirely of metal, a thousand tons of steel being used. From then on, Lord Northcliffe and the *Daily Mail* virtually took charge of the whole business, carrying out the final negotiations between the British and French Governments and arranging the date for the airship's delivery. On 16 October 1910 the Clément-Bayard took off from Compiègne with a crew of seven on board: Alphonse Clément, the designer; Baudry, the pilot; Leprince, the second pilot; flight engineer Sabatier; mechanics Dilasser and Daire; and William du Cros of the *Daily Mail*. There was a strong tailwind and the ship made good progress, averaging 41 m.p.h. on the 246-mile flight to Wormwood Scrubs. She set up a record on the way by becoming the first airship to cross the Channel, but it was to be her one and only success. On arrival at Farnborough, where she was taken by road from Wormwood Scrubs, it was found that her envelope was in a state of rapid disintegration—the result of the severe mauling it had received during trials and manœuvres with the French Army during the preceding months. A critical examination by experts at the Balloon Factory resulted in the decision that the ship was unfit for further service, and she was dismantled—a white elephant that had cost a total of £18,000, nearly £6,000 of it in the form of public donations.

The Lebaudy airship, on which so many hopes were now pinned, seemed far more promising. Commanded by L. Capazza, she took off from Moisson on the flight to England on 26 October. There were seven people on board, including Major Sir Alexander Bannerman, who had recently taken command of the military side of the Balloon Factory following the transfer of Colonel Capper, the latter having moved on to a higher post and promotion. In spite of a light headwind, the airship reached a speed of 36 m.p.h. during the Channel crossing, outpacing a destroyer which had been detailed to escort her. After a flight of five and a half hours she arrived at Farnborough, where a ground crew of 160 guardsmen and sappers was standing by to manhandle her into her airship shed. Watched by a number of VIPs, including Lord Roberts, the ship was walked cautiously into her berth. When she was almost halfway inside, the officer in charge of the ground crew noticed with alarm that the entrance to the shed appeared to be too small, and ordered his men to stop work while he took a closer look. Almost immediately, the order was countermanded by a Brigadier on Lord Roberts's staff, who shouted imperiously to the men to carry on. The result was disastrous: the top of the airship's envelope caught the roof of the hangar and ripped wide open, sending the ground crew scattering for safety as the writhing mass of fabric deflated in a hiss of escaping gas. The damage was so serious that the Lebaudy had to be completely reconstructed. A subsequent investigation into the accident revealed that the diameter of the airship had exceeded the manufacturer's figure by ten feet.

On 1 April 1911 the Air Battalion of the Royal Engineers came into being under the command of Major Bannerman. It consisted of two companies: No. 1 (Airship, Balloon and Kite) and No. 2 (Aeroplanes). No. 1 Company was commanded by Captain E. M. Maitland, formerly of the Essex Regiment. The establishment of the Battalion was fixed at 14 officers and 176 men, but it was some time before full strength was attained.

In May, an attempt was made to recommission the ill-fated Lebaudy airship, which had been completely rebuilt—much to the detriment of her aerodynamic qualities, as the French crew who came over to test her soon discovered. When they took her up on the morning of 4 May, they found her sluggish and almost uncontrollable and brought her hurriedly down to land after only a few minutes in the air. The approach, however, was too fast and the Lebaudy skimmed rapidly over the field a few feet above the ground, the ground crew running along behind and making desperate attempts to catch hold of the trail ropes. The ship's career was brought to an abrupt halt by a house on the field boundary, into which the Lebaudy slammed with engines running flat out. The envelope burst and an explosion was averted in the nick of time by a sapper who ran forward at considerable risk and turned off the fuel. The remains of the airship were subsequently scrapped.

Meanwhile, construction of another Army dirigible—the *Delta*—was under way at Farnborough. It had actually begun over a year earlier, in February 1910, and the ship was laid down as a semi-rigid with a capacity of 160,000 cubic feet. Serious snags were encountered in the basic design, however, and the whole project was hampered by lack of funds. In April 1912 the ship was completely redesigned as a non-rigid, and it was in that form that the ship finally began test-flying the following October. She entered service a few weeks later along-side *Beta* and *Gamma*, forming the equipment of No. 1 (Airship) Squadron of the Royal Flying Corps—the old No. 1 Company of the Air Battalion, which had changed its name when the RFC was constituted on 13 April 1912. No. 1 Squadron was part of the RFC's Military Wing; the Naval Wing had only one lighter-than-air craft at this time, the non-rigid *Willows Naval Airship No. 2*, which was used for training purposes. Later, when the Royal Naval Air Service was formed out of the Naval Wing on 23 June 1914, all airships in British military service were turned over to the Royal Navy.

For several years, the Admiralty had been following the de-velopment of airships in Germany and elsewhere with far more interest than the War Office. The Navy's leading advocate of the airship was Captain R. H. S. Bacon, DSO, the Director of Naval Ordnance, who in July 1908 proposed that the firm of Vickers Sons and Maxim should be asked to submit a design for a rigid-type airship for use by the Royal Navy. This proposal was supported by Admiral Sir John Fisher and the Admiralty Board, who in turn submitted it to the Imperial Defence Committee. After a delay of six months, the Committee finally agreed—in January 1909—to ask for £35,000 to be set aside in the Naval Estimates of 1909–10 for the building of a Naval airship. The tender submitted by Vickers was eventually accepted on 7 May 1909, and construction of the airship—known as *Rigid Naval Airship No. 1*, or more popularly as the *Mayfly*—began almost immediately in a special floating shed at Barrow-in-Furness.

The ship, which was 512 feet long with a diameter of 61 feet 10 inches and a capacity of 663,518 cubic feet, was eased out of her shed for the first time on 22 May 1911 and moored to a specially constructed mast, where she remained for two days—successfully withstanding wind speeds of up to 45 m.p.h. After further tests inside her hangar, preparations were made for the *Mayfly*'s maiden flight—but as she was being manhandled from her shed on 24 September, a strong gust of wind flung her against the entrance and she broke her back. She was never rebuilt, and further airship development was abandoned by the Admiralty.

While one mishap after another combined to destroy the already shaky faith of British Government circles in the value of airships, manufacture on the other side of the Channel had been proceeding at a rapid rate—almost entirely as a private venture, for the French Government showed even more reluctance than its British counterpart to finance an airship construction programme. One of the most successful manufacturers in the early years of the twentieth century was the *Société Astra des Constructions Aéronautiques*, founded by Edouard Surcouf to manufacture balloons. The company's breakthrough into airship design came when it carried out reconstruction work on the original Lebaudy airship under contract, and not long afterwards an order for an Astra-designed ship was placed by Henri Deutsch de la Meurthe. This craft, named *Ville de Paris,* made its first flight on 11 November 1906. Damaged in a landing accident during a subsequent flight, it was rebuilt in 1907 and enjoyed a highly successful career. Thirteen more airships of this type were built before the end of 1912, and at least two were exported—one to Spain and the other to Russia. In 1911, the company's airships began to incorporate a new, internally braced envelope which afforded a significant reduction in air resistance. It had been invented by a Spaniard, Torres Quevedo, who gave his name to the line of Astra-Torres airships which later saw war service in France and Britain. The craft were built at four factories—Pau, Meaux, Rheims and Issy-les-Moulineaux—which enabled as many as six airships to be under construction at any given time.

Two more French airship companies were started as private ventures: one was *Maison Clément-Bayard*, whose first dirigible flew on 29 October 1908. It came to grief on 23 August the following year, when—after an altitude test—it made a forced landing in the Seine. One of the men on board was a Colonel Nash, a Russian officer who had been evaluating the airship for possible use by the Russian Army. The second Clément-Bayard airship was the one purchased with disastrous consequences for service with the British Army. *Airship No. 3* was more successful: on 20 April 1912 it established a new airship altitude record of 9,500 feet.

The other French firm, *Société Zodiac*, was primarily concerned with the manufacture of balloons, but it produced a series of small airships for sporting and publicity purposes which were exported to Holland, Russia and South America. The first one flew on 29 November 1908, piloted by a M. de la Vaulx.

Early in 1906, a very wealthy American named Walter Wellman arrived in France and began to take a serious interest in airship design, visiting Santos-Dumont and other pioneers. At that time, the United States was not even in the running as far as airship development was concerned. In fact, despite the exploits of the Wright brothers, few Americans had any interest at all in aviation—apart from ballooning—and those who were interested had to come to Europe in search of technical knowledge and instruction.

Wellman had a dirigible built in France to his own specification, and in June 1906 it was shipped to Virgo Bay in Spitzbergen from where the American planned to make the most ambitious airship flight attempted so far—a voyage over the North Pole. It was from this forbidding spot, nine years earlier, that the Swedish engineer and explorer Salomon August Andrée and two companions had ascended in their French-made free balloon on a similar attempt, and had vanished without trace. It was to be another twenty-four years before the details of their flight were finally known, when Andrée's diary was found beside his frozen body in August 1930.

Wellman's attempt was held up for over a year, and it was not until 2 September 1907 that his dirigible—christened *America*—took off on the first stage of what was to be the most epic flight in history. Besides Wellman, there were three others on board: his colleagues Melvin Vaniman and Louis Loud, and a Russian named Nikolai Popov. The hydrogen-filled airship, with a length of 228 feet and a capacity of 350,000 cubic feet, was powered by two 90-h.p. engines. It was capable of carrying a crew of six, but Wellman had decided on a four-man crew in order to carry extra fuel and supplies. They were not needed. After a flight of only three hours, the ship ran into very strong headwinds and began to develop engine trouble, compelling the crew to return to base. During the days that followed the weather grew steadily worse, and, with the prospect of making a second attempt before the following year becoming increasingly remote, the venture was abandoned.

Wellman, however, lost no time in organizing another project: a flight across the Atlantic from west to east. The *America* was subjected to a number of modifications, including the addition of a 300-foot steel cable to which several floats were attached. The idea was that the airship would tow these floats over the surface of the water, using them to stay at a constant altitude of 300 feet. If she rose above that height, the floats would lift clear of the water and their weight would pull the ship down again—in theory, at least.

The *America* took off from Atlantic City on 10 October 1910 and set course eastwards, trailing her floats behind her. On this occasion, the ship carried a crew of six: Wellman, Vaniman, J. R. Irwin, Loud, Aubrey and an Englishman, Captain

1. A 'dirigible' built and flown by the Russian engineer Dr K. I. Danilevsky in 1898. Powered by the oar arrangement shown in the photograph, the machine was a failure —although its inventor claimed to have made progress against a headwind during one flight in August 1898

2. The British *Nulli Secundus*, which first flew on 10 September 1907, seen after its rebuilding

5. The Lebaudy airship *Morning Post,* ordered by the British Government and paid for by public subscription, makes its first flight at La Roche Guyon on 14 September 1910

4. The maiden flight of the Lebaudy dirigible *République,* on 24 June 1908. It was 200 feet long and powered by a 4-cylinder, 70-h.p. Panhard engine

3. The Zeppelin *LZ.3* in October 1909, newly fitted with a third car and a third pair of propellers

6. The ill-fated Vickers Rigid Airship No. I—the *Mayfly*. Riding on the surface of the water in Cavendish Dock, Barrow (summer, 1911)

7. The end of the *Mayfly*. Its back broken, it lies half in its shed and half in the water (September 1911)

8. The Zeppelin *LZ.8 Ersatz Deutschland,* one of the first commercial Zeppelins, built in 1911

9. The DELAG Zeppelin *LZ.11 Viktoria Luise,* in 1912

10. The *Willows Dirigible No. I*, seen in December 1912, with the *Beta* in the background

11. The French *Clément-Bayard VII*

12. The German Army Zeppelin *Z.4* (*LZ.16*), seen on a visit to France in 1913

13. An experimental French airship of 1913: the Spiess rigid

14. A mechanic checks an engine in flight on board a French Navy Astra-Torres

15. Convoy protection during the First World War: an early British Submarine Scout dirigible approaches a convoy, its crew on the lookout for the tell-tale wake of an enemy periscope

16. The destruction of the Zeppelin *L.31*, commanded by Kapitänleutnant Heinrich Mathy, at Potter's Bar on the night of 1–2 October 1916

17. The end of the Zeppelin *L.34*, commanded by Kapitänleutnant Max Dietrich, over Hartlepool on the night of 28–9 November 1916

18. The Zeppelin *L.20* wrecked on landing in Norway, 3 May 1916

19. The remains of the Zeppelin *L.33* after a compulsory landing at Little Wigborough, Essex, on 23 September 1916

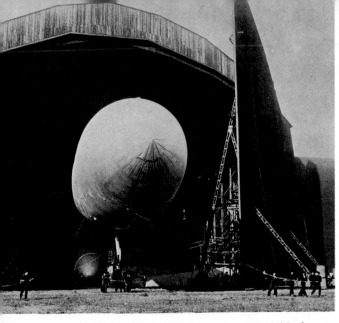

20. The British *SS.4* being towed out of its hangar

21. A British NS (North Sea) non-rigid airship

22. A British SS-type coastal non-rigid in service with the French Navy in 1917. The combined control and engine gondola is nothing more than the fuselage of a B.E. 2C aircraft

23. View aft from the cockpit of a French Navy Astra-Torres dirigible, in 1918

24. The crew of an Astra-Torres dirigible make identification of a freighter in the Mediterranean, 1918

25. 26. 27. A Royal Naval Air Service blimp undergoing mooring trials in 1918. A gust of wind hits it . . . a spar breaks . . . and the ship collapses. Such experiences led to more sophisticated methods of mooring

28. The British *R.33* about to land

29. Part of the ground equipment at Pulham Airship Station, Norfolk: a tank used to tow open the doors of the big hangar

Murray Simon, who was acting as navigator. Apart from some trouble with the engines, the flight appeared to be going well until, several hours after take-off, the ship ran into bad weather. She was buffeted by severe turbulence, and as the storm lashed the sea into a fury the trailing floats made matters worse by causing a violent pitching motion. For eighty-six hours the crew endured misery, saturated and racked with sickness, as the airship was swept along at the mercy of the wind. At last, off the coast of New England, they sighted a ship; she was British, the RMS *Trent*. Taking advantage of a short lull in the storm, the crew brought the airship down to the surface and ditched her, launching their small lifeboat. Wellman and his colleagues were picked up safely, but the *America* was a total loss.

After this abortive attempt, Wellman lost interest in long-distance airship flights. Not so his engineer, Melvin Vaniman, who believed that the flight could have succeeded if a more advanced airship had been available. Vaniman drew up plans for a new ship with a capacity of 400,000 cubic feet, the biggest non-rigid craft designed up to that time.

The problem was to find a fabric light and strong enough to provide a suitable envelope for the new ship. From various sources, Vaniman learned that such a fabric was being produced by the Goodyear Tire and Rubber Company at Akron, Ohio. Several months earlier, a Goodyear representative had visited the North British Rubber Company in Edinburgh, which had invented a method of insulating fabric by coating it with layers of extremely thin rubber film, applied by a machine to ensure even distribution. Negotiations were immediately opened which resulted in the British company being licensed to use certain Goodyear tyre patents, in return for which Goodyear acquired American rights to the rubberizing process. One of the machines was shipped to Akron, together with an experienced operator named Charles Ferguson. Fabric treated with this process did not absorb moisture, which meant that there was no tendency for it to rot. Tensile strength was increased by 10 per cent without any increase in weight. On an aircraft's wing the fabric stayed tight and reduced surface resistance, and initial tests in the air showed an average speed increase of 5 per cent. The Wright brothers were the first to order the new fabric, and by the end of 1911 most of the country's leading aviators were using it. Its success was finally assured when it became a requirement for US Army and Navy aircraft.

Vaniman went to Akron and managed to persuade Goodyear's president, F. A. Sieberling, to finance the new airship. Work on the envelope began in June 1911, while Vaniman—assisted by several Goodyear engineers—built the gondola in Atlantic City. The ship, named *Akron*, was of the semi-rigid type and had a near-perfect cigar shape. A long cylindrical fuel tank comprised the keel; attached to it was a V-shaped structure of lightweight tubular steel, covered in fabric, which served the dual purpose of providing rigidity for the envelope and forming the airship's gondola. The ship was powered by two main Stearns-Knight automobile engines, specially modified, and a third auxiliary motor purchased from France. The engines were mounted sideways on the frame, the crankshafts being extended several feet on both sides to drive the airship's three sets of twin propellers. The rear propellers, driven by the auxiliary engine, were mounted on a swivelling axis. The 285-foot ship was completed in the autumn of 1911 and made a short trial flight on 4 November, after which it was laid up in its hangar until the following year. During this time several modifications were made, including the installation of new gas valves.

The *Akron* had been the subject of a great deal of publicity during its construction, and as the months dragged by without any attempt to make a second flight the public and the Press began to grow restless and highly critical. As a result of this pressure, Vaniman decided to make a demonstration flight before tests on some of the airship's equipment had been completed. On 2 July 1912 the *Akron* rose from her moorings at Atlantic City and headed out to sea, watched by an enormous crowd. Fifteen minutes later, a terrific explosion ripped through her and she plunged seawards, a blazing wreck. Horrified, the spectators saw the bodies of the four-man crew drop clear and tumble into the water like broken dolls. The cause of the disaster was never fully established, but it was thought that the new gas valves had been too tight, causing the envelope to burst under pressure as the ship ascended. Another contributory factor may have been the hydrogen itself, which was produced with the aid of a very ancient generator and, according to a French engineer who assisted Vaniman, was full of impurities. Whatever the true facts may have been, the loss of the *Akron* marked the end of serious airship work in the United States for several years to come. The Goodyear Company, however, still convinced that lighter-than-air travel had a future, did design several airships for commercial use during 1912–13— but plans to build these were frustrated by the outbreak of war in Europe, as a result of which the company's facilities were fully committed in other directions. It was not until 1917 that airship production in the USA really began to get into its stride.

In 1912, with ominous storm-clouds gathering over Europe, Germany held an undisputed world lead in the development of airships for military purposes. Yet it was not in Europe that the airship received its baptism of fire, nor was the craft of German design.

In October 1911 an Italian expeditionary force had landed in North Africa with the task of establishing full Italian sovereignty over Tripoli by force of arms. The invasion met with fierce resistance from Arab guerrillas, actively supported by the Turkish Government, and Italy found herself involved in a war with Turkey that was to end only a year later, when Turkey became fully committed to the Balkan conflict. In the meantime, thousands of Italian troops became hopelessly bogged down in Tripoli, making hardly any progress in the fight against an elusive enemy.

Early in 1912, the Italian Expeditionary Force received air support in the shape of two recently acquired Army dirigibles, the *P.2* and the *P.3*. Both were small non-rigid types, designed by an engineer named Forlanini. Their first operational mission was flown on 10 March 1912, when they carried out a reconnaissance over Arab positions and dropped several grenades, without doing any damage. On 13 April, during another reconnaissance mission, they remained airborne for thirteen hours, their crews spotting for the Italian artillery. Several more reconnaissance and bombing sorties were flown by the two ships before they were withdrawn in June. Some of the later bombing missions were highly successful, the airships' crews breaking up concentrations of Arab tribesmen with well-directed grenades.

The contribution made by the two airships in Tripoli was in no way decisive, and it was severely restricted by weather and technical troubles. In a small way, however, it was a foretaste of things to come.

5 The Airship at War

At the outbreak of war on 4 August 1914, the German Army possessed five Zeppelin airships, numbered *Z.4* to *Z.9*. On 6 August, one of these craft the *Z.6 (LZ.21)*, flew the first German airship combat mission of the war when it dropped 500 pounds of bombs on Liège. The ship was damaged by anti-aircraft fire on its way back from the target, and crashed on landing at Bonn.*

The German Navy's Airship Division was in no position to mount any such offensive operation. It still possessed only one airship, the *L.3*, and its personnel strength of 12 officers and 340 men fell a long way short of the authorized establishment of 414. The big new airship base at Nordholz was as yet only partially completed, which meant that missions over the North Sea had to be flown from the rented DELAG base at Fuhlsbüttel. Any such missions would be limited to reconnaissance, for no bombs of any kind had so far been delivered to the Airship Division.

Two days after the outbreak of hostilities, an urgent conference was called at the Admiralty to lay down the basis of a crash expansion programme. This resulted in an immediate order for the production of a series of Zeppelins with a capacity of one million cubic feet and for the setting up of hangars to accommodate them. Unfortunately, the Zeppelin Company was in no position at that time to meet the demand; the largest airship that could be constructed in the existing shed at Friedrichshafen was of the 800,000 cubic foot *L.3*-type. Work on a new construction shed, financed by Navy funds, was begun at once, but in the meantime the Admiralty was forced to order

* For details of all airship operations during the First World War see Appendix II.

ten *L.3*-type airships to fill the gap until the more advanced Zeppelins came along. Two more new construction sheds—one belonging to the Army at Löwenthal, the other converted from the DELAG hangar at Potsdam—were also taken over by the Navy.

With a delay of several weeks anticipated before delivery of the first *L.3*-type craft, the Navy requisitioned a non-rigid Parseval airship, the *PL.6*, on 9 August 1914. She was found to be unsuitable for operations in anything but the calmest weather, and was finally relegated to a training role. A second Parseval, the *PL.19*—one of four originally ordered by the British Admiralty, three of them having been turned over to the German Army when war broke out—was loaned to the Navy on 19 September and subsequently made many patrol flights over the Baltic from Kiel, flown by an Army crew. She carried up to 1,260 pounds of bombs and had a duration of over eleven hours. A third Parseval airship, the *PL.25*—which was being built under an Army contract at the start of the war—was also turned over to the Navy for operations over the Baltic at a later date.

The Army's own Zeppelin airships, meanwhile, had been suffering heavily in action. Following the loss of the *Z.6* on the third day of the war, the *Z.8* was destroyed on 22 August by a French 75-mm. artillery battery, and on 28 August the crew of the *Z.5* was forced to surrender to Russian troops after the ship was badly damaged near Mlava. A shell put the *Z.5*'s rudders out of action, and she drifted helplessly over the heads of a Russian cavalry brigade. The crew took the opportunity to drop a couple of bombs, which killed twenty-three Russians, before the airship came down in a nearby wood. The Russians captured the whole crew with the exception of the commander, Captain Grüner, who had been killed by small-arms fire. A fourth airship, the *Z.9* (*LZ.25*), was destroyed on 8 October, when aircraft of the Royal Naval Air Service raided the Zeppelin sheds at Düsseldorf. It was the *Z.9* which, on 25 August, had started a big atrocity outcry against the Germans by dropping nine bombs on Anvers in Belgium, killing or injuring twenty-six civilians and damaging the royal palace.

The first of the Navy's new airships, the *L.4* (*LZ.27*) was completed on 28 August, the same day that the Army's *Z.5* was lost. She was followed by the *L.5 (LZ.28)* on 22 September. All ten craft in this series were completed by February 1915 and were quickly pressed into service, the Admiralty successfully resisting attempts by the General Staff to acquire the ships for Army use. During the first two months of the war, the German Navy's airship operations were carried out single-handed by the *L.3*. For much of the time she was employed in training, but during the first week of the war she made two coastal reconnaissance flights over the German Bight, on the lookout for marauding British warships. The Admiralty expected the British to mount a full-scale naval attack in the Bight without delay, and when two unidentified vessels were sighted off the Dutch coast by a unit of the High Seas Fleet on 11 August, the airship was immediately sent out to investigate. Off the island of Terschelling, after a flight of 170 miles, the crew of the *L.3* sighted the Dutch battleship *De Zeven Provincien* with an escort of four destroyers, and reported their position.

Six days later, on 17 August, the *L.3* flew a reconnaissance mission over the Skagerrak, 300 miles from her base at Fuhlsbüttel, on the orders of Konteradmiral Franz Hipper, who commanded the scouting elements of the High Seas Fleet. British warships had been reported in the area, but none was sighted by the *L.3*'s crew.

Several more fruitless patrols were flown during the days that followed. Then, early in the morning of 28 August, the alarm suddenly went up. Warships of the Royal Navy's Harwich Force had entered the German Bight and were dealing out severe punishment to patrolling German destroyers. The *L.3* was hastily ordered to proceed to the scene of the action, and at 8.40 a.m. her crew sighted the first German destroyers, scurrying eastwards for the shelter of Heligoland. On the horizon, almost hidden by the morning mist, the airshipmen caught a glimpse of the British warships. At that moment, one of the *L.3*'s engines started to give trouble and her commander decided to return to base. Had he been able to continue the flight, he would almost certainly have spotted the battle cruisers *Lion*, *Queen Mary* and *Princess Royal*, and so averted a massacre; as it was, the British warships succeeded in trapping three German light cruisers and destroying them.

As more Zeppelins came into service, the Airship Division was able to extend its scouting operations considerably. On 19 October the *L.5*, commanded by Oberleutnant zur See Hirsch, made a sixteen-hour reconnaissance flight over the North Sea to within sixty miles of Great Yarmouth without sighting any British warships, and as a result of his report a force of German battle cruisers made an ineffective raid on the port a week later. On 25 October Zeppelin *L.4*, commanded by Graf von Platen, flew a scouting mission in the vicinity of the islands of Borkum and Norderney, narrowly missing a sighting of the Harwich Force. The latter was escorting three seaplane carriers—converted cross-Channel packets—whose task was to launch an air raid on the German airship base at Cuxhaven. The attempt was frustrated by bad weather, but a month later—on 21 November—three Avros of the Royal Naval Air Service attacked the Zeppelin factory at Friedrichshafen, their bombs narrowly missing the shed containing the partly completed *L.7*.

On the night of 24 December the Harwich Force again penetrated the German Bight, together with the seaplane carriers *Empress*, *Engadine* and *Riviera*, carrying nine Short seaplanes between them. The force, which was sighted and shadowed by a German submarine, hove-to at 7.00 the following morning and the carriers hoisted out their aircraft. Two of them failed to get off the water, but by 8.00 the remaining seven were on their way to the target—Cuxhaven. As soon as the submarine's report was received, the Naval Airship Division was ordered to take offensive action against the British ships. Only the *L.5* and the *L.6* were operational—the *L.3* was undergoing modifications to her control surfaces and the *L.4* was grounded by dense fog at Fuhlsbüttel—and they took off from Nordholz within just over an hour of each other and headed westwards.

At 9.12 the *L.5* sighted three of the British seaplanes over the River Weser and alerted Nordholz, which by this time was also shrouded in fog. At 9.25 one of the British aircraft was spotted through a gap and fired on by machine guns. The aircraft came

94

down to a thousand feet and released two bombs at a big gaso-meter, but they missed and exploded harmlessly in a nearby wood.

Meanwhile, shortly after 8.30, the *L.6*—commanded by Ober-leutnant zur See Horst Baron von Buttlar—had arrived over the Harwich Force and begun its attack. One 100-pound bomb was released at the *Empress*, missing the target by a good hundred feet, after which von Buttlar sheered off into the clouds as anti-aircraft fire began to come up thick and fast. When he landed at Nordholz, having lost contact with the enemy, he found ten bullet holes in the ship's gas cells.

At 11.30, three of the British seaplanes, out of fuel, landed near the British submarine *E.11*. The submarine had just picked up the crew of the last aircraft when the silver shape of a Zeppelin appeared overhead. It was the *L.5*, and she dropped two bombs—both of which missed—as the *E.11* started to sub-merge. After shooting up the three abandoned seaplanes with his machine guns the Zeppelin's commander, Hirsch, continued his patrol westwards, shadowing the British warships until they withdrew over the horizon at 12.25.

Experimental in nature though they still were, the Navy's Zeppelins were beginning to prove their worth, and a plan now formed to extend their role to offensive operations over the British Isles. The plan had actually originated some three weeks after the war began, but it had to be shelved because the handful of Navy airships available during the last months of 1914 were fully committed to patrol and reconnaissance duties. Early in October the Army General Staff also indicated its intention to mount Zeppelin raids on England from bases in the occupied areas of France and Belgium, but since these bases would not be ready for another six months, and because combat losses had by this time reduced the Army's effective Zeppelin force in the west to the old ex-DELAG ship *Sachsen*, the plan came to nothing. A suggestion by General Erich von Falkenhayn, the Chief of the Army General Staff, for a joint Army and Navy bombing offensive against the British Isles in December 1914 was not viewed with favour by the Admiralty. The lack of interest was understandable, for the Army's idea of joint co-operation involved the turning over of the seven Navy Zeppelins that were then under construction, together with complete crews, for their own use.

The Army's airship losses were made good to some extent in the autumn of 1914, with the entry into service of Zeppelin *Z.10* (*LZ.29*) and the transfer of the Schütte-Lanz airship *SL.2* from the Eastern Front, where it had been operating in support of Austrian ground forces in the Krasnik sector. Strength was increased still further in November and December, when the *Z.11* and the *Z.12* also became operational.

On 25 December the Army used its small fleet of airships to raid the French towns of Nancy, Dunkirk and Verdun. The German Navy immediately requested the release of its own airships to attack selected targets on the east coast of England, but the request was turned down by Tirpitz, who believed that the bombing of these targets by single airships would have little or no material effect. He advised Admiral Hugo von Pohl, the Chief of Naval Staff, to defer such a move until both Army and Navy were in a position to mount a maximum-effort raid on London with all available airships.

Another serious obstacle to the Navy's plans at this time was the Kaiser himself, who was unwilling to authorize the bombing of targets in Britain—and particularly in London. To be fair to the German Emperor, he had no wish to see the destruction of historic places in Britain's capital, and the idea that such raids might result in death or injury to his 'royal cousins'—the British King and Queen—horrified him.

It all added up to frustration for the crews of the Airship Division. By the middle of December the Division had enough airships to carry out both the primary task of reconnaissance in co-operation with the High Seas Fleet and long-range special missions over England, and every new delay in obtaining authority to undertake the latter type of operation meant that favourable weather conditions were being allowed to slip by. There was also the danger that the Navy's new airships might be destroyed in enemy air attacks before they could be used to good effect, and this fear was expressed in a letter to von Pohl from Konteradmiral Philipp, the Chief of German Naval

Aviation. Pressure from Philipp and other senior naval commanders finally resulted in von Pohl seeking an audience with the Kaiser on 7 January 1915, in which the Admiral stressed the importance of attacking military objectives in England during the months of January and February, when weather conditions for long-range airship operations would be at their best. He requested the Kaiser's approval to attack targets of military importance on the lower Thames and in London itself, giving his assurance that the airship crews would take great pains to spare historic buildings and private property.

Reluctantly, the Kaiser gave his consent to air attacks on docks and military installations on the lower Thames and the east coast of England—but not in London itself. After months of waiting, the Airship Division could at last go ahead with its plan, already worked out in minute detail by Peter Strasser. The plan, submitted to von Pohl on 10 January 1915 for his final approval, involved attacks on Tynemouth, the Humber, Great Yarmouth, Lowestoft, Harwich and the Thames Estuary by three airships, which would bomb their targets at dusk after a daylight flight over the North Sea and return to their bases under cover of darkness.

The first attempt to raid England, made on 13 January, was abortive. Four airships actually set out—the *L.3* and the *L.4* from Fuhlsbüttel, the *L.5* and the *L.6* from Nordholz—but they ran into heavy rain and were forced to turn back. The second attempt was made on the 19th, when the *L.3,* the *L.4* and the *L.6* took off under the command of Strasser himself. The first two airships were to raid the Humber, while the *L.6*'s objective was the Thames. Five hours after take-off, the *L.6*—with Strasser on board—developed serious engine trouble off Terschelling and was forced to turn back. The other two Zeppelins, each carrying a load of eight 110-pound explosive bombs and ten 25-pound incendiaries, crossed the English coast at 8.50 p.m. and 9.30 p.m. respectively. An unexpectedly strong wind had caused them to drift a long way south of their intended track and they made landfall over Norfolk. The *L.3*'s commander followed the coast and dropped his bombs on Great Yarmouth, causing some damage and killing two people, while the *L.4*

97

released her load on King's Lynn, killing a woman and a small boy.

Three aircraft of the Royal Naval Air Service had been on readiness at Great Yarmouth air station when the Zeppelins made their attack, but they never took off. Even if they had done so, they could not have gained height quickly enough to effect an interception. Both airships consequently returned to base completely unscathed.

On 12 February 1915 the following Imperial Directive was issued to the German Naval Staff and the Army General Staff:

1. His Majesty the Kaiser has expressed great hopes that the air war against England will be carried out with the greatest energy.

2. His Majesty has designated as attack targets: war material of every kind, military establishments, barracks, and also oil and petroleum tanks and the London docks. No attack is to be made on the residential areas of London, or above all on royal palaces.

This was interpreted by both Army and Navy as an authorization to attack targets in East London, and considerable rivalry developed between the two services for the honour of being the first to bomb the British capital. In the event it was the Navy who made the first attempt, using Zeppelin *L.8*. Commanded by Kapitänleutnant Helmut Beelitz, the airship took off from Düsseldorf on 26 February, only to be forced down at an army base near Ghent by violent headwinds. On 1 March, Beelitz was ordered to return to Düsseldorf. On his own initiative, he decided to make a second attempt to fly to England from the Belgian base, and on 4 March the *L.8* set course for the Essex coast with a war-load of 70 incendiaries. At Nieuport, on the Belgian coast, Beelitz came down through the overcast to get his bearings and the *L.8* was promptly greeted by a storm of small-arms fire from the Belgian trenches directly beneath. Beelitz hurriedly jettisoned all his ballast and bombs, together with a large quantity of fuel, and headed away from the danger area at top speed. Eighty-five miles from Düsseldorf, the airship's engines suddenly failed. Losing hydrogen rapidly through dozens of bullet-holes in her gas cells, she slid stern-first towards the ground and crashed into a row of trees. Only one member of the crew was killed, but the ship was totally wrecked.

A few days after the loss of the Navy's *L.8*, the Army moved several of its airships to advanced bases in Belgium and France from their permanent stations in the Rhineland. The ships involved were the Schütte-Lanz *SL.2* and the Zeppelins *Z.10*, *Z.12* and *LZ.35*. (After the *Z.12*, the Army had reverted to the Zeppelin factory designation for their airships. The reason was mainly one of superstition: under the old system, the *LZ.34* would have become the *Z.13*.) These airships took off in an attempt to raid England on 17 March, but the island was covered in dense fog and they turned back with their bombs still on board. The *Z.12* dropped her load on Calais on the way home, but was damaged on landing at her base and was out of action for two weeks afterwards.

Preparations to make another attempt were thwarted when, on 18 March, the Kaiser issued an Imperial Directive vetoing any air attack on London for the time being. No such directive was extended to Paris, however, and on 20 March the three remaining Army airships set out to raid that city. The *SL.2* never reached the capital; she developed engine trouble and dropped her bombs on Compiègne. Of the other two airships, the *Z.10* was shot down near Saint-Quentin on her way home. Only the *LZ.35* bombed the target successfully and returned home safely, but she too was destroyed in a forced landing on 13 April, after being hit by French anti-aircraft fire near Ypres. As the *SL.2* had been withdrawn for reconstruction after the raid of 20 March, this left the Army with only one airship, the *Z.12*, on the Western Front, effectively destroying their hopes of any further operations against England for some weeks to come.

On the morning of 14 April the naval airship *L.9*, commanded by Kapitänleutnant Heinrich Mathy, set out on a reconnaissance flight to the west of Terschelling. She carried ten 110-pound explosive and 40 incendiaries, and after flying all day without sighting any British ships Mathy obtained permission to carry out a raid on a British coastal target before returning to base. The objective Mathy had selected was Tynemouth, with its complex of shipyards, but landfall was made at Blyth, some miles to the north, and the *L.9*'s commander mistook the River Wansbeck for the Tyne. Most of his bombs fell harmlessly in open country around the area's mining villages, although two people were injured at Wallsend when a near-miss damaged their house. Convinced that he had inflicted considerable damage on the Tyne's shipyards, Mathy steered for home.

Encouraged by what he believed to be *L.9*'s successful mission, Peter Strasser ordered another raid on Britain the following day. The three airships involved on this occasion were the *L.5*, the *L.6* and the *L.7*, with Strasser himself flying as a passenger in the latter aircraft. The old *L.5*, commanded by Kapitänleutnant Alois Böcker, dropped her bombs on Lowestoft and set fire to a lumber yard, while von Buttlar in the *L.6*—with no idea of his position—released his load on a town that later turned out to be Maldon in Essex. The *L.7* returned to base without sighting any kind of target, although the ship had actually crossed the darkened English coast without the crew knowing it.

Böcker and the *L.5* almost came to grief a few weeks later, on 12 May, while attempting to raid England again. Flying towards the Humber at just under 5,000 feet, the ship ran through a shower of sleet which coated her envelope with a layer of ice. Then two of her engines failed and the overladen ship stalled, dropping rapidly towards the sea. Böcker saved the situation just in time by jettisoning the whole bomb-load, the airship righting herself a few hundred feet above the sea. Fighting a strong headwind, with only two engines working, the *L.5* limped homewards and finally came down near Namur, where she remained for a week until she was made sufficiently airworthy to fly back to Nordholz.

As a result of this near-disaster, Strasser decided to withdraw the older *L.3*-type Zeppelins from long-range raiding operations and confine them to scouting duties in support of the fleet. The decision was further strengthened by the fact that both the *L.3* and the *L.4* had been destroyed within hours of each other off the Danish coast in February, fortunately with only small loss of life, after a spate of mechanical troubles had developed during a reconnaissance flight along the Norwegian coast.

From now on, the air raids on England would be carried out by the improved Zeppelin types which were being completed at Friedrichshafen. The first of these, the *L.10*, entered service on 17 May 1915 and was the forerunner of nine more airships of a similar class, all with a capacity of 1,126,000 cubic feet, which were to be purchased by the Navy before the end of the year. The ships were 536 feet 5 inches long, with a diameter of 61 feet 4 inches, and they were powered by four Maybach C-10 engines of 210 h.p. They could cruise at 11,000 feet and fly as far as the west coast of England with two tons of bombs on board.

The advent of the new Zeppelins, however, came too late to enable the Navy to strike the first blow against London. Early in May, the first of the Army's new airships—the *LZ.37*, the *LZ.38* and the *LZ.39*—joined the *Z.12* in Belgium, and after one or two probing attacks on Southend, Ramsgate and Bury St Edmunds, the *LZ.38* flew to London on the night of May 31 and dropped 3,000 pounds of bombs on the north-east sector of the capital, killing seven people and causing damage amounting to over £18,000.

The Navy's first attempt to reach London was made on 4 June, using the *L.10*. The ship ran into strong headwinds over the English coast and her commander, Hirsch, decided to bomb what he believed to be the naval base at Harwich instead of the primary target. In fact, his bombs went down on Gravesend; he could easily have reached London before dawn, but he had mistaken the lights of the capital for those of Ipswich. This attack was made in conjunction with a raid by the Schütte-Lanz airship *SL.3*, which had entered naval service a few weeks earlier. The airship crossed the coast near Flamborough Head, with Hull as its objective, but its bombs fell harmlessly in open country.

Hull was raided successfully on 6 June by Heinrich Mathy in the *L.9*, which released ten explosive and fifty incendiary bombs on the town. Several fires were started, causing damage amounting to £45,000. It was the most destructive raid carried out over England so far.

The three new Army Zeppelins also took off that same night to attack London, but none of them reached England. The *LZ.38* developed engine trouble and had to return to her base at Evère, near Brussels; she had only been back in her shed a matter of hours when two RNAS aircraft from Dunkirk swept down out of the darkness and dropped their bombs through the roof, totally destroying the airship.

Meanwhile, the *LZ.37* had also run into trouble. Over Ostend, she had been sighted by Flight Sub-Lieutenant R. A. J. Warneford, who had been on his way to bomb the enemy airship sheds when the Zeppelin loomed out of the clouds ahead of him. The RNAS pilot stalked the airship in his little Morane Parasol, climbing until he was directly above her. Taking careful aim, he released his bombs, which ripped through the Zeppelin's envelope. The ship burst into flames and dropped like a stone, exploding in the grounds of a convent near Ghent, killing all her crew. The *LZ.39* was also attacked by an aircraft near Ghent, but she escaped in cloud and returned safely to base.

Following the loss of the two Army ships, a tentative plan by the Navy to stage its own airships at forward bases in Belgium was hurriedly abandoned and the next raid on Britain was made from Nordholz by the *L.10* on 15 June. The objective was Tynemouth, and the ship profited from unexplained inactivity on the part of the defences to inflict considerable damage on industrial installations, many of which were brightly lit. During this raid, for the first time, the airship made use of radio bearings, direction-finding signals being transmitted from Borkum and Nordholz.

Because of the limited period of darkness, no further raids were made on British targets until 9 August, when the *L.9*'s bombs killed sixteen people at Goole, in Yorkshire. Four other airships—the *L.10*, the *L.11*, the *L.12* and the *L.13*—also set out that night to raid London, but all of them failed to reach their objective. The *L.13*, commanded by Mathy, was forced to turn back with engine trouble and the others, defeated by dense rainclouds, dropped their bombs haphazardly. The *L.12* was

hit by a three-inch anti-aircraft shell at Dover and came down
in the sea off the Belgian coast. She was towed into Ostend by a
patrol boat, and survived an attack by three RNAS aircraft
the following morning. As the ship was being dismantled, her
forward section caught fire and was totally destroyed; fortunately her after section was still in the water and did not burn,
enabling at least part of the wreck to be salvaged.

Another abortive raid was made on 12 August, when four
airships set off for London. Only two reached England, and
only one, the *L.10*, found a target to bomb, causing slight damage
in Harwich. The other, the *L.11*, turned back with her bombs still
on board and nearly came to grief when she ran through a violent thunderstorm over the sea. It was almost the same story
on 17 August, when another four-Zeppelin mission set course
for England; two of the airships developed mechanical trouble
and had to turn back, while a third—the *L.11* again—dropped
her load on Ashford and Faversham. The fourth airship, however, succeeded in reaching London and dropped her bombs on
the north-east suburbs, causing considerable damage and killing
ten people. The ship was the *L.10*, and her commander, Ober-
leutnant zur See Friedrich Wenke, became the first Naval officer
to bomb the British capital.

The *L.10* was normally commanded by Klaus Hirsch, and it
was he who was on board when the ship set out on a North Sea
reconnaissance on 3 September. On her way back to Nordholz,
she exploded near Neuwerk Island and crashed in the sea with
the loss of all nineteen crew.

On 7 September 1915 it was once again the Army's turn to
raid London. The ships involved were the new *LZ.74* and the rebuilt *SL.2*. The latter bombed Millwall, Deptford, Greenwich
and Woolwich docks, causing a great deal of damage, while the
LZ.74 released most of her load on Cheshunt. She dropped one
incendiary—all she had left—on the City of London. Targets
in Britain were attacked again the following night, but only one
ship managed to reach London; she was Mathy's *L.13*, and her
bombs started a huge fire among the textile warehouses to the
north of St Paul's. In this one raid, Mathy caused one-sixth of
the total damage inflicted on Britain during all the air raids of

the First World War; the total loss amounted to over half a million pounds.

Mathy's success was followed by a raid on 13 October which, although it inflicted less material damage, was the most devastating of the whole war in terms of human life. Five airships took part: the *L.13* and the *L.16* from Hage, and the *L.11*, the *L.14* and the *L.15* from Nordholz. The *L.11* dropped her bombs soon after crossing the coast and did little damage, but the others went on to bomb London and its docks, killing 71 people and injuring 128.

It was the last airship raid made on Britain during 1915. For the remaining weeks of the year, the Navy's Zeppelins were either employed on co-operation work with the Fleet or were grounded by bad weather. When operations began again in January 1916, they were directed against targets spread along the whole length of England—and even further, for Edinburgh was bombed for the first time on the night of 2 April by the *L.14*, sending £44,000-worth of whisky up in flames when a warehouse was hit. The first raid of the year, on 31 January, was made on Liverpool by nine Naval airships; one of them, the *L.19*, came down in the North Sea and was lost with her entire crew.

Up to the beginning of 1916, the air defence of Britain had been the task of the Royal Naval Air Service, which was ill-equipped to deal with the Zeppelin threat. Early in February 1916, however, the air defence role was turned over to the War Office, which took immediate steps to counter the night raiders by increasing the number of anti-aircraft batteries up and down the country and forming a number of Royal Flying Corps squadrons whose primary role was that of night fighting. Nevertheless, the British airmen failed to make contact with the Zeppelins during the spring raids of 1916, and on 2 May— the day after a raid by five airships on east-coast targets— the Royal Navy attempted to launch an air strike on the Zeppelin sheds at Tondern. The raid was a complete failure from the start, eight out of eleven new Sopwith Baby seaplanes failing to get off the water, but the warships escorting the seaplane carriers *Engadine* and *Vindex* succeeded in shooting down the Zeppelin *L.7*, which had been detailed to shadow the British force off the island of Sylt.

The five-airship raid of 2 May was the last for nearly three months, for the Navy's Zeppelins were now almost entirely committed to scouting operations over the North Sea in preparation for the emergence of the High Seas Fleet from its base at Wilhelmshaven—an offensive foray that was to culminate in the Battle of Jutland on 31 May. The airships, however, were prevented from playing a vital part in the battle by bad weather and poor visibility.

On 30 May 1916 the Airship Division received the first of a new class of Zeppelin—the *L.30*. Powered by six Maybach HSLu engines, she had an overall length of 649 feet 7 inches, a diameter of 78 feet 5 inches and a capacity of 1,949,600 cubic feet. Her maximum speed was 62 m.p.h., and her ceiling over 17,000 feet. She could carry five tons of bombs, and had a defensive armament of up to ten machine-guns.

The *L.30* and her sister ships formed the spearhead of a new striking force with which the Naval Airship Division began a renewed air offensive against Britain in July 1916. With eighteen airships at his disposal, Strasser—for the first time—was able to plan the raids from a position of moderate strength, and this was demonstrated on 24 August when thirteen airships—including the Schütte-Lanz craft *SL.8* and *SL.9*—set out to attack southern England. Only Mathy in the *L.31* reached London; the others either turned back for various reasons or dropped their bombs on the east coast.

On 2 September the biggest raiding force of airships assembled during the entire war left their bases and set course for England. There were sixteen of them: eleven Navy craft and five Army, the *LZ.90*, the *LZ.97*, the *LZ.98*, the *SL.8* and the brand-new *SL.11*, completed only a month earlier. As the ships droned out over the sea, their crews could not know that this mission would mark the death-knell of the hope so fondly cherished by Strasser and other airship advocates in the German Navy: that England could be beaten to her knees by Zeppelin-borne fire from the skies.

Two of the attackers—the *L.17* and the Army's *LZ.97*—ran

into bad weather and had to turn back. The other Army ships crossed the English coast at various points some way ahead of the Navy craft; the *LZ.90* dropped her bombs on Norfolk before sheering off seawards once more, while the *LZ.98* and the *SL.11* approached London from the south and north respectively. Flying over the capital's northern suburbs, the *SL.11*'s commander, Hauptmann Wilhelm Schramm, released his bombs singly on landmarks which, as a boy, he had known well—for London had been his birthplace. Past Tottenham the airship came under heavy fire and Schramm changed course abruptly, heading northwards once more to drop bombs along the Enfield Highway. Minutes later—shortly before the *SL.11* dropped the last of her load on Forty Hill and Turkey Street—she was sighted by three Royal Flying Corps pilots of No. 39 (Home Defence) Squadron; they were Lieutenant William Leefe Robinson and Second Lieutenants J. I. Mackay and B. H. Hunt. All three went after the ship, and Leefe Robinson was the first to catch up with her. After a long climb to get within range of the airship, he stalked her as she slipped in and out of the probing searchlight beams. Then, from a distance of 800 feet, he emptied two drums of explosive ammunition into the silvery envelope. Away in the distance, the crews of the Naval airship droning steadily towards London saw a sudden brilliant light burst across the sky. Horrified, they watched the burning mass that had been the *SL.11* slide towards the darkened earth. One ship, the *L.16*, was close enough to be lit up by the lurid flames and was pursued by another RFC pilot, but she got away and headed for the coast at full speed. Two of the other airships aborted because of bad weather, but the remainder succeeded in bombing their respective targets.

The wreckage of the *SL.11* fell at Cuffley, where the remains of her crew were buried with full military honours. Her passing marked the end of the German Army's participation in the raids on Britain.

The Navy was not so ready to admit defeat, although Strasser's operational plans suffered a serious setback when the *L.6* and the *L.9* were destroyed in a hangar fire at Fuhlsbüttel on 16 September. Both these airships had been employed on training duties, and their loss meant a serious delay in the training of new crews.

The loss of the *SL.11*, although it had not deterred the Navy from mounting further raids, nevertheless persuaded Strasser to act with more caution. Although the older types of Zeppelin continued to raid targets in the provinces, subsequent attacks on London itself were carried out by the new 'Super-Zeppelins' operating in small numbers, and they too began to suffer as the British defences grew more organized. During the next raid, on the night of September 22–3, two of them were shot down. The *L.33*, damaged by anti-aircraft fire and air attack, crash-landed virtually intact in a field near West Mersea, while the *L.32* was sent down in flames near Billericay by Second Lieutenant Sowrey, flying a B.E. 2C. Heinrich Mathy in the *L.31* was more fortunate: he bombed London, killing twenty-two people and injuring seventy-four, before making his escape pursued by heavy gunfire. But even Mathy's days were numbered: on the night of 1–2 October 1916 he and his crew were killed when the *L.31* was shot down at Potters Bar by Second Lieutenant W. J. Tempest. The first people to reach the wreckage found Mathy's body sunk into the ground; he had chosen to leap clear rather than die in the inferno of blazing hydrogen.

Before the end of the year two more airships went down over England, bringing the total loss to six—all within four months of operations. The day of the large-scale Zeppelin raids was over, and from the beginning of 1917 the air offensive against London and the south of England was progressively taken over by heavier-than-air machines such as the big Gotha G and Zeppelin R types, which were reaching the squadrons of the German Flying Corps in increasing numbers by the winter of 1916–17.

Operations against more distant British targets, out of range of the bombers, were still undertaken by the Airship Division, although such raids had little more than a nuisance value. The majority of raids were made with a new generation of Zeppelins known as 'height climbers', which made their appearance early in 1917. These ships had a capacity of two million cubic feet and were 682 feet in length. They were powered by five (later six) Maybach engines, and—stripped of machine-guns and other heavy equipment—were capable of climbing to over 20,000 feet, far above the maximum ceiling of the aircraft used by the RFC for home defence up to the end of 1917.

The last major raid on Britain by the 'height climbers'—known as the 'Silent Raid' because the ships flew at maximum altitude—was carried out by seven Zeppelins on 19 October 1917. The raid was a disaster, with five out of the eleven airships that set out being lost. From then on, the number of airships operating over Britain on any one raid never exceeded five. The last raid of the war was made on 6 August 1918, and was intercepted by aircraft from Great Yarmouth air station. Zeppelin *L.70* was shot down by Major Egbert Cadbury, flying a DH.4, and fell blazing into the sea with the loss of all her crew. Among them was the man who had upheld the Naval Airship Division through four years of war, often in the face of bitter criticism: Peter Strasser.

Between January 1915 and August 1918, the German airships had made a total of fifty-one raids on Britain, dropping 196 tons of bombs. They had killed 557 people and injured 1,358, as well as inflicting damage amounting to £1,527,585—£850,109 of it in the London area. Most of the damage had been done during 1915, when the Zeppelins were able to roam virtually at will over England with little fear of the defences; during that year 27 airships had actually raided England out of the 47 that set out, and between them they caused £815,865-worth of damage for the loss of one of their number. During 1916 111 airships had attacked British targets, but the damage they caused was only £594,523, and six of them had been destroyed. From then on, the damage toll dropped steadily and airship losses increased. Towards the end of the war there was a marked drop in efficiency when useful load had to be sacrificed in favour of ballast, to enable the ships to climb above the worst anti-aircraft fire. If the airships had not achieved Strasser's aim of inflicting crippling material and psychological blows on Britain, however, they had made a considerable contribution to the German war effort in an indirect way: by the end of 1916, the Zeppelin threat had tied down in Britain twelve RFC squadrons and 110 aircraft, not to mention hundreds of guns and searchlights. The total number of personnel involved was 17,341 officers and men—and this at a time when both men and equipment were desperately needed in France.

Yet throughout the war, the primary task of the Naval airships had remained reconnaissance, although such operations were severely curtailed by adverse weather conditions and tailed off drastically towards the end of hostilities. Far more could undoubtedly have been achieved if the Navy had exploited the capabilities of its airships to the full; the later craft were capable of remaining airborne for 100 hours and enjoyed a range of 3,000 miles with a full fuel load. Operating in conjunction with submarines, they could have wrought havoc on the Allied convoys in the North Atlantic.

Such was the weight of propaganda surrounding the airship raids on Britain that it is for this type of operation that the Zeppelin is best remembered. The hardships and losses suffered by the Naval airship crews, however, were greatly overshadowed by those experienced by their counterparts in the Army Airship Service, in the early part of the war at least. Many of the missions they flew were suicidal, the airships operating at low level over enemy concentrations despite the hideous vulnerability of the hydrogen-filled gas cells to small-arms fire. Apart from that, the Army Airship Service suffered from a complete lack of any central command, and was dogged by more than its share of bad luck: several of its craft were lost in accidents, not all of them attributable to bad handling.

The Army made extensive use of Schütte-Lanz airships, despised by the Navy because of the vulnerability of their wooden structures. The first of the Army's wartime Schütte-Lanz craft, the *SL.5*, was destroyed on the ground by a thunderstorm following her last trial flight before acceptance on 4 July 1915, and her crew was assigned to her sister craft, the *SL. 7*, which—after suffering severe damage during her trials in the autumn of 1915—finally entered service in November. On 21 February 1916, together with three other Army airships, she bombed railway junctions around the fortress of Verdun; two of the accompanying airships were shot down, one—Zeppelin

LZ.77—coming down in flames over Brabant with the loss of all her crew.

Most of the Schütte-Lanz ships were subsequently sent to the Eastern Front, leaving the Zeppelins—with their higher ceiling—to carry out air operations over the improved defences of the Western Front. In the northern sector, several of the Army's ships were placed under Naval command and used for scouting flights over the Baltic. They included Zeppelins *LZ.130* and *LZ.120*, the only six-engined, 2,000,000-cubic foot craft to serve with the Army. Other Army airships on the Eastern Front operated as far afield as Ploesti and Bucharest before the Army Airship Service was finally disbanded on 1 August 1917. On its dissolution, most of the airships were either dismantled or handed over to the Navy.

When the Armistice came in November 1918, control of the German airship bases was seized by revolutionary seamen of the 'Sailors' Soviet', who plundered vast quantities of supplies and sold them on the black market in Sweden. The airships themselves were hung up in their sheds and deflated. Not all the men of the Airship Division, however, were in the grip of revolutionary fervour; the flight crews remained loyal to the Kaiser almost to a man, as did many of the veterans among the ground crews, and when the German Fleet was scuttled in Scapa Flow on 21 June 1919 a long-standing conspiracy to destroy the remaining airships was translated into action. On the morning of 23 June groups of conspirators entered the airship sheds at Nordholz and Wittmundhaven and destroyed seven Zeppelins by allowing them to fall from their suspension ropes on to the concrete hangar floors.

To frustrate further attempts, the Inter-Allied Control Commission demanded the immediate surrender of the eight remaining airships. Orders were also issued for the demolition of the Zeppelin works at Friedrichshafen: the Allies were determined that the German airship industry should not be resurrected. The factory was in the event saved by the intervention of the United States Government, which—annoyed that none of the airships seized as war booty had been allocated to it—demanded that the Zeppelin facilities be used for the construction of an *L.70*-type airship for the US Navy. It was this demand alone that saved the Zeppelin Company from extinction during the immediate post-war years, and paved the way for the expansion that resulted in the giant passenger-carrying ships that were to carve out new air routes across the world in the years to come.

BRITISH AIRSHIP OPERATIONS

The loss of the *Mayfly* in September 1911 and the Admiralty's subsequent loss of enthusiasm left Great Britain with no rigid airship, either building or projected. Interest in other circles, however, was still very much alive, and in June 1912 the Imperial Defence Committee sent Murray Sueter and Mervyn O'Gorman on a tour of France, Austria and Germany to study airship development in those countries. At Friedrichshafen the two men were given a demonstration flight in the airship *Viktoria Luise*, and came away suitably impressed. On their return to Britain, they reported that 'German airships have, by repeated voyages, proved their ability to reconnoitre the whole of the German coastline on the North Sea. In any future war with Germany, except in foggy or stormy weather, it is probable that no British war vessels or torpedo craft will be able to approach within many miles of the German coast without their presence being discovered and reported.' Although this report was treated seriously by the Defence Committee, a strong case submitted by Sueter and O'Gorman for the immediate building of another rigid airship was rejected on the grounds that no Naval personnel were suitably trained to operate it. As a first step towards putting this state of affairs to rights, however, the Naval Airship Section—disbanded after *Mayfly* was wrecked —was reformed and attached to the Military Wing of the Royal Flying Corps, which was then operating the non-rigids *Beta, Gamma* and *Delta*.

In 1913, Captain Sueter's persistence paid dividends when he was finally authorized to order two airships for Naval use. The first of these was one of the well-tried French Astra-Torres non-rigid types of 350,000 cubic feet capacity; she was followed shortly afterwards by a German Parseval airship, ordered as a second choice when the Germans refused to part with one of their Zeppelins. An Italian semi-rigid craft designed by Forlanini was also evaluated, and one was ordered. So were four more Parsevals, but the outbreak of war prevented their sale to Britain. The Parseval ships were retained by Germany, and the Italian craft was requisitioned for service with the Italian Army.

On 23 June 1914 the Royal Naval Air Service was formed, and the small number of airships serving with the RFC were turned over to the Navy. On the outbreak of war, the Astra-Torres and the Parseval were immediately allocated to coastal patrol duties. The average length of each patrol was twelve hours, and the first under war conditions was flown on 10 August. These early patrols were not without incident: on more than one occasion, the British airships were mistaken for Zeppelins and fired on by friendly forces.

Four more airships were ordered towards the end of 1914: one a Parseval, built under licence by Vickers, and the others Astra-Torres types. It would be some time, however, before they were ready to enter service, and in the meantime the German submarine threat was assuming grave proportions. In October 1914 the Germans had captured Ostend and Zeebrugge, and from these bases U-boats were beginning to make things unpleasant for Allied shipping in the Channel. Three ships were sunk by submarines in the Channel area before the end of 1914, and in the first hours of 1915 the battleship *Formidable* was torpedoed off the coast of Devon.

In an attempt to counter the new menace, seaplane bases were hurriedly established at Dover and Dunkirk, and from these a number of air attacks were made on the German bases. Then, early in 1915, came the disturbing information that a new type of German submarine, ninety feet long and designed to operate in coastal waters, was under construction at Antwerp. Bombing raids on the shipyards had little effect, and it soon became clear that the only immediate solution to the threat was to set up an efficient network of air patrols over home waters.

On 28 February 1915 the First Sea Lord, Admiral of the

Fleet Lord Fisher, recommended the construction of a large number of fast, inexpensive airships for coastal patrol work. The prototype for these craft was the *Willows No. 4*—known as *Naval Airship No. 2* in Admiralty service—and her conversion had been completed by 18 March 1915; she entered service under the designation *SS.1* (*Submarine Scout No. 1*). Twelve more non-rigid ships were ordered from Airships Ltd—a company formed by the amalgamation of a raincoat-manufacturing firm, which made the envelopes, and a firm of furniture manufacturers, who built the gondolas. The first ship to be produced, *SS.2*, was a failure, but subsequent craft were successful, and the Admiralty placed follow-on orders for thirty-eight more. The crafts' instruments and valves were produced by Short Brothers, the aircraft manufacturers who were at that time employed in the construction of a highly successful series of seaplanes for the RNAS. Shorts in fact designed and built an airship of their own—the *SS.3*—as a contender for the SS order, but although she did well in her acceptance trials at Kingsnorth the order went to the other company. The *SS.3* had a capacity of 60,000 cubic feet, and, like the *SS.1* (*Willows No. 4*), her gondola consisted of the fuselage of a B.E. 2C aircraft, with its wings removed.

By the end of July 1915, airship bases had been set up at Polegate and Folkestone and at Marquise near Calais, and a few weeks later an additional station was established at Anglesey. From these bases, daily patrols were flown when weather permitted. The task of the airship crews was far from easy: it was almost impossible to spot a submerged submarine beneath the murky waters of the Channel and the Irish Sea, and only experience could teach the crews what tell-tale signs revealed a U-boat's presence.

The SS ships had a capacity of 70,000 cubic feet and were powered by a single engine varying in power from 75 to 100 h.p. They carried a crew of two, and their endurance was up to sixteen hours at a speed of 40 m.p.h. Altogether, 150 ships of the SS type were built; the standard SS type was later progressively replaced by more advance variants, the SS 'P', the SS 'Zero' and the SS 'Twin'. The 'P' type was driven by a pusher propeller, and had an endurance of seventeen hours at 43 knots. The 'Twin' carried a crew of five, while one of the 'Zeros' demonstrated its endurance capability by making a flight lasting 50 hours 55 minutes.

Towards the end of 1915, by which time the initial order of fifty airships had been completed, the SS craft were joined in service by a vastly improved airship known as the C (Coastal) Type. Very similar to the Astra-Torres, the C Type had a capacity of 160,000 cubic feet and was powered by two 180-h.p. Sunbeam engines. A crew of five was carried, one of them manning a machine-gun mounted on top of the envelope. Endurance was more than twenty-four hours, which allowed a substantially wider radius of action. Twenty-four C Type airships were built, and they were followed in turn by a still larger version. This was the C*, a ship of 200,000 cubic feet capacity with a length of 218 feet and a speed of just under 60 m.p.h. Like the basic C Type, the C* carried a crew of five. Ten of these ships were built.

The last and most successful of the British non-rigid airships was the NS (North Sea) Type, which entered service in 1917 and was still in use after the war. The NS ships had a length of 262 feet and a capacity of 360,000 cubic feet. They were powered by two 240-h.p. engines and the enclosed gondola had accommodation for a crew of ten, the latter split into two watches. Two hundred NS ships were built and on operations they logged patrol flights of fifty hours or more. In December 1918 one of these ships, the *NS.11*, made a record flight for a non-rigid airship by staying airborne for 61 hours 30 minutes while sweeping an area of the North Sea for mines. On 17 July 1919 this airship was destroyed when she fell into the sea in flames after being struck by lightning.

For most of the time, the job of patrolling the sea approaches to Britain was one of sheer monotony. There were occasional breaks in the boring routine: on the night of 28–9 August 1916, for example, III Army Corps asked the Navy to carry out a reconnaissance flight over the Somme in an area where the Germans were believed to be preparing a large-scale counter-attack. The *SS.40* was sent out, her underside painted black, but

because of the danger from anti-aircraft fire her crew were forbidden to fly lower than 8,000 feet over the enemy lines, and
nothing of significance was reported.

There were hazards, too; the majority encountered during
routine flights but others while new methods of making the
airship a more effective weapon were being tested. Early in
1916, with the British defences still completely unable to cope
with marauding Zeppelins, two Naval officers—Commander
N. F. Usborne and Lieutenant-Commander de Courcy W. P.
Ireland—began to experiment with the idea of an SS-type craft
being used as a 'mother ship' for a B.E. 2C aircraft. The idea
was that the aircraft would be carried aloft by the airship, which,
with its greater endurance, would be able to cruise around for
several hours on the lookout for incoming Zeppelins. When one
of the latter was sighted, the aircraft would be released from its
position under the airship's hull to make its attack on the raider.
It was an excellent idea in principle, but in practice it ended in
disaster. During a trial flight on 21 February 1916 the aircraft
became detached prematurely and went out of control, crashing
and killing both its occupants.

On other occasions, the airship proved to its naval crews that
it could be brutally unmanageable at times. On one such occasion, an SS airship was flying from its base on the South Coast to
another in the Midlands when it ran into thick fog and the pilot
decided to land. Bringing the ship down to within a few feet of
the surface, he ordered two crew members to jump out and
secure the trail rope. As they did so, the ship's engine cut out
without warning and the craft shot up rapidly to 5,000 feet, drifting out to sea. After forty-five minutes of frantic effort—which
involved clambering along the outside of the engine gondola and
swinging the propeller by hand—the pilot managed to restart
the engine and regain control, after which he headed for dry
land again and made a safe landing.

Another Naval airship pilot, Flight Lieutenant E. F. Monk,
was faced with considerably worse an ordeal. On 15 September
1916 he brought his ship, the *SS.42*, back to her station after a
patrol in bad weather off Lundy Island. As the craft was being
moored, a sudden squall dashed her violently against the ground

and tore away most of the gondola's port suspension ropes. The wireless operator was thrown out, but Monk hung on as the gondola turned almost upside down. The airship was whisked into the air again, and Monk caught a fleeting glimpse of Caldy Island before the clouds enveloped him at 3,000 feet. The next land he saw was Lundy Island, which the airship skirted at a height of about 7,000 feet. A few minutes later, without warning, the forward starboard suspensions—which had been supporting most of the weight of the engine—also snapped and the gondola dropped sickeningly into a vertical position. Somehow, Monk managed to retain his grip as the gondola swung down, and he now scrambled forward to a position of temporary safety on the undercarriage axle. At 2 p.m., three hours after her runaway flight began, the airship—now at 8,000 feet—started to fall. She dropped slowly at first, but her speed gradually built up and by the time she fell out of a cloud bank over the Devonshire countryside she was spinning quite rapidly. A second or two before the *SS.42* crunched to earth in a field near Ivybridge, Monk jumped clear and escaped with only slight back injuries.

It was not until June 1917 that the convoying of merchant ships as protection against submarines became an established practice, and the British airships were used extensively for this type of work. Although opportunities for attack were few and far between, the presence of airships over the Western Approaches, the Channel and the Scandinavian shipping routes forced the U-boats to travel submerged, with a consequent reduction in speed and the time spent on station.

The most active airship base in Britain was at Mullion, in Cornwall. During 1917, when the convoy protection system was getting into its stride, the Mullion airships flew a total of 2,845 hours. One of them, the *C.9*, covered more than 70,000 miles on patrol between her commissioning in July 1916 and the end of the war. One of her most adventurous patrols occurred on 3 October 1917. Together with other airships from Mullion, she was heading for home in the teeth of a rising gale when her captain, Flight Commander Struthers, saw an Italian freighter burst into flames about six miles astern. Struthers at once turned the airship and sped downwind towards the stricken ship, arriving overhead in a matter of minutes. Almost immediately, he spotted the periscope of a U-boat, lying just under the surface about half a mile away. Sailing overhead, the *C.9*'s commander dropped all his bombs, straddling the U-boat, and called up a pair of destroyers, which plastered the area with depth-charges. There was no time to watch the result; the airship was now battling against the full force of the gale, and as she struggled homewards winds of up to sixty miles an hour reduced her ground speed almost to nothing. It took her six hours to cover the forty miles back to base.

In all, nearly four hundred non-rigid airships of all types were produced in Britain during 1915–18, and the record they achieved was quite remarkable. Together, they covered more than two and a quarter million miles on patrol, losing only forty-eight officers and men through all causes, including enemy action. The task of the Naval airship crews had seemed unrewarding: cruising for long hours over grey seas and under grey skies had been a job far removed from that of the Navy's heavier-than-air pilots, whose exploits had been much publicized. It was only after the war, when the records of the German Navy—including the reports of submariners who had operated in British waters—were made available that the full contribution made by the airships in keeping open Britain's lifelines at last became known.

Meanwhile, work on rigid airships in Britain had languished since the loss of the *Mayfly*. In 1914 Vickers had started work on another rigid design, the *R.9*, and everything was ready for the building of the prototype when war broke out and the funds allocated were diverted to what were considered more urgent priorities. The project was revived towards the end of 1915, and the airship was completed in November of the following year. She was not, however, delivered to the Naval Air Service until April 1917, following extensive modifications.

In January 1916, the Admiralty invited Short Brothers to build two rigid airships based on the *R.9*'s design. After a number of programme changes, the firm eventually received a firm contract to build the *R.31* and the *R.32*, both of which were the

creation of the designers of the Royal Corps of Naval Constructors. Prominent among these designers was a Swiss named
Müller, who had worked for Schütte-Lanz, and the influence
of the German design was apparent in the wooden framework of
the two British airships.

To build the new ships, Short Brothers received a government
loan of £110,000 towards the construction of a 700-foot double-
bay airship shed at Cardington, near Bedford. The first airship
to be completed was the *R.31*; she made her first flight in August
1918 and reached a speed of 70 m.p.h., faster than any other
airship then flying. Powered by six 275-h.p. Rolls-Royce Eagle
engines, the ship was 615 feet long and 65½ feet in diameter, with
a capacity of 1,547,000 cubic feet. The control cabin was fitted
well forward, flush under the hull, giving access to a walkway
stretching along the inside of the hull to the tail. A metal ladder
from the control car led to the machine-gun positions on top of
the hull; there were more machine-guns under the tail-cone,
in the gondolas and along the walkway.

During initial trials, it was found that the *R.31*'s fuel con-
sumption was unexpectedly high, and it was decided to remove
one of her engines; this resulted in a drop in speed of only 5
m.p.h. The airship was finally commissioned on 6 November
1918, having logged a total flying time of nine hours on her
trials. During her delivery flight to East Fortune that same day,
some of her glued joints began to come apart and she had to be
hastily docked at Howden in Yorkshire, in a shed whose roof
had been destroyed by fire. A downpour of rain did the rest;
within a matter of days, she had been damaged beyond repair.
Her remains were subsequently sold to a coal merchant for £200.
The man thought he had a bargain, but complaints from dozens
of angry customers soon showed him otherwise: the airship's
wooden framework, specially treated with fireproof chemicals,
stubbornly refused to burn.

During the last year of the war five Vickers-built rigids entered
service. They were all modifications of the basic *R.9* design, and
they saw little active service. The first three, the *R.23*, the *R.24*
and the *R.25*, were 535 feet long, with a capacity of 997,500
cubic feet and a speed of 55 m.p.h. The other two were known as

the 23x Class; they had a maximum speed of 57 m.p.h. and carried a useful load of 7½ tons. Four were ordered, but only two—the *R.27* and the *R.29*—were completed. The *R.29*, commanded by Major G. M. Thomas, DFC, of the RAF, assisted in the sinking of a German submarine during the last weeks of the war and logged flights of up to 32 hours' duration. The *R.27* enjoyed a less fortunate career: in August 1918 she was destroyed in a hangar fire at Howden—the same hangar in which the *R.31* was docked, to her cost, three months later.

Several other British rigid airships, laid down during the war, were not completed until after hostilities had ceased; they included the *R.32*, the *R.31*'s sister ship, and they will be described in a subsequent chapter.

FRENCH AIRSHIP OPERATIONS

On the outbreak of war, the French Army had fifteen non-rigid airships, mostly of Astra-Torres or Clément-Bayard design. The total also included two ships produced by the Zodiac company and a small non-rigid, the *Fleurus*, built by the State Airship Factory at Chalais-Meudon.

It was the *Fleurus*, commanded by Captain Tixier, which made the first Allied airship raid of the war on 9 August, operating out of Verdun. That same day, another French airship—the Clément-Bayard *Conté*, commanded by Captain Frugier—ran into a storm of French machine-gun fire that lasted ten minutes and limped back to base with 1,300 bullet-holes in her envelope; she was out of action for three months. Another Clément-Bayard, the *Dupuy-de-Lôme,* made two short forays into Belgium from her base at Maubeuge during the early days of the war, and on 20 August she dropped six bombs near Genappe and Louvain. Four days later, on the 24th, she was fired on by French troops as she flew low over Reims. She was hit hundreds of times, and one of her crew members, Lieutenant Jourdan, was killed. The airship crashed near Courcy, the remaining crew members escaping with only slight injuries.

A third Clément-Bayard, the *Montgolfier*, had been stationed at Maubeuge alongside the *Dupuy-de-Lôme*. A small craft of only

233,000 cubic feet capacity, she was powered by two 70-h.p. engines giving her a maximum speed of 36 m.p.h. and a ceiling of 7,700 feet. She, too, fell foul of trigger-happy French gunners; on 20 August she was hit by French artillery fire and forced to land, but she was quickly repaired and made a reconnaissance flight over the enemy lines the following night. Soon afterwards Maubeuge was overrun by the Germans and the airship was transferred to Saint-Cyr, from where she made a twelve-hour flight on 13 October. Her last operational mission was flown from Toul on 26 December 1914; together with the *Fleurus*, she was subsequently relegated to a training role and remained in service until 1918.

Meanwhile, the *Conté* had been repaired and was back in service at the beginning of November. On 8 November she was ordered to attack German rolling stock at Tergnier railway junction. Crossing the front line at a safe height under cover of darkness, she hovered over her objective and dropped her bombs, inflicting considerable damage, and returned to base safely.

The French airships were still being fired on regularly by their own troops; the crews had already been forbidden to fly daylight missions because the ships' low ceilings made them easy targets, and now, in January 1915, operations were suspended altogether until more advanced airships arrived at the front. The break lasted until April, during which time the Army evolved a system of signalling which, it was hoped, would enable the French troops to recognize the friendly airships without difficulty.

In April 1915, the *Conté*—which had been the only French airship at the front in an operational condition for the past four months—was joined by two more Clément-Bayard craft, the *Adjudant Vincenot* and the *Commandant Coutelle*. The *Conté* flew one more mission before being deflated because of trouble with her envelope, and the *Coutelle* made only two operational flights before being shot down on the French side of the lines on 22 September 1915. The *Adjudant Vincenot* went on to become the most successful French Army airship of all, making a total of thirty-one operational flights.

In September 1915, an improved Astra-Torres airship—the *Alsace*—arrived at the front. She had a capacity of 530,000 cubic feet, and her two 120-h.p. engines gave her a speed of 43 m.p.h. and a ceiling of 13,000 feet. During September this airship carried out a series of raids at night in Champagne, but on the night of 2 October she was hit by anti-aircraft fire while flying low over the lines in bright moonlight and forced down. One crew member jumped clear before the impact and was killed; the other six were taken prisoner.

Shortly after the loss of the *Alsace*, two Zodiacs—similar in size and performance to the Astra-Torres—were sent into action. The first, the *D'Arlandes*, was stationed at Verdun and her sister, the *Champagne*, was sent to Toul. The Zodiac ships were 335 feet long; they could carry a ton and a half of bombs and were armed with machine-guns mounted on top of the envelope. Three more airships were also nearing completion at this time, two of them enlarged *Fleurus* types, the *Tunisie* and the *Lorraine*, and the third an Astra-Torres named the *Pilâtre de Rozier*. Only the latter was destined to see service at the front; of the others, the *Lorraine* became a training ship at Saint-Cyr and the *Tunisie* was handed over to the French Navy, together with her crew.

Of the three airships already at the front during the first half of 1916, the *Champagne* was severely damaged by a shell on 21 May and the *Adjudant Vincenot* was put out of action by small-arms fire on the night of 2–3 June. That left the *D'Arlandes* as the only ship at the front until the autumn of 1916, when the *Champagne* re-entered service after being repaired and the *Pilâtre de Rozier* arrived. The latter was already outclassed by the German anti-aircraft defences, and it was clear that the Army needed still larger and more powerful ships. But the French Navy also had an urgent requirement for airships, and the constructors found themselves unable to meet the demands of both services for new ships and the sheds necessary to house them, mainly because of an acute shortage of steel. In December 1916, therefore, it was decided to turn the remaining Army airships over to the Navy for anti-submarine patrol duties over the Mediterranean early in the New Year.

When the deadline for the handover arrived on 24 February 1917, however, the Army only had one operational airship left. The previous day, the *Pilâtre de Rozier*—commanded by Captain Prêcheur—had left Epinal to make a ten-hour reconnaissance flight, but over the village of Voellerdingen she had caught fire and exploded in mid-air, killing all her crew; while the *Champagne*, no longer considered airworthy, had been withdrawn from service on 22 February.

The remaining airship, the *D'Arlandes*, was subsequently based on Corfu for minesweeping duties, and operated until the end of 1917. On one occasion, in October, she located no fewer than eighteen mines while sweeping ahead of a convoy.

The French Navy had received its first airship in January 1916, some two months after the French Admiralty had decided to form a naval airship service along similar lines to that of the RNAS. The first airships to enter French Naval service were three SS-types, purchased from Britain; they were followed by the ex-Army *Tunisie* shortly afterwards. Airship stations were set up at Le Havre, Rochefort, Aubagne, Cherbourg, Brest, Oran and Algiers during 1916, and these were joined by four more at Corfu, Paimboeuf, Arachon and Ajaccio the following year. The three SS ships were based on the Channel, where they were joined in April by two more SS 'Zeros'. The SS-types shared the task of patrol and anti-submarine reconnaissance with several small Zodiac 'vedettes', with capacities of 90,000 and 110,000 cubic feet. Their two 80-h.p. engines gave them a speed of up to 50 m.p.h., and their endurance was twelve hours.

The *Tunisie*, meanwhile, had been sent to Bizerta on the North African coast. A fortnight later another airship also arrived; she was the *T.1*, a product of the Airship Factory at Chalais-Meudon. Commanded by Captain Caussin, she disappeared with all hands off the coast of Sardinia in May 1917. Her successor, the *T.2*, had a capacity of 312,000 cubic feet and a length of 267 feet; she was powered by twin 240-h.p. engines giving her a speed of 50 m.p.h. Throughout her career she was based at Paimboeuf under the command of Captain Leroy.

The Chalais-Meudon factory subsequently built four more

non-rigid airships for the French Navy, all of them with a capacity of 194,000 cubic feet. The *Société Astra-Torres* built a series of much larger craft; the first four, designated *AT.1* to *AT.4*, had a capacity of 230,000 cubic feet and an endurance of twenty-four hours, and they were followed by five more craft (*AT.5* to *AT.9*) of similar design but with an increased capacity of 260,000 cubic feet. One of the Astra-Torres ships made the longest flight of any French airship during the war, remaining airborne for 37 hours 15 minutes. Five other airships of 260,000 cubic feet capacity were built by the Zodiac Company; some of these were armed experimentally with a 75-mm. gun in the bows for the purpose of attacking submarines on the surface.

Many of the larger airships were based in North Africa until the end of the war, employed on convoy surveillance duties. Unfortunately, very little information exists about their operational service. Most of them were deflated shortly after the end of hostilities, although at least two Astra-Torres and a small number of Zodiac 'vedettes' were retained in service for several years after the war.

UNITED STATES AIRSHIP OPERATIONS

In 1916, influenced by reports of the success then being enjoyed by British non-rigid airships on patrol duties around the coasts of Britain, the US Navy began developing a similar type of craft. It was originally intended that only one small non-rigid airship should be built and used for experimental purposes, but in February 1917—with the possibility of the USA's entry into the war looming closer—the Navy Department ordered sixteen non-rigid airships to be built immediately. The Goodyear Company were awarded a contract to build nine of the ships and to erect a testing and training establishment at Wingfoot Lake, not far from Akron.

The first ship, the B Type, was completed within two months and made her maiden flight in May 1917, two weeks after the United States declared war on Germany. She made several trial flights, including one of twelve hours' duration, and work went ahead on her sister ships at a rapid rate. Meanwhile, the first of 600 volunteers for the Navy's airship service had begun their training at Wingfoot Lake.

The last of the nine airships ordered from Goodyear was delivered in June 1918 and joined the others in service at various patrol air stations along the Atlantic coast of the United States from Chatham, Massachusetts, to Key West in Florida. Up to the end of the war the airships spent 13,600 hours in the air and covered over 400,000 miles on patrol duty. Although they had been designed with a maximum endurance of sixteen hours, some of them logged flights of up to forty hours' duration. In the summer of 1918, when the Germans stepped up their U-boat campaign against shipping off the Atlantic coast, the airships sighted and bombed enemy submarines on at least two occasions, and on another they drove off a U-boat which was attemping to lay mines in the shipping lanes off New York Harbour.

In 1918 Goodyear received a Navy contract to design and build a more advanced airship known as the C Type. It incorporated numerous improvements, including twin engines that gave it a top speed of 60 m.p.h. The first of thirty ordered under the Navy contract was completed in September 1918 and carried out a series of successful trial flights, but with the signing of the Armistice a few weeks later the Navy Department cancelled twenty of the new ships.

No American-built airships were sent overseas during the First World War, but in October 1917 an agreement between the French and United States Governments was made whereby the French Naval Base at Paimboeuf was to be handed over to the US Navy as soon as sufficient American airship crews had completed their training. The handover took place in March 1918, the French giving two of their naval ships—the Astra-Torres *AT.1* and the Zodiac 'vedette' *VZ.3*—to their American allies. In April, the US Navy asked for ten more French airships to equip three additional bases at Gujan, Rochefort and Guipavas. In the event, only four ships were delivered: these were the Zodiac 'vedette' *VZ.7*, delivered in June, the Astra-Torres *AT.13* in August, and the *VZ.13* and the Chalais-Meudon *T.2* in October. The last never became operational with the Americans, suffering a series of accidents during her acceptance trials;

of the remainder, the *AT.1* was shipped to the United States and the *VZ.3* returned to the French Navy after the Armistice.

The French-built non-rigids based on Paimboeuf had the task of patrolling coastal waters and escorting convoys off the mouth of the Loire, in conjunction with seaplanes. The only sighting of an enemy submarine took place on 1 October 1918, when the *AT.13* located a U-boat on the surface between La Pallice and Quiberon Bay. The airship commander elected to turn back and warn the convoy he was escorting of the submarine's presence, and no attack was made.

AIRSHIP OPERATIONS IN OTHER COUNTRIES

After Germany, Britain and France, the only other European belligerent to use airships in any number was Italy. At the outbreak of war the Italian Army had two main types of airship in service, one built by the Corps of Engineers under the direction of Ricaldoni and Crocco and the other, a semi-rigid type, designed and built by Forlanini. At the beginning of 1915 there were eleven airships in service, eight of them non-rigids with a capacity varying between 150,000 and 420,000 cubic feet, and the other three semi-rigid Forlaninis with a length of 234 feet, a capacity of 400,000 cubic feet and a useful lift of four tons. The latter were powered by twin 80-h.p. engines, giving them a speed of 40 m.p.h.

Although a few of the Italian airships were used for anti-submarine patrol work, the majority were employed on reconnaissance missions over the Austrian lines throughout the war. Most of these missions were flown in daylight, and the losses sustained were fearful, several of the airships being shot down by Austrian aircraft. The first to be destroyed in this manner was the *M-2*, commanded by Felice di Pisa, which was shot down in flames by an Austrian aircraft while returning from a bombing raid over Trieste on 8 June 1915. A sister airship, the *M-4*, was shot down on 4 May 1916 by two Brandenburg C.1s and a Fokker monoplane near Gorizia. A month later, on 3 June, the airship *M-5* was destroyed in an unfortunate accident involving a collision with a Caudron aircraft of the Italian Air Corps.

The year 1917 was a particularly black one for the small Italian Airship Service. On 22 May the *M-12* was hit by Austrian anti-aircraft fire and fell into the Adriatic, two of its crew being drowned, and the following day the *M-3* was also shot down. In September, the *M-8* and the *M-13* were destroyed when their hangar at Campalto was bombed by an aircraft of the Austro-Hungarian Air Service, and on the 22nd of that same month the *P-10* was shot down near Latisana. The Italians, however, stubbornly refused to alter their tactics and airship operations continued in broad daylight until the end of hostilities, by which time at least a dozen ships and their crews had been lost.

The Austrians, for their part, made little use of airships during the war, relying on heavier-than-air machines for reconnaissance and bombing tasks. The only airship operations in support of Austro-Hungarian ground forces were flown by German Army craft, mainly Schütte-Lanz types.

The remaining belligerent, Russia, is known to have used at least two airships—both of French origin—during 1915. The first was the former *Clément-Bayard I*, known as *Kommissionny* in Russian Army service, and the other was a Lebaudy craft named *Lebed*. Details of their operational careers, and their eventual fate, are not known.

6 Post-War Development in Europe

Count Ferdinand von Zeppelin never lived to see the defeat of his country in 1918, or the post-war struggle for survival of the company he had created two decades earlier. Following the Count's death in 1917, control of the company had been taken over by Zeppelin's nephew, Baron Gemmingen, and at the end of 1918—working in close conjunction with Hugo Eckener—he laid plans to renew the Zeppelin Company's efforts in the commercial field. At the time of the Armistice, one Zeppelin—the *L.72*, originally destined for the Navy—had just been completed at Löwenthal, and a proposal that she be used to make an attempt on the first air crossing of the Atlantic received considerable support from the board of directors. It was, however, opposed by Eckener and Gemmingen, who felt that a successful transatlantic flight by the *L.72* would probably result in a wave of anti-German feeling at this early stage after the war. Instead, Eckener proposed the building of two new commercial airships for use on internal German services by a reconstituted DELAG, and after some discussion this plan was adopted.

The first post-war commercial Zeppelin, the *LZ.120*, or *Bodensee* ('Lake Constance'), made her first flight on 24 August 1919. She was small by the standards of the wartime Super-Zeppelins, having a capacity of only 706,200 cubic feet. She was powered by four 240-h.p. Maybach engines which gave her a speed of 82 m.p.h. and she was luxuriously equipped for her day, having a refrigerator and a fully electric galley. The *Bodensee* entered service on the Berlin–Friedrichshafen run, covering the distance in six hours. During her first three months of service she flew on 82 days, carrying 2,380 passengers, 30 tons of freight and 5 tons of mail and logging a total of 533 flying hours. She also made two experimental flights to

Stockholm, and the success of these resulted in a plan to inaugurate a regular service to the Swedish capital with the aid of the second commercial airship.

The new craft, named the *Nordstern* ('North Star'), was ready for service in January 1920; she was larger than the *Bodensee*, and hopes ran high that she would be the successful forerunner of a series of Zeppelins that would soon be operating on a network of routes all over Europe. But it was not to be; soon after her maiden flight, the Inter-Allied Commission of Control—which had already seized the surviving Navy Zeppelins, but had spared the *L.72*, the *Bodensee* and the *Nordstern* because they were regarded as commercial property—demanded the surrender of the three ships. The Germans argued and pleaded, but it was useless; the *L.72* went to France, where she became the *Dixmude*, and the French Navy also received the *Nordstern*, which was used as a training ship under the name *Méditerranée*. The *Bodensee* went to Italy.

It looked like the end for the Zeppelin Company, particularly since the Allies were demanding a considerable sum of money in compensation for the Naval Zeppelins which had been destroyed by their crews before they could be handed over. It was then that the directors had the flash of inspiration that was to save the Company from complete extinction. Instead of paying the American share of the compensation—800,000 dollars—in gold, they approached the American Military Commission and offered to build an airship for service with the US Navy. The Americans were immediately interested, since none of the airships seized as war booty had been allocated to them. The condition was that the ship's airworthiness had to be proved by a delivery flight across the Atlantic, and here a snag arose. To make such a flight, the airship would need to have a capacity of at least 2,500,000 cubic feet, and the Germans were forbidden to build a ship exceeding 1,100,000 cubic feet in volume. Also, such a ship would cost at least 900,000 dollars to build, which meant that 100,000 dollars would have to be provided by the US Navy Department. The question of funds did not present an insurmountable problem, as the Americans agreed to pay the additional amount quite readily. The problem of the ship's size, however, was a different matter; France and Britain insisted that the Americans could not own an airship larger than those shared out among the victorious powers, and it was not until 16 December 1921 that they reluctantly gave their approval for construction to begin of an *L.70*-type airship, with a volume of about 2,600,000 cubic feet.

Once approval had been obtained, the Zeppelin Company lost no time in starting work. The ship, the *LZ.126*, was to have a capacity of 2,542,320 cubic feet and was to be powered by five 350-h.p. Maybach engines. She was eventually completed in September 1924, and on the 25th of that month, after a short trial flight over Lake Constance, she flew from Friedrichshafen to Malmö and back with 73 passengers and crew on board, covering the 2,150 miles in 32 hours 30 minutes.

On the morning of 13 October 1924, with Hugo Eckener in command, the *LZ.126* took off from Friedrichshafen and broke through a thin layer of cloud, heading across France in bright sunshine on a course that would take her to the Azores. She crossed the coast of Spain at sunset, and her crew's last sight of land for four thousand miles—apart from the northern tip of the Azores—was the lighthouse on Cape Finisterre, blazing like a beacon in the gathering darkness.

At 10 p.m. on the 15th, Eckener sighted the lights of Halifax, Nova Scotia, away to the north, and in the early hours of the following morning Boston was overflown to a chorus of whistles and sirens. At dawn, 77 hours after she had started her epic flight, the airship approached New York, which was reached at an altitude of 10,500 feet. At 9 a.m. the *LZ.126* touched down at Lakehurst, New Jersey, where a vast crowd of spectators and an official US Navy delegation were waiting to greet her. There, in a special ceremony, she was named the *Los Angeles*; her service designation was *ZR-3*. She was to serve the United States Navy well, and her career is described in Chapter Ten.

The successful construction and delivery of the *LZ.126*, alias the *ZR-3*, meant that the Zeppelin Company was back in business. Plans were immediately made to build an even bigger airship capable of regular trans-oceanic flights, and Eckener and his colleagues embarked on a massive publicity campaign to raise the necessary funds—just as they had done nearly twenty years earlier, when the company had been dogged by one misfortune after another. Ultimately, they succeeded in raising the equivalent of 750,000 dollars, and a further contribution from the German Government raised the sum to the million dollars necessary to develop the ship. The new craft was to have a capacity of 3,707,550 cubic feet, a length of 775 feet and a diameter of 100 feet. She was to be powered by five 530-h.p. Maybach engines giving her an estimated maximum speed of 81 m.p.h.

On 8 July 1928, when the ship—the *LZ.127*—was complete except for her fittings, she was christened by the Countess von Brandenstein-Zeppelin, daughter of the late Count. The name given to the ship had been chosen by Eckner; a name that reflected past achievements, and promised still greater successes to come. *Graf Zeppelin*.

In Britain, meanwhile, determined efforts had been made in the year following the war to build a fleet of rigid airships for military use. When the war ended, ten Zeppelin-type rigid airships were either building or projected. The first in the numerical series, the Short-built *R.32*, was almost identical with her sister craft *R.31* (destroyed in her hangar by bad weather in 1918). She was commissioned on 3 September 1919 and, based at Howden in Yorkshire, was engaged in experimental work with the National Physical Laboratory, flying a total of 84 hours up to October 1920. For the next six months she was used as a school ship, training US Navy crews on attachment to the RAF; she was afterwards intentionally tested to destruction on 27 August 1921 and broken up.

The design of the *R.33* and the *R.34* had originated towards the end of 1916, and was based on that of Zeppelin *L.33*, which had crash-landed in East Anglia on the night of September 23–4 that year. Both entered service in 1919. They had a length of 643 feet, a diameter of 79 feet and a capacity of two million cubic feet. Each was powered by five engines, giving a speed of 65 m.p.h. The *R.33* was perhaps the most successful rigid airship ever built in Britain; based on Pulham in Norfolk she carried out several flights to the Continent in 1919, and also participated in fleet manœuvres from Howden and East Fortune. During this time she survived a number of potentially dangerous situations, including being struck by lightning. During 1921, with future commercial flights in mind, she carried out a series of mooring experiments in all weathers at Pulham and Howden, spending a total of 150 days moored at a masthead and proving conclusively that this method was far more satisfactory than accommodating a rigid airship in a shed. Experience had shown that a rigid could not be safely manhandled into or out of a shed when the wind speed exceeded 20 m.p.h., but on one occasion, following a flight from Croydon in pouring rain, the *R.33* moored safely at her Pulham mast in a wind gusting at 40 m.p.h.

In the autumn of 1921 the *R.33* was flown to Bedford, where she was deflated and slung, and for a time it looked as though she would be scrapped. Then, in May 1924, she was reconditioned and returned to Pulham to carry out further trials in connexion with two new ships of 5,000,000 cubic feet capacity which were then on the drawing board and which were to emerge as the *R.100* and the *R.101*. One night the *R.33* broke away from her moorings in a gale and drifted astern over the North Sea, with her two forward bays and gas cells severely damaged. Her commander, Flight Lieutenant R. S. Booth, AFC, was on board with a skeleton crew; realizing that it would be impossible to make headway into the gale with the bows damaged, he allowed the ship to drift until the wind dropped and eventually brought her back safely to Pulham after a flight of thirty hours. At times during the flight, the ship had come down so low that she had been lashed by spray, and with hardly any ballast on board the crew had been powerless to do anything. Booth had considered the possibility of heading for Holland, where he could have brought the ship down low enough to allow the crew to jump to safety, but that would have meant the ship being wrecked and he had rejected the idea.

After repairs, the *R.33* was used for a wide variety of experimental tasks. During one experiment, on 21 October 1926, she carried two Gloster Grebe fighters slung under her keel. The aircraft, piloted by Flying Officers R. L. Ragg and C. Mackenzie-

Richards, were released at 2,000 feet and dived away, flying around the airship for several minutes before hooking-up again successfully. The first 'hook-up' experiment involving the *R.33* had in fact been made a year earlier, on 15 October 1925, when the airship had carried and successfully retrieved a de Havilland Humming Bird, and several similar experiments had been made during the months that followed. The trial of October 1926— the first involving two aircraft—was the last of its kind; an examination of the *R.33*'s framework afterwards showed signs of metal fatigue, and further experiments were discontinued. Although the airship's useful life was by no means at an end, she was scrapped the following year.

Although the *R.33* and the *R.34* were of similar design, they were not sister ships in the true sense of the word, because they came from different stables, the *R.33* being built by Armstrong-Whitworth at Selby and the *R.34* by the Scottish engineering firm of Beardmore. The two ships were, however, exactly similar in dimension and were both powered by five 275-h.p. Sunbeam engines.

The *R.34* is best remembered for her transatlantic flight, the first by a lighter-than-air craft, which she made in July 1919. Even so, the feat was overshadowed by the non-stop flight of Alcock and Brown, made only a fortnight earlier, which won them the Britannia Trophy and the *Daily Mail* prize of £10,000. The *R.34* took off from East Fortune at 1.24 a.m. on 2 July 1919, bound for New York. Her commander was Major G. H. Scott, AFC. On board were Brigadier-General E. M. Maitland, CMG, DSO, the officer commanding the British Military Airship Service, a crew of thirty, a kitten and a stowaway—an airman named Ballantyne. The airship carried 4,900 gallons of petrol. Apart from a minor malfunction in one of the *R.34*'s engines, the flight westwards across the Atlantic was uneventful. Heavy rainclouds were encountered early in the evening of 3 July, but the airship climbed above them easily. At 12.50 p.m. on 4 July the *R.34* crossed the coast of Nova Scotia, 59 hours into the flight and with 900 miles still to go. Soon afterwards, she ran into severe storms and received a bad buffeting, the crew clinging to girders and stays as lurid electrical discharges flickered around the ship. The fuel situation, too, was beginning to cause some concern and Major Scott was beginning to doubt that the ship would be able to reach her destination. As a precaution he radioed Chatham, Massachusetts, and prepared to make an emergency landing there if things got really bad. As it turned out, this step was not necessary; soon after the signal was sent, the *R.34* encountered more favourable winds and continued towards New York with her engines throttled well back to conserve fuel. At 1.54 p.m. on 6 July, 108 hours and 12 minutes after she had left East Fortune, the *R.34* arrived over Mineola airfield near New York. As she cruised overhead, one of her crew, Major J. E. M. Pritchard, jumped from her by parachute to supervise the landing.

On the night of Wednesday 9 July, after three hectic days of celebrations and Press interviews, the *R.34*'s crew re-embarked and prepared for the return flight. The stowaway, Aircraftman Ballantyne, was not on board; he had been sent home by sea. On arrival back in Britain, Ballantyne received only a reprimand for his clandestine flight; Brigadier-General Maitland was conscious of the fact that the man had been bitterly disappointed at not being selected as one of the *R.34*'s crew, and since the stowaway's presence had never endangered the flight he was inclined to be lenient. Ballantyne stayed in the RAF; he was later commissioned and became a pilot.

The airship took off from Mineola at 3.54 a.m. on 10 July, lit up by a cone of searchlights as she flew over New York. Just over two hours later she crossed the coast of Newfoundland, heading out across the Atlantic at a steady 83 m.p.h. During the first day, one of the engines in the aft gondola broke down and could not be repaired in flight, but the crew found that the airship could make satisfactory progress on her four remaining motors. During the flight, the ship was constantly in touch with various radio stations, and as the craft approached the south-west coast of Ireland a favourable weather report was received which made Scott abandon his original intention of making for London and instead turn the ship's bows towards East Fortune. The forecast turned out to be correct: after flying through fog and cloud during much of Friday night, the *R.34* suddenly burst out into a brilliant sunrise and the crew scanned the horizon for the first glimpse of the Irish coast. It was sighted at 7.25 p.m., ten miles away on the starboard bow, and thirty minutes later the airship made landfall at Clifden—the spot where the record flight of Alcock and Brown had ended in an Irish peat bog. As the *R.34* cruised on across Ireland in brilliant moonlight, heading for Belfast, the wireless operator received a signal from the Air Ministry instructing her captain to change course and land at Pulham. The Norfolk base was reached at 6.56 on Sunday morning, after a flight of 75 hours 2 minutes; another engine broke down during the final hours of the voyage, which was completed on the remaining three.

The *R.34* was the first aircraft ever to cross the Atlantic from east to west, and also the first to make the round trip. Her career ended tragically eighteen months later, on 28 January 1921, when she flew into a hill in Yorkshire. Although badly damaged she was able to limp back to her base at Howden, but a storm broke and she was damaged beyond repair.

The next airship in the numerical series, the *R.35*, was cancelled under Britain's post-war economy programme. The *R.36* and the *R.37*, however, were both built; the former by Beardmore and the latter by Short Brothers. Both ships were based on the design of the Zeppelin *L.48* and were larger than the *R.33* and the *R.34*; their length was 675 feet and their diameter 78 feet 8 inches, capacity being 2,101,000 cubic feet. The ships were powered by four 350-h.p. Sunbeam Cossack engines in single gondolas. Construction was begun in 1917, but slowed down markedly after the Armistice, when funds were drastically reduced. In January 1921 construction of the *R.37* was practically complete when, through lack of funds, the Airship Service of the Royal Air Force was disbanded and the programme under which one new rigid airship was to have been completed every two years was abandoned. All work on the *R.37* was stopped and she was dismantled soon afterwards.

The *R.36*, however, had already begun her trials, and after the disbanding of the RAF's Airship Service she was used to explore the commercial possibilities of airships in various roles. One of the experiments she carried out was traffic control, her crew 'spotting' for the police and passing information on traffic congestion over an air-to-ground radio link. The airship, however, had an unfortunate career right from the start. During her delivery flight to Pulham in May 1921, two of her fins broke and she went out of control, losing a thousand feet of height and just managing to limp home. She was repaired and made several successful flights, but in August she overshot the mooring-mast while landing at Pulham and the mooring cable pulled backwards into her nose, causing severe damage. The situation was serious, for the sheds at Pulham were occupied and there was no possibility of the damaged airship reaching Howden. Neither, with the wind rising, could she remain at the mast. The only solution was to make room in one of the Pulham sheds by breaking up its occupant—the surrendered Zeppelin *L.64*. By dawn the work of destruction was complete; the mangled remains of the *L.64* were towed out of one end of the shed and the *R.36* was towed in at the other, but not before the wind had caused more damage to her structure. She never flew again, remaining a 'hangar queen' until she was broken up in 1926.

Meanwhile, the Short-built airship *R.38* had begun her trials. Her design had originated in 1918 as a result of an Admiralty requirement for a craft with a range of 3,000 miles and an endurance of 211 hours, and Shorts' answer was an airship with a length of 699 feet, a diameter of $85\frac{1}{2}$ feet and a capacity of 2,750,000 cubic feet—tailored, in fact, to fit inside the 700-foot airship shed at Cardington. The *R.38* had a useful lift of $45\frac{1}{2}$ tons and a ceiling of 22,000 feet; she was powered by six 350-h.p. Sunbeam Cossack engines in three twin gondolas, giving her a maximum speed of just over 70 m.p.h. and a duration of 65 hours at 65 m.p.h.

A firm Admiralty order had been placed with Shorts in September 1918, at a time when the firm's future in airship construction appeared rosy. The Admiralty had plans to take over the factory at Cardington, but Shorts were to be left in charge and were to build a series of airships for commercial use. With the coming of peace, however, the Admiralty's interest appeared to wane and Shorts asked for an assurance that the original plan would go ahead. They also asked for better financial terms in future contracts. The Admiralty's answer, in January 1919, was to cancel the *R.38* order and to nationalize Cardington under the Defence of the Realm Act. Shorts received compensation to the tune of £40,000, but it was a bitter pill to swallow; in view of these circumstances, it was remarkable that Shorts allowed a number of their designers to remain at Cardington to assist in the development of the *R.38* when the airship was reinstated as a project of the Royal Airship Works, as Cardington had now become.

The fact that the *R.38* project was allowed to proceed at all after the war was due to the Americans, who shortly before the end of hostilities had ordered a rigid airship from Britain based on the design of one of the later Zeppelins. The *R.38* met this requirement, and construction went ahead—partly paid for in advance in US dollars. While the ship was building, the American crews destined for her underwent intensive training aboard the *R.32*. Because of various technical snags, construction of the *R.38* was not completed until June 1921, and the airship's seven-hour maiden flight on the 23rd of that month revealed still more troubles, particularly control overbalance. After a second flight, made on 28 June, a number of modifications were carried out; these included the strengthening of the fin and the reduction of all control surface areas by ten per cent. During this time the ship was given United States Navy markings and the serial *ZR-2*.

The third flight, on 17 July, almost ended in disaster. Commanded by Flight Lieutenant Pritchard, the ship reached a speed of $57\frac{1}{2}$ m.p.h.—and then, without warning, she began to pitch alarmingly. Two girders failed amidships and the ship would almost certainly have broken up within minutes if Pritchard, seizing the helm from the coxswain, had not regained some measure of control. Still pitching, but less violently, the airship limped back to Howden and moored safely.

After repairs to her structure, she took off on another test flight on 23 August, this time with Flight Lieutenant A. H. Wann in command. This time everything appeared to go well, but when the *R.38* reached her destination at Pulham her crew found the base shrouded in dense fog. They were unable to locate the mooring-mast, and, with darkness approaching rapidly, Wann decided to stand off over the North Sea all night. Early the following morning the *R.38* came in over the Suffolk coast near Thorpeness; everything was still functioning normally and Wann ordered the test flight to continue with more high-speed trials. In the afternoon, the airship's engines were opened up and she maintained a steady 69 m.p.h. for fifteen minutes, heading northwards for Howden. At 5.20 p.m., over Hull, Wann started a series of yawing manoeuvres at a height of 2,500 feet and a speed of 62 m.p.h. Seventeen minutes later the *R.38* broke in half and fell into the Humber, the forward section being destroyed by fire and explosion. Out of the forty-nine people on board, only five survived; they were Wann and three other crew members (including one US Navy observer) and a cameraman from the National Physical Laboratory named H. Bateman. Among those who died were Air Commodore Maitland and the ship's designer, C. I. Campbell.

A subsequent Court of Inquiry concluded that the airship's structure had failed because it had been too weak to withstand the high control forces exerted during the yawing tests, but the technical findings were incomplete. When the *R.38*'s design was compared with that of the captured Zeppelin *L.71*, the British ship was found to be the stronger of the two—but the pressure on the German airship's controls at high speeds was found to be considerably heavier, providing a built-in protection against possible over-stressing of the airframe as a result of violent manoeuvres.

The disaster had one immediate result: several projects for a British commercial airship, which were being considered at that time, were abruptly cancelled. They included a design put forward by Shorts for a commercial airship of 4,450,000 cubic feet, capable of carrying a payload of 20 tons (including 50 passengers) over a still-air range of 6,000 nautical miles at a speed of 50 knots. The ship was to have been powered by five Rolls-Royce Condors of 550 h.p. each. Further development came to a virtual standstill until 1924, when the Labour

Government sanctioned further experiments to assess the prospects of the airship as a commercial vehicle. As we have seen, most of these experiments were carried out with the aid of the *R.33*, and their success resulted in the initiation of two large commercial airship designs: the *R.100* and the *R.101*. Their story will be told in Chapter Nine.

Three other British projects for rigid military airships were begun during the First World War. Two of them, the *R.39* and the *R.40*, fell victim to the post-war economy axe and were never built. The third, the Vickers *R.80*, entered service in 1921 and had a relatively short life. She was the only British rigid started during the First World War whose design owed nothing to the German airships, and she was smaller than the *R.31–R.33* class ships, with a capacity of 1,250,000 cubic feet and a useful lift of 15 tons. She was powered by four 240-h.p. Maybach engines and carried a crew of twenty at a maximum speed of 60 m.p.h. For a short period, she took over the training of American airship crews from the *R.32*.

It was an airship disaster, too, that wrote finis to French hopes of developing the airship for commercial use. After the war, as was mentioned earlier, the French had received three Zeppelins: the *L.72*, the *LZ.113* and the smaller commercial *Nordstern*. The *LZ.113* was eventually broken up, but the other two entered service; the *Nordstern* as a training ship, the *Méditerranée*, and the *L.72* as a Naval survey craft, the *Dixmude*. The latter made several long voyages, including a world record endurance flight of 118 hours in September 1923. Then, on 18 December that same year, the airship left her base at Cuers-Pierrefeu, near Toulon, and set course out over the Mediterranean. She was heading for Algeria, from where she was to carry out a series of survey flights over the Sahara. She carried a complement of fifty-two officers and men.

On 20 December radio contact was made with her and her commander—Lieutenant de Vaisseau du Plessis de Grenedan—was informed that a severe storm was crossing his track. The airship was then about fifty miles south of Biskra, and de Grenedan immediately changed course to try and avoid the worst of the weather. At two o'clock in the morning of 21 December, he radioed that the ship was battling against a furious gale, and that fuel was getting dangerously low. At 3.30 p.m. there was another short radio message, indicating that de Grenedan was going to attempt an emergency landing. Then there was complete silence.

Ships and aircraft scoured the Mediterranean in the biggest air and sea search history had yet seen in peacetime. The northern fringe of the Sahara was covered, too, for there were rumours that the airship had been seen drifting in over the North African coast. Then came some concrete news: the body of the *Dixmude*'s commander had been found by some Sicilian fishermen, floating in the sea. Questions were asked in fishing villages along the coast of southern Sicily, and several villagers declared that the sea and sky had been lit up by a glare in the early hours of the morning. No trace of the ship herself, however, was found —and de Grenedan's body was the only one recovered. The exact cause of the disaster remained a mystery, but the most likely theory was that the *Dixmude*'s framework—made as light as possible, since the ship had been designed as a 'height climber'—had broken up in the gale and the escaping hydrogen had ignited.

Whatever the real truth, airship development came to a complete halt in France. The remaining ex-German ship, the *Méditerranée*, was broken up in 1925. Two Astra-Torres airships, the *E.5* and the *E.6*, remained in service with the French Navy for some years, together with one Zodiac Vedette, but they were withdrawn in the late 1920s.

Apart from Britain and Germany, the only other European country to continue with the development of airships after the First World War was Italy. Like Britain and France, Italy had received her share of surrendered Zeppelins; the three that went to her were the *L.61*, the *LZ.120* and the commercial *Bodensee*, the latter being test-flown extensively at the hands of an Italian crew. Italy's own wartime airship designs, however, had not been very successful, and the first Italian post-war venture into the commercial airship field was far from encouraging. The ship, named the *Roma*, was a semi-rigid built under an American contract. The creation of an Italian designer named Usuelli, the *Roma* was transported across the Atlantic in sections and assembled at Langley Field, making her first flight in the United States on 15 November 1921. She was powered originally by six Ansaldo engines, but the Americans removed two of them and substituted a pair of 240-h.p. Liberties. It was lucky that they did so: on the airship's first long-distance flight, made on 21 December from Langley Field to Washington, all four of the craft's Italian engines broke down and she completed the journey on the power of the two American motors. Nevertheless, the addition of the more powerful American engines meant that the ship was subjected to stresses for which she had not been designed, and on 21 February 1922 this resulted in tragedy. While undergoing high-speed tests at 1,000 feet, the *Roma*'s structure began to break up and she went out of control, crashing into a hillside at Hampton Roads. Thirty-four of her occupants were killed, the remaining eleven being seriously injured.

The *Roma* tragedy gave Italian airships an undeserved reputation for being unsafe and poorly built. It was to be four years before the black cloud was lifted to a certain extent. The man who raised it was Colonel Umberto Nobile, and he did it in the most dramatic way possible. For it was an airship of his design, the *N.1*, that in 1926 was to carry a handful of intrepid men on the first air crossing of the North Pole.

7 Voyages of Discovery

At 5.10 p.m. on 21 May 1925 two Dornier Wal flying boats took off from Ny Aalesund in Spitzbergen and headed out into the long shadows of the Arctic. The expedition was commanded by the famous Norwegian explorer Roald Amundsen. Eight hours later, the two aircraft touched down on the sea at 87° 43' North, 10°20' West; one of them was damaged in the landing and had to be abandoned. At 10.30 a.m. on 10 June the surviving Dornier took off and returned to Spitzbergen, landing safely eight and a half hours later.

It was Amundsen's second attempt to fly over the North Pole. The first, made in 1923, had never really got off the ground; the aircraft, a Junkers, had been written off during a test flight. On the second abortive attempt, Amundsen had been accompanied by a rich American named Lincoln Ellsworth and two Scandinavians, Lief Dietrichson and Hjalmar Riiser-Larsen. The latter was a qualified airship pilot; part of his training had been carried out in Italy, and while he was there he had made the acquaintance of Umberto Nobile. Soon after Amundsen's second attempt at a Polar flight, Riiser-Larsen learned that Nobile's latest semi-rigid airship, the *N.1*, was up for sale and he suggested that she might be the ideal craft to use on a third try. The airship had already proved herself: on 20 May 1925, together with the Italian airship *Esperia* (the former *Bodensee*) she had taken off on a two-day cruise over the Mediterranean with twenty-five people on board, calling at Barcelona, Cuers and Pierrefeu.

Amundsen agreed and negotiations got under way for the purchase of the airship, the project being financed by Lincoln Ellsworth. Amundsen's team had to overcome a good deal of opposition from Mussolini, who did not exactly favour the idea of all the credit going to the Norwegians; in the end, it was

agreed that although Amundsen would be in overall command
of the expedition, Nobile himself would command the airship.
Some of Amundsen's colleagues saw trouble ahead: the Norwegian explorer possessed a volatile temperament and so did
Nobile, and there were likely to be times when the two would be
pulling in opposite directions. On 29 March 1926 the *N.1* was
christened *Norge* in an impressive ceremony in Rome. She was
350 feet long, with a capacity of 653,000 cubic feet, and her three
250-h.p. Maybach engines gave her a maximum speed of 70
m.p.h. She was essentially a functional ship, with few refinements and no living-quarters as such.

On 10 April the *Norge* took off from Ciampino and set course
for her first port of call: Pulham, in England. She carried a
crew of sixteen. Pulham was reached at 3 p.m. the following day
and the ship was bedded down alongside the *R.33* until the 13th,
when conditions were favourable for the next stage of the flight—
to Oslo. Taking off at 11 a.m. on the 13th, the *Norge* crossed the
Danish coast early the following morning and reached Oslo at
three o'clock in the afternoon. The weather was still good and
it was decided to continue with the minimum delay; the airship
was replenished and was on her way again at 1.20 a.m. on 15
April, this time heading for Leningrad. The *Norge* arrived over
the Russian city at 9.38 that evening, any further hope of rapid
progress being shattered by the onset of bad weather. Amundsen and his team were forced to remain at Leningrad for nearly
three weeks, waiting for a break. Finally, on 5 May, they were
able to continue to Vadsö on the northern tip of Norway, remaining there only a few hours before setting off on the last
lap to King's Bay, Spitzbergen.

Their destination was reached at 6 a.m. on 7 May, and the
final preparations for the Polar flight began immediately. The
Norge was thoroughly overhauled and the necessary equipment
stowed on board, after which the airship's fuel tanks and hydrogen cells were topped up. On 9 May, while preparations were
still under way, Amundsen's team received a bitter disappointment: at 4.30 p.m. GMT a Fokker F.VII monoplane, fitted with
skis, touched down at King's Bay and its two-man crew climbed
stiffly from the cockpit. They were Commander Richard Byrd,

USN, and his co-pilot Floyd Bennett, and they had left King's Bay shortly after midnight that same day. Now, after a flight lasting sixteen hours, they were back—with the news that they had become the first men to see the North Pole from the air. It was a blow for Amundsen and his men, but they were consoled by the hope that they would still be the first to make the complete air crossing of the Polar icecap. On the morning of 11 May everything was ready, and at 9.55 a.m. the Norge lifted from the snow of King's Bay and climbed away towards the north. Throughout the day she ran through patches of thick fog, but this caused no navigational problems and the ship held a steady course for the Pole. The navigator was Riiser-Larsen, and at 1.20 a.m. on 12 May he made the final calculations designed to bring the *Norge* accurately over her target. As members of the crew stood by to drop Norwegian, Italian and American flags, Riiser-Larsen knelt by an open window and took several sightings with his sextant. Suddenly, he called, 'Ready with the flags!' and a moment later, 'Now—we're here!'

The Norwegian flag was thrown out first, fluttering down on its aluminium staff towards the crinkled expanse of snow and ice which, according to Riiser-Larsen, was Latitude ninety degrees North—the Pole. The flag landed upright, standing firm despite a stiff breeze; it was followed a moment later by the flags of the other two nations. Wordlessly, Roald Amundsen turned and shook the hand of his coxswain, Oscar Wisting. Together, these two men had planted another Norwegian flag at the North Pole fourteen years earlier, on 14 December 1911. It was a proud moment.

The voyage went on, the *Norge*'s crew in high spirits now as radio messages congratulating them on their success came flooding in. The weather was growing steadily worse, however, and by 8.30 that morning the airship was flying through a blanket of thick fog. Ice began to build up on the craft's exposed metal parts; it flew off the propellers like shrapnel, ripping through the lower part of the envelope and giving Nobile serious cause for concern. The crew managed to repair the worst of the holes, however, and by nightfall the weather had taken a turn for the better, with vastly improved visibility. At 6.45 a.m. on 13 May land was sighted on the port bow, and the crew felt that the worst part of the journey was over; the vast unexplored region of the Arctic was safely behind them and they were more or less on course for Nome, Alaska. Riiser-Larsen announced that the landfall was Point Barrow, and this was borne out a few hours later when the airship flew over a small settlement which Amundsen identified as Wainwright. He and a fellow explorer, Oskar Omdal—also a member of the *Norge*'s crew—had stayed there in 1922.

The weather, however, had not yet finished with the *Norge*. In the early hours of 14 May a gale came howling down from the north and the dense fog came rolling down again, forcing the ship to fly at high altitude over the mountainous terrain. Navigation became extremely difficult, but periodic glimpses of the ground enabled the crew to follow the coastline along the Bering Straits. Both Amundsen and Nobile agreed that they would have to land soon; they were now uncertain of their position and there was a danger that the gale would drive them out over the Straits. Moreover, the crew had been on continuous duty for seventy hours; all of them were suffering badly from cold and fatigue, and some were experiencing hallucinations.

At 7 a.m. on 14 May an expanse of reasonably flat ground and a cluster of houses were sighted. Slowly, Nobile inched the ship down towards a knot of spectators, heading into wind and all too conscious that the landing—with no skilled ground crew and in gale conditions—was likely to be a nightmare. The crew tensed, ready to leap overboard into the snow if the ship struck hard and started to collapse. Then the miracle happened: when the *Norge* was only seconds away from the ground, the wind suddenly dropped to a dead calm and the ship touched down with hardly a bump, her trail ropes held fast by those on the ground. It was 7.30 a.m. GMT, and the *Norge*'s epic voyage of three thousand miles had ended at Teller, Alaska, only fifty-five miles from her planned destination at Nome.

It was only now that the clash of personalities between Amundsen and Nobile developed into a series of bitter arguments as both men fought for their share of the limelight. The unfortunate and childish squabble went on for nearly two years, marring what was otherwise a very noteworthy achievement. Angrily, Nobile returned to Italy, determined to launch his own Polar expedition. He returned to his country a public hero, a fact that was to lead indirectly to considerable frustration—for Benito Mussolini had no love for public heroes other than himself, and he refused to lend further support to Nobile in case the pilot's future ventures led to still higher pinnacles of fame. It was the city of Milan that came to Nobile's rescue, the townspeople subscribing sufficient funds to enable the designer to build another airship. Named the *Italia*, the second craft had approximately the same dimensions as the *Norge*, but her design incorporated a number of improvements and her useful lift was increased by 2,900 pounds.

The *Italia* made her maiden flight in March 1928, and a subsequent series of short test flights proved highly successful. Nobile decided to wait no longer before launching the Polar expedition; airship stations along the route were prepared to receive his craft, and the crew was ready to go at short notice. The crew had been carefully selected, and their qualifications were impressive: four of them besides Nobile had had considerable airship experience, and the ship's two radio operators were among the best to be found. The rest were made up of engineers, scientists and meteorologists; one of the latter, Professor Malmgren, had been on the *Norge* expedition.

In all, there were eighteen personnel on board the *Italia* when she took off from Milan at 1.55 a.m. on 15 April; two more scientists were scheduled to join her later. Nobile had decided to take a more easterly route to the Arctic than that followed by the *Norge* and the airship now set course for Stolp in northern Germany, where an old German Army airship station had been placed at her disposal. The weather during this first leg was atrocious, the ship encountering rain, fog, snow, hail, lightning and strong winds. By the time the *Italia* landed at Stolp at 7.50 a.m. on 16 April, she had no ballast left and one of her fins had sustained some damage. This was quickly repaired, however, and the flight was resumed on 3 May. The *Italia* took off from Stolp

145

at 3.28 a.m., heading for Vadsö in the teeth of a strong northerly wind. This leg of the flight was made on two engines, the third being started only when bad weather was once more encountered shortly after midnight on 4 May. Navigation was hampered by thick fog, but in spite of this Vadsö's mooring mast was sighted at 8.55 a.m. and the airship landed safely fifteen minutes later.

The *Italia* left for King's Bay at 8.34 p.m. on 5 May. As she approached Spitzbergen she ran into violent winds and driving snow, and the crew prepared to stand off until the surface wind at King's Bay dropped. The weather was not a serious problem at this stage, as the ship had sufficient fuel for 70 hours' flying. However, the radio station at King's Bay reported more favourable wind conditions on the morning of 6 May, and the airship landed at 12.45 p.m. on two engines, the third having broken down. The wind was still too strong to allow the airship to be walked into her shed and she was moored at the nearby mast, the crew taking turns to stand watch aboard her in pairs. Preparations for the Polar flight lasted four days, and included the changing of the faulty engine No. 3. The expedition in fact planned to make a series of flights over the Arctic, the proposed programme being to explore Nicholas II Land, which was then largely uncharted, to make two flights over the Pole and to carry out an air survey of an unexplored area of Greenland.

The *Italia* took off to carry out the first part of this schedule at 7.55 a.m. on 11 May, but bad weather forced her to return to King's Bay at 4.10 that same afternoon. The next two days were anxious ones, for layers of snow piled up on the exposed envelope of the *Italia* faster than it could be removed and for a time it looked as though the weight might break her back. Then a thaw set in, the snow turning to ice which covered the airship in a glistening shroud. Fortunately the crew were able to break this off without too much difficulty, and from then on the danger lessened as the weather improved steadily.

At 1 p.m. on 15 May the *Italia* once again set off for Nicholas II Land, carrying a load of almost twelve tons, much of it made up of survival equipment, a crew of sixteen and 1,500 gallons of fuel, enough for a flight of 4,300 miles. The weather at first was near-perfect, and the crew were able to obtain some excellent photographs of the little-known west coast before passing on into an unexplored area known as Gillis Land. Here, the airship encountered snowstorms and thick fog, but at no time did the weather give rise to any thought of the flight being abandoned. When the *Italia* finally landed at 10.20 a.m. on 18 May, after 69 hours in the air, she had completed the most comprehensive aerial survey flight ever made, having covered a total of 15,400 square miles in the unexplored regions between Spitzbergen and Franz Josef Land, the Eastern Islands and Franz Josef's Archipelago, North East Land and Nicholas II Land.

Compared to this marathon, the Polar flight itself—preparations for which now went ahead—seemed relatively easy. The *Italia* took off at 4.28 a.m. on 23 May, carrying 1,500 gallons of petrol, and set course for the Pole. At 6.50 the airship ran into thick fog which lasted throughout the morning, but shortly after 1 p.m. it started to clear a little and at 1.45 the coast of Greenland was sighted on the port bow. With the wind behind her the *Italia* made good progress, and the Pole was reached at 12.20 a.m. on 24 May. Nobile threw down an Italian flag and a wooden cross given to him by the Pope at the start of the expedition, then throttled back and brought the ship round in a slow circle. The *Italia* carried a waterproof car and the scientists had hoped to descend to the ice in this to make some observations, but the wind proved too strong and the plan was abandoned. At 2.20 a.m., after radio messages had been sent to the Pope, the King of Italy and Mussolini, Nobile reluctantly turned the ship's bow towards Spitzbergen once more.

An hour after leaving the Pole the airship again encountered fog, and severe icing began to develop. Up to this time the ship had been cruising on two engines, but now—with the headwind growing steadily stronger—the third motor was started. Even so, progress was painfully slow and the weather continued to deteriorate, making it hard for the two coxswains, who were by this time very tired, to maintain an accurate heading. At 8 a.m. on the 25th, the crew had to face up to the unpleasant fact that the ship was lost. Hopefully, they scanned the horizon for a glimpse of Spitzbergen, which should have been in sight some time ago, but there was nothing but an endless vista of pack-ice beneath and a grey blanket of fog above. They managed to establish radio contact with King's Bay, but received no information that enabled them to fix their position.

Then, at 9.25 a.m., the coxswain shouted in alarm that the elevator wheel would not move. Nobile tried it, and found that the elevators were solidly jammed. There was no alternative but to shut down the engines and allow the *Italia* to drift while repairs were carried out. The ship was light and, deprived of her power, she rose steadily. At 3,000 feet she burst through the layer of fog into a brilliant sky and hot sunlight. The repairs to the elevators were finished by 9.55 and Nobile brought the ship down through the fog again to 1,000 feet. While up above the murk, the crew had been able to get a rough idea of the *Italia*'s position with the aid of the sun; they calculated that the airship was now 45 miles north-east of the Ross Islands and 180 miles north-east of King's Bay. If this was correct, it meant that they could expect to land at base between 3 and 4 o'clock that afternoon.

The wind was dropping now, and the crew were in good spirits as the airship cruised on. Suddenly, the coxswain reported that the ship was becoming stern heavy. Power was hastily increased to improve dynamic lift, but the stern-heavy tendency continued and the *Italia* began to slide relentlessly towards the ice. It was exactly 10.30 a.m. Nobile rushed forward to take the wheel, but it was too late. There was time only for a last horrifying glimpse of a field of jagged ice, rushing up to meet the ship, before she struck with a fearful crash. Something hit Nobile on the head and then a massive weight descended on him, crushing him. He felt an arm and a leg snap like matchwood. The next instant he was flung out on to the ice as the control car smashed open, scattering occupants and equipment in all directions. Relieved of their weight, the *Italia* shot up rapidly, disappearing in the fog with six crew members still on board. Neither they nor the airship were ever seen again.

Slowly, stunned by the impact, the nine survivors on the ice took stock of their situation. They were surrounded by a mass of wreckage and odds and ends of equipment; fortunately, it included a tent, some sleeping-bags, food and a radio set that was still in working order. Most of the men were injured in varying degrees; Nobile appeared to be the most badly injured, with two broken limbs. Only one member of the crew, in fact, had escaped completely unharmed: Nobile's dog Titina.

At noon, a distorted distress message from the stranded party was picked up by the King's Bay radio station. It gave no indication of the survivors' position, and further attempts to establish contact failed. A big air and sea search was started, but with no real idea where to look the searchers drew a complete blank. Then, on 9 June, another distress signal was picked up, and this time a position was given: 80°30′ North, 28°00′ East. Aircraft covered the new search area, but still failed to find any sign of life. In the meantime, three of the survivors, Professor Malmgren, Mariano and Zappi, had decided to trek across the ice in the hope of finding help. After three days, Malmgren—a sick man—collapsed and was unable to go further. He begged the others to leave him and save themselves. They did so, knowing that he was dying, after leaving him some of their scant provisions. Mariano and Zappi were lucky: on 12 July, after suffering incredible hardships, they were rescued by the Russian ice-breaker *Krassin*, one of two Soviet vessels taking part in the rescue operation.

On 23 June the other survivors were located by the Italian pilot Umberto Maddalena, flying a Savoia, and provisions were dropped to them. On the 24th Captain Lundborg, a Swede, landed at the spot in a D.H. Moth fitted with skis and flew out Nobile and his dog. Lundborg returned the same day, only to suffer an engine failure and find himself stranded with the others. Some were eventually rescued on 5 July by another Swedish airman, Schyberg, and the remainder were flown out on 12 July. In all, ten aircraft had taken part in the rescue operation. These were two Junkers G.24s (pilots Nielsen and Chuknovsky); one Savoia (Maddalena); one Dornier Wal (Penzo); a mixed Norwegian-Swedish formation, commanded by Tornberg, consisting of two Heinkel He 5 floatplanes, one Fokker C.V.D., one Moth and one Klemm; and a French Latécoère seaplane, the *Latham*. The air search brought its own share of drama and tragedy: apart from Lundborg, one other search crew, Van Dongen and Sora, had to be rescued themselves when their Fokker crash-landed. The greatest tragedy of all, however, surrounded the French *Latham*. On 16 June it took off from Caudebec in France, heading northwards for Spitzbergen to take part in the search. In addition to the four-man crew—Guilbaud, Cavelier de Cuverville, Valette and Brazy—the flying-boat carried two distinguished passengers: Roald Amundsen and Lief Dietrichson. Characteristically, Amundsen had cast aside his differences with Nobile and was now throwing himself wholeheartedly into the rescue operation. The aircraft staged through Bergen, arriving at Tromsö on 17 June. The following day it took off on the last lap of its journey to Spitzbergen. It never arrived. Somewhere beyond North Cape, in the freezing waters of the Arctic Circle, it vanished without trace.

The tragedy of the *Italia* marked the end of airship development in Italy. Nobile was accused—completely without justice—of neglect, and resigned from the Italian Army soon afterwards. Disillusioned, he went to the Soviet Union, where for a time he became deputy director of an airship research programme. He returned to Italy in 1935, however, and was appointed Professor of Aeronautical Construction at Naples University. He later became director of the Institute of Aeronautics in that same university, a post which he was to hold for the best part of forty years.

8 The Saga of the *Graf Zeppelin*

On 18 September 1928, while the survival story of the *Italia*'s crew was still being told in the world's newspapers, a new era dawned in the story of the commercial airship. At eight o'clock that morning the gleaming 775-foot length of the new *Graf Zeppelin* lifted away from Friedrichshafen, and after circling over Lake Constance the airship set course northwards towards the Rhine valley. Her maiden flight was to last thirty-five hours, taking the airship out over the North Sea before returning to her base via Hamburg, Kiel and Berlin. Hugo Eckener was well pleased with the result: every item of equipment on board the big airship had functioned perfectly. The stage was now set for the real test of the *Graf Zeppelin*'s capabilities: a flight across the Atlantic. With a fine sense of drama, Eckener had planned that the flight would begin on 10 October—the anniversary of the discovery of the New World by Columbus. The weather, however, failed to respect Eckener's publicity plans; on 9 October the North Atlantic was swept by violent storms. Reports of ships in distress kept coming in, and westerly gales were delaying west-bound sea traffic by as much as twenty-four hours.

Anticipating more bad weather, Eckener decided to abandon the steamer route across the Atlantic—the track which the airship had originally been intended to follow—and to select one of two alternatives: the shorter route over northern Scotland and past the south coast of Iceland, or the longer 6,000-nautical mile haul via Gibraltar, Madeira and Bermuda. In the end, Eckener settled for the latter; with air navigation still very much in its infancy, the northern route, with its fogs and the danger of icing, seemed too risky. Because of the weather situation, take-off was postponed for twenty-four hours. At 7.30 a.m. on 11 October the airship's thirty-seven crew and twenty passengers—including four VIPs from the German Air Ministry and six leading newspaper correspondents—boarded the airship with their luggage, and half an hour later the ship was airborne. At maximum speed the *Graf Zeppelin* droned down the Rhine and skirted the Black Forest, passing Basel on her course for the Saone valley. The passengers sat glued to the windows as the landscape unfolded beneath them: picturesque Burgundy on the right and the towering Alps on the left. The airship slid over the Mediterranean coast at noon, and Barcelona's lights were sighted ahead shortly after dark. Skirting the south-east tip of Spain, Eckener brought the *Graf Zeppelin* on a westerly heading towards Gibraltar, which was reached at dawn. The airship nosed out over the Atlantic in almost perfect conditions; the sky was cloudless and a stiff north-easterly breeze pushed her along at a ground speed of 80 knots as she held her heading for Madeira. The favourable conditions stayed with the ship for several hours; Madeira was passed at 1.30 p.m. local time and radio contact was made with a station in the Azores.

It was from this station that Eckener received the first hint of possible trouble ahead. The southern fringe of a deep Atlantic depression was approaching the Azores, and the airship was likely to run into it. As it grew dark, the *Graf Zeppelin*'s crew and passengers saw lightning flickering across the northern sky, but the hours of darkness went by and still the airship flew on in relatively calm conditions. Then, at about 6 a.m., a long line of black cloud came marching towards the ship over the north-west horizon, approaching with frightening speed. The *Graf Zeppelin* drove into the squall at 75 knots and immediately began to pitch alarmingly in severe turbulence, sending cups and plates crashing from the breakfast tables. The buffeting went on for several minutes, but Eckener ordered the engines throttled back to half power and soon had the ship firmly under control again. For an hour, the *Graf Zeppelin* flew through lashing rain, but this eventually stopped and the airship emerged into clear skies once more.

The squall had done some damage, however. A few minutes later, Eckener's Flight Chief reported that the fabric covering the under-surface of the port stabilizing fin had torn away and was flapping in the breeze, threatening to jam the elevator. As a safety precaution, Eckener radioed the US Navy Department and asked them to divert a destroyer to the airship's position. There was no immediate danger, but Eckener was determined to take all necessary steps to ensure the safety of his passengers, some of whom had been frightened by the storm and needed a little reassurance. Within an hour and a half the crew had carried out temporary repairs to the fin, enabling the airship to proceed at 45 knots, and over the next three hours more thorough repairs were made which ensured that the fabric would hold so long as the *Graf Zeppelin* did not run into any really violent weather. Eckener's own son, Knut, was among the gallant handful of men who clambered out on to the framework of the fin, braving the slipstream to mend the damage.

The flight continued in good weather, although there were reports of more squalls on the way. In spite of the reduced speed good progress was made during the night and the following day, but as the *Graf Zeppelin* approached the Bermuda island group towards evening the threatening clouds once more appeared on the horizon. Eckener, with supreme faith in his ship and in the skill of the men who had repaired the fin, took her right through the heart of the squall; after an hour of buffeting and torrential rain she was through the worst and the fin covering had held, the only damage being a small tear which was spotted at first light.

At 10 a.m. on 15 October the great airship cruised serenely over Chesapeake Bay and headed for Washington, flying low over the city before continuing northwards. Soon after dark she landed safely at Lakehurst, sixty miles south of New York, to a tumultuous reception from a crowd of over twenty thousand people. The flight had lasted 111 hours 43 minutes.

The return flight from Lakehurst began at 2 a.m. on 29 October. On this occasion, as well as twenty-four passengers, the airship carried over 100,000 letters and postcards to a total stamp value of 75,713 dollars. This time, Eckener had decided to fly via the northern route—but soon after daybreak the ship ran into increasingly vile weather and he began to doubt the wisdom of his choice. In the afternoon the *Graf Zeppelin* was hit by a series of vicious squalls, rain and hail lashing down on her envelope with a fearful racket. By 3.45 p.m., however, the airship had put the worst of the weather behind her and was once again sailing serenely along in a clear, blue sky, making a groundspeed of over 80 knots. But not for long: soon after 4 p.m. the ship ran into fog, patchy at first but soon forming an opaque wall extending from sea level up to more than 3,000 feet. To climb above it would have meant valving off gas, and this Eckener did not want to do so early in the flight. Accordingly, after fixing the airship's position at 43° 00′ North, 56° 00′ West, he took her into the grey wall. Eckener hoped to emerge from the fog still on course, about 170 miles south of Cape Race—but at 6 p.m. the ship began to pitch and roll as she passed through areas of turbulence, and the commander knew that she must be somewhere over land. The question was, where? Half an hour later he had his answer. Through a gap in the murk he caught sight of rocky terrain below: it was Newfoundland, and the ship was well to the north of her required track. Making some hasty calculations, Eckener and his officers worked out that they were some 210 miles off course and altered the *Graf Zeppelin*'s heading accordingly. In fact, the error had been 300 miles; for the past few hours, unnoticed by the crew in the fog, the ship had been driven steadily northwards by a Force 11 southerly gale, a product of the violent weather conditions caused by the mingling of the warm Gulf Stream and the cold Labrador Current.

At 4 a.m. the ship's position was fixed accurately at 52° 00′ North, 48° 00′ West. In order to escape the southerly wind as quickly as possible, Eckener held a steady north-easterly course. Dawn revealed a sea dotted with great icebergs and floes, drifting south on the Labrador Current. The wind had now dropped considerably and the airship was making a ground speed of 50 m.p.h. by the time she reached the 54th Parallel. Eckener now turned south-east, heading for the mouth of the English Channel. By midnight the airship was crossing the 20° West meridian, and the crew hoped that with a favourable wind they would be home within twenty-four hours. At 7 a.m. the following morning, however, the ship's radio operators picked up a weather forecast which indicated stormy weather at the mouth of the

Channel, and to avoid it Eckener elected to steer a more southerly heading towards the Bay of Biscay. At 6 p.m. the *Graf Zeppelin* crossed the French coast at the mouth of the Loire and Eckener laid off a course for Dijon and Basel. The last stage of the journey was flown through thick fog, and it was with considerable relief that the crew saw the brightly lit airship shed at Friedrichshafen appear dead ahead through a rift in the grey curtain.

It was now 4 a.m. and Eckener decided to stand off until first light. At 7.06 a.m., 1 November 1928, the *Graf Zeppelin* came safely to earth after a record-breaking flight lasting 71 hours and 7 minutes.

Although the flight had been amazingly successful, Eckener knew only too well that the *Graf Zeppelin* had made it with one major disadvantage: lack of speed. If the commercial airship was to compete with the much faster heavier-than-air machine, it must be bigger and more powerful. But the Zeppelin Company needed capital in order to build such a ship, and meanwhile the *Graf Zeppelin* had to break more records if public interest in the passenger airship was to be maintained. To keep the *Graf Zeppelin* flying required operating funds, which had to be raised somehow. For weeks, Eckener racked his brains in an effort to find new ideas; he was reluctant to approach the German people for help yet again, and the Government, while outwardly showing considerable interest in the Zeppelin enterprise, politely refused to commit itself.

Eventually, Eckener hit upon the notion of inviting a group of Government officials and other influential people to go on a long-distance flight aboard the *Graf Zeppelin* so that they might have an opportunity of sampling the comfort and safety of the airship at first hand. The goal of the flight would be the eastern Mediterranean, with a landing in Egypt, and Eckener planned that it would take place in February 1929—taking his passengers out of the cold of a northern winter into the sunshine of a Mediterranean spring in a matter of hours.

Because of bad weather—it was one of the worst winters in living memory—the flight was postponed until 21 March, and even then it was bitterly cold until Marseilles was reached. One by one, the passengers began to put aside their winter overcoats, and Eckener exploited their high spirits to the full by taking the *Graf Zeppelin* down low and giving them a grandstand view of the Riviera as it unfolded beneath them. Turning south, the airship cruised past Corsica and Elba, heading for Rome; the Italian coast was crossed at Ostia and then the *Graf Zeppelin* was over Rome itself, the passengers looking down in awe on the Vatican, the ruins of a bygone age and the teeming streets of the modern capital. After sending a signal to Mussolini, and receiving one in return, Eckener took the ship southwards again, following the coast to Naples. Soon after dark the airship left Messina, on the southern tip of Italy, and nosed out into the Ionian Sea. The passengers were treated to a sumptuous meal by candlelight and afterwards turned in, well satisfied with their day.

The rest of the flight unfolded like a dream. The following morning the airship passed Crete and Cyprus, crossing the coast of Palestine at Haifa and heading for Jerusalem. Approaching the city, Eckner brought the *Graf Zeppelin* down low over the Dead Sea, and at dinner informed his astonished passengers that they had been flying at about 1,000 feet below sea level. Then the ship climbed over the heights on the west side of the Dead Sea and cruised over the plateau of Jerusalem, bathed in moonlight.

The original plan had been to fly as far as the Pyramids, but the German Foreign Office had—for an unexplained reason—forbidden the *Graf Zeppelin* to fly over Egyptian territory, and Eckener had to be content with following the coastline as far as Port Said before turning out over the Mediterranean, on course for Athens. The Greek capital was reached at dawn and the airship sailed on over the Isthmus of Corinth, following the Adriatic coast as far as Spalato. The idyll was almost over now; every passing hour was bringing the *Graf Zeppelin* closer to the wintry skies of Europe. Eckener was now faced with three alternatives: he could navigate the ship to the Riviera and bring her back to Friedrichshafen by her outward route; cross the Brenner Pass and follow the valley of the Adige; or cross the outer fringes of the Dinaric Alps to Pressburg (Bratislava) and Vienna.

The third route was finally chosen as being the least of three evils; everything depended on clear weather, for if the cloud came down over the mountain passes Eckener would have to take the ship up to 6,500 feet to clear the higher peaks, and that would mean valving off precious gas.

The *Graf Zeppelin*'s luck held: there was just enough visibility to enable the great airship to thread her way between the peaks. It was not until she was through the mountains that she ran into bad weather, fighting her way towards Vienna against a strong wind that carried showers of sleet with it. The blizzard got steadily worse and a layer of ice a quarter of an inch thick formed on the windows of the control car, making it almost impossible to see out. By a combination of luck and accurate guesswork Eckener kept the ship on her course along the Danube valley, and by the time Ulm was reached the blizzard was almost over. At 8 a.m. on 24 March the huge airship shed at Friedrichshafen was sighted and the *Graf Zeppelin* landed safely thirty minutes later, having been airborne for eighty-one hours.

Stimulated by the success of the flight to the eastern Mediterranean, with the support of the passenger VIPs now assured, Eckener and his colleagues began to dream of an even more ambitious project: a flight around the world. Such a flight had already been made by heavier-than-air machines in March 1924, but it had been accomplished only after 175 days and innumerable stops—and even then, only two of the four Douglas DT.2 machines which had set out had completed the journey. Eckener's plan, on the other hand, envisaged a global flight with only three stops—and it would be a flight on which the *Graf Zeppelin* would carry a normal load of passengers and mail.

In the meantime, while preparations for the world flight went ahead, Eckener decided to take the *Graf Zeppelin* on another passenger-carrying round trip to America. The airship left Friedrichshafen on 16 May 1929 and set course over France, but almost immediately she encountered a setback in the shape of the Mistral, the wind that sweeps up the Rhône valley. With her ground speed reduced considerably the airship pushed on over southern France, but then two of her engines broke down with damaged crankshafts and the power of the remaining motors was just sufficient to enable her to hover, completely immobilized, over the town of Bellegarde. There was nothing for it but to make an emergency landing at Cuers-Pierrefeu— a hazardous undertaking, for a power failure had plunged the French base into complete darkness. However, Eckener handled the ship brilliantly and she moored without trouble, eventually returning to Friedrichshafen on 23 May after the engines had been repaired. It was the only time during her long career that she suffered a serious mechanical defect.

The cost of the round-the-world flight was raised in record time—partly from newspapers and magazines anxious to secure reporting rights on the trip, and partly from the sale of commemorative stamps—and on 1 August 1929 the *Graf Zeppelin* left Friedrichshafen and headed out over the Atlantic towards Lakehurst, where the global flight was to begin in earnest. The trip westwards across the Atlantic was uneventful and Lakehurst was reached on 5 August, after a flight of 95 hours 26 minutes.

The great voyage began at 5.42 a.m. on 8 August, when the *Graf Zeppelin* lifted away from Lakehurst to the cheers of the spectators and set course back out over the North Atlantic.* This time, the winds were really in her favour and she made the crossing in 55 hours 22 minutes, arriving at Friedrichshafen on 10 August. She departed again at 4.30 a.m. on the 15th, heading north on the start of her longest flight yet: a flight that would end only in Tokyo, on the other side of the world. After six and a half hours she was over Berlin; Stettin and Danzig followed and then she was crossing the Baltic, heading for the Russian border. The frontier was crossed at about 6 p.m., the airship steering north before a freshening south-west wind. Early on the 16th the city of Vologda was reached and the ship now turned due east, cruising towards the Ural mountains on the power of four engines. The Urals were sighted later that day, stretching across the *Graf Zeppelin*'s path, and she crossed them at 3,300 feet north of Perm. There were some moments of anxiety when the hydrogen-filled ship passed over several forest fires that were raging on the slopes below, but nothing happened and the flight

* For details of freight, passengers and crew, see Appendix III.

went on as planned, passing over Sverdlovsk and heading towards the heart of Soviet Asia. Gradually, the primitive villages became fewer as solid ground gave way to vast swamps. For fourteen hours, between 7 p.m. on 16 August and 9 a.m. on the 17th, the airship pressed on at a steady 70 m.p.h. over the multi-coloured expanse of watery nothingness. Some of the passengers marvelled at the scene's wild beauty; others were appalled by the utter desolation. Even the *Graf*'s crew had some forebodings as the terrain unfolded beneath: they knew only too well that if the airship had to make an emergency landing in this, one of the remotest places on earth, there would be little hope of survival.

Later that morning, they picked up the first landmark in the endless sea of swampland: the mighty Yenisei River, with the small village of Verkne Imbatskoe nestling in one of its bends. As they cruised overhead, they saw people hurl themselves to the ground in abject terror at the sight of the gigantic silver cigar in the sky.

Two hundred miles farther on the *Graf Zeppelin* reached Tunguska. It was in this area, twenty years earlier, that something had hurtled down from outer space and exploded with the force of a multi-megaton hydrogen bomb, flattening the forest for miles around. The flash had been seen 250 miles away in broad daylight. The vast area of destruction had never been seen from the air, and the *Graf*'s crew were anxious to obtain some photographs which would be of great interest to the world's scientists. But they failed to locate the point of impact: they were too far to the north. Bitterly disappointed, they flew on.

At four o'clock that afternoon they ran into the first bad weather of the flight, with heavy, ominous black clouds stretching down almost to the treetops of the primeval forest below. The airship plunged into the pitch darkness, rolling and yawing a little in the turbulence. Once, she dropped violently as a down-current gripped her—and then, after ten minutes, passengers and crew were relieved to find themselves in clear skies and bright sunshine once more.

The airship cruised serenely on over primitive settlements where peasants eked out their miserable lives in a land where the earth froze as solid as iron for months every year, and where the winter temperature sometimes fell to ninety degrees below zero. The contrast between such an existence and life aboard the luxury airship, with her brightly lit passenger lounges filled with the strains of an orchestra, her tables groaning under the weight of choice foods and wines, was incredible. But the *Graf Zeppelin* still had to negotiate the most dangerous part of her trans-Siberian journey: the uncharted Stanovoi Mountains, running parallel to the eastern coast of Siberia and plunging steeply into the Sea of Okhotsk.

Once again, all sign of life disappeared as the height of the ground below rose steadily. At 2,500 feet the *Graf Zeppelin* slid into a valley which, according to the scant information on the maps available to the crew, led to a pass that cut between the mountain peaks. But the maps were uncertain, to say the least: the valley could just as easily end in a mountain wall. Cautiously, Eckener eased the airship on the winding flight along the canyon. Below, jagged rocks jutted up like clutching fingers. The canyon floor sloped upwards gradually, forcing the *Graf Zeppelin* to climb to 3,000 feet and then 3,500. The canyon was growing narrower, the rocky walls closing in as though bent on crushing the airship in a deadly grip. At 4,000 feet, the massive bulk of the *Graf* was almost scraping the jutting rocks, and still the ship was being forced higher. At 5,000 feet the crew could see the entrance to the pass, above and ahead of them; but the airship was rapidly approaching her ceiling and the rock walls were terrifyingly close. To make matters worse a gusty wind had sprung up, making it hard for the helmsman to keep the craft steady. One really violent gust would be enough to hurl the *Graf* against the mountain crags, ripping her apart.

Five thousand, five hundred feet. With only feet to spare, the *Graf Zeppelin* scraped over the ridge that ran along the crest of the mountains. Ahead lay the Sea of Okhotsk, blue and sparkling in the sunlight—and beyond it, Japan. The world's first non-stop flight across the length of Russia's mighty land mass was over.

The *Graf Zeppelin* landed in Tokyo on 19 August, having covered 7,000 miles in 101 hours 44 minutes. During the last part of this stage, she successfully weathered the fringes of a typhoon off Sakhalin. Three-quarters of the flight had been made on four engines, and when she landed in Japan the *Graf Zeppelin* had enough fuel and supplies on board to take her non-stop to Los Angeles; the stop at Tokyo, however, had to be made for political reasons.

At 3 p.m. on 23 August the great airship lifted away from the Japanese capital and set course east-south-east over the Pacific. Once again, she narrowly missed being caught up in the fury of a typhoon that swept across her track. Skilfully, Eckener made use of the strong winds encountered in the typhoon area to aid the ship's progress. Soon afterwards, the *Graf Zeppelin* ran into a far worse enemy: fog. For twenty-four hours she nosed through banks of dense white cotton-wool, the crew plotting her position as accurately as possible. Emerging from the fog on the third day of her flight, her crew sighted a ship—the Japanese steamer *Hakutatsu Maru*. When the vessel and the airship compared positions, Eckener was delighted to learn that, thanks to a more favourable wind than he had expected, the *Graf Zeppelin* was actually 170 miles farther along her track beyond the position calculated by her navigators.

At 4 p.m. on 25 August the American coast was sighted, and an hour later the airship was cruising over San Francisco Bay. It was just sixty-seven hours since she had left the coast of Japan behind her. Now, accompanied by squadrons of aircraft that buzzed like hornets around her massive shape, she droned over San Francisco in the setting sun and headed for Los Angeles, 450 miles away. The city was reached at 1 a.m., but because of an arrangement with the US Navy the ship could not land before dawn. For four hours, while the passengers and part of the crew slept, the ship cruised around in circles until Eckener was finally able to bring her in for a landing at 5 a.m. local time. The landing was not easy: as the *Graf Zeppelin* descended into a layer of cooler air which hung over the surface she became about 4,000 pounds lighter, and the crew had to valve off more than 35,000 cubic feet of gas before the ship could be moored safely.

This temperature inversion—a regular night-time phenomenon

around Los Angeles because of ground radiation and cold air flowing down from the mountains—created an even bigger problem when the *Graf Zeppelin* took off the following evening on the last stage of her journey. During the day, exposure to hot sunshine had resulted in a considerable quantity of gas being valved off automatically, with the result that the ship was dangerously heavy. To make matters worse, the ship's gas cells had been refuelled earlier in the day, and the airfield's gas supplies were now exhausted—which meant that there was no possibility of the cells being topped up before flight.

To reduce the *Graf Zeppelin*'s weight, Eckener decided to leave some of the crew behind to finish the journey to Lakehurst by rail. Fuel and water ballast were also reduced to the barest minimum. Even so, when the ship finally took off it was found that although she floated quite well in the cool ground layer, she became heavy as soon as she rose into the warmer layer above. To overcome the problem, Eckener ordered all engines running at flank speed so that the airship nosed forward just above the ground, in order to bring her up into the warmer layer very gradually. At first, everything seemed to go well. The ship ran forward, her elevators up to elevate the bow into the climbing attitude. She was so low that the angle of climb brought her tail into contact with the ground, causing the lower rudder to drag along the surface for a few feet. The ship bounced and hit the ground again, gouging a furrow. She became fully airborne again, but now a new danger loomed up in the shape of high tension wires, running across her path on the airfield boundary. With her speed increasing steadily, the *Graf Zeppelin* raced towards the red obstruction lights that marked the poles and their wires. Everything now depended on the coolness of Hugo Eckener. The bows and the forward car of the ship cleared the wires by several feet, but she was still in a twelve-degree climbing angle and the remainder of her 700-foot length was still below the level of the cables. Judging the right moment with a skill born of long years of experience, Eckener gave a signal to his son Knut, who spun the elevator wheel. The nose went down sharply towards the ground, bringing the tail up rapidly to clear the cables by three feet. With the danger past, Knut reversed the elevators and the *Graf Zeppelin* resumed her climb. Eckener later confessed that he suffered from reaction for some time afterwards; he knew only too well that if she had torn through the cables, the resulting electrical discharge would have turned her into a gigantic funeral pyre.

The *Graf Zeppelin* landed at Lakehurst at 6.40 a.m., local time, on 29 August, after a flight across the American continent lasting 51 hours 13 minutes. Her round-the-world voyage had been completed in 21 days, 7 hours and 34 minutes, of which 7 days, 5 hours and 54 minutes had been spent on the ground at her ports of call.

On 1 September, with Dr Lehmann in command—Eckener having stayed behind to take part in various civic functions on behalf of the crew—the *Graf Zeppelin* took off on the return flight to Friedrichshafen, arriving at 8 a.m. on 4 September after a flight of 67 hours 20 minutes. On this last stage of her long journey, she carried 63 passengers and crew and 800 kg. of mail and cargo.

Back in the United States, Hugo Eckener used his fame to good effect in American business circles, raising funds for the establishment of a regular airship service across the Atlantic. He realized, however, that it would be necessary for the *Graf Zeppelin* to make more prestige flights if public interest was to be maintained, and he lost no time in planning the next project: a flight to South America. This eventually took place on 18 May 1930, when the *Graf Zeppelin* left Friedrichshafen *en route* to Pernambuco, arriving at the Brazilian city on the 24th after one stop at Seville. The airship left Pernambuco four days later, returning to Europe by way of Lakehurst. Apart from a violent rainstorm encountered over the south Atlantic, the flight was completely uneventful and pioneered a highly successful regular service to South America which began in earnest in 1932. The *Graf Zeppelin* made nine flights across the south Atlantic during that year, three of them as far as Rio de Janeiro. An airship shed was built at Rio by a firm of German contractors and was ready for use in 1935. Meanwhile, the *Graf Zeppelin* had made nine more flights to South America in 1933, followed by twelve in 1934 and sixteen in 1935; and in

1936, when she was joined in service by the airship *Hindenburg*, the number of flights made by both airships on the South American service rose to nineteen. During the later trips the *Graf Zeppelin* was carrying 800 pounds of mail on each run; and in 1935, she carried a total of 31,000 pounds—some 900,000 items. Seven hundred and twenty passengers were also carried during this year, compared with five hundred in 1934 and four hundred in 1933. With the arrival of the *Hindenburg*, the future seemed bright; no one could have foreseen the tragic accident which, in 1937, would sound the death-knell of the passenger airship.

For some time—even before the flight round the world—Hugo Eckener had been keenly interested in taking the *Graf Zeppelin* on a flight to the Arctic. The germ of the idea had been sown by the famous Norwegian explorer Fridtjof Nansen, who in 1926 had founded an 'International Association for Exploring the Arctic by Means of Airships'. In 1928, Nansen got in touch with Eckener and the two men had long discussions on the possibility of using the *Graf Zeppelin* on an extensive Arctic survey, but Eckener was reluctant to commit himself because of what he considered to be more urgent priorities.

In 1929 Nansen died, and Eckener was once again approached by the directors of the International Association. Their argument was strengthened by the Polar explorer Sir Hubert Wilkins, who put forward what at the time seemed an incredible proposal: he planned to take a submarine under the Arctic icecap, boring his way up through the ice to rendezvous with the *Graf Zeppelin* at the North Pole. The venture had the backing of the newspaper millionaire William Randolph Hearst, who agreed to pay 150,000 dollars for reporting rights if the airship and submarine succeeded in meeting at the Pole and exchanging passengers and mail; if the two met somewhere in the Arctic other than at the Pole, he would still pay 30,000 dollars.

Wilkins, however, was dogged by bad luck right from the start. The submarine he intended to use, an obsolete US Navy type, first of all experienced several breakdowns during trials in American coastal waters; he managed to limp across to Norway, only to break down again in Trondheim harbour. It was now the early summer of 1931, and Eckener knew that if the flight was going to take place that year it would have to be made in July, before weather conditions in the Arctic began to deteriorate. Attempts to repair Wilkins's submarine before the deadline were unsuccessful, and the plan to use the craft was abandoned. Instead, it was decided that the exchange of passengers and mail would take place between the *Graf Zeppelin* and the Soviet icebreaker *Malygin*, which was due to leave on a scientific expedition to Franz Josef Land at the beginning of July.

The *Graf Zeppelin* left Friedrichshafen on 24 July 1931, heading for Leningrad via Berlin. At 9 a.m. on 26 July the airship, carrying enough fuel for 130 hours' flying and 650 pounds of mail, took off from the Russian city and set course over northwest Russia towards the Barents Sea. Over Archangel she turned due north, running into steadily decreasing temperatures as she headed for the edge of the Arctic icefield. The rendezvous with the icebreaker was made at 5 p.m. GMT on the 27th in a part of Franz Josef Land called Quiet Sound, and the airship landed on the water close to the *Malygin*. The exchange of mail was carried out quickly and the airship took off again thirty-seven minutes later. The take-off was rather hasty, for Eckener had noticed several large ice-floes drifting towards the airship and he was afraid that one of them might damage her hull.

The *Graf Zeppelin* subsequently carried out a survey of Franz Josef Land and Severnaya Zemlya. For the geographers on board it was an exciting journey, and one which led to considerable revision of existing maps of the area. Landfall on the coast of northern Siberia was made at the mouth of the Yenisei and the airship now changed course again, heading for the northern tip of Novaya Zemlya, which was sighted at 2 a.m. on 29 July. At noon that same day, after a flight along the full length of Novaya Zemlya, the *Graf Zeppelin* reached the Barents Sea and pointed her nose towards Leningrad. On arrival over the city, Eckener found that even after a flight lasting ninety hours the *Graf Zeppelin* still had enough fuel on board to reach Friedrichshafen, so he decided to press straight on. Later, in response to a radio appeal from the Mayor of Berlin, he changed his plan and landed at the German capital's Tempelhof airfield at 5.37 p.m. on 30 July.

During the year of delay that had preceded the Arctic flight, Eckener and the *Graf Zeppelin* had been far from idle. In July 1930, two months after the pioneer flight to South America, Eckener took the airship to Norway and Spitzbergen, returning to Friedrichshafen via the Orkneys, Aberdeen, Edinburgh, the North Sea and Amsterdam. Eight days later the *Graf Zeppelin* was once again heading north into the Arctic Circle, this time to Iceland. During the next two years the ship visited London, Helsinki, Stockholm, Copenhagen, Rome, Budapest and several other foreign capitals, and in August 1931 she made a flight around the British Isles—all in addition to her regular flights across the Atlantic.*

Storm-clouds, however, were gathering rapidly on the horizon ahead of Eckener and his enterprises. In 1933 Adolf Hitler became Chancellor of Germany and almost at once Eckener was ordered to paint large swastikas on the fins of the *Graf Zeppelin*. He flatly refused, and persisted in his refusal; to the end of her days the airship never carried the Nazi emblem. It was a courageous stand on Eckener's part: others had been sent to a concentration camp for less. As it was, the Nazis made several attempts to efface Eckener's popularity: the Propaganda Minister, Goebbels, even considered ordering the German press not to mention his name or publish his photograph.

The *Graf Zeppelin* continued in service until 1937. During her nine years of life, she made 650 flights and carried more than 18,000 passengers over a million miles. Then came the *Hindenburg* disaster—the tragic outcome of using inflammable hydrogen. Attempts were made to obtain helium from the United States, the only natural source of the gas, but the Americans refused to supply any to Hitler's Germany. The *Graf Zeppelin* now became a huge white elephant, forbidden to fly by the German Air Ministry so long as she was filled with hydrogen. There could only be one outcome. Early in 1938 she was broken up—a sad end to the majestic craft that had done so much to open up air routes to remote corners of the globe.

* For details of passengers carried, miles flown etc., see Appendix III.

9 Britain's Last Airships—
Triumph and Tragedy

In 1924—after discussions that had dragged on for two years—Ramsay MacDonald's Labour Government initiated an airship research programme which was to prove once and for all whether the large rigid airship would be a worthwhile commercial enterprise. The programme, which was to be spread over three years at a cost of £1,350,000, was to lead to the construction of two experimental airships capable of carrying a large payload on intercontinental flights. The ships, designated *R.100* and *R.101*, were to be built respectively by the Airship Guarantee Company—a subsidiary of Vickers—and the Air Ministry establishment at Cardington. Both Cardington and Pulham—virtually unused since the *R.38* disaster of 1921—were to be retained by the Government and placed in commission once more, and airship bases were to be built by the Air Ministry in Egypt, Canada and India.

The civilian Airship Guarantee Company was hampered from the start by shortage of money, but the lack of funds was more than compensated for by the genius of the men in control of the enterprise. Commander Dennis Burney, RN, was responsible for the company's general administration and control; he was the man who, when the *R.38* tragedy had seemed certain to mark the death of rigid-airship development in Britain, had pounded desks for two years in Government circles until a Cabinet Committee had been appointed to reconsider the whole question. On the company's technical side, the chief designer was Dr Barnes Wallis—a man of great talent and revolutionary ideas, with a vast amount of design experience on earlier Vickers rigid airships, whose work in this field was to be overshadowed by later fame in connexion with the bombs that smashed the Moehne and Eder dams in 1943, and a host of other brilliant projects. His chief calculator was a young man who was also to earn fame, but in a different sphere: Nevil Shute Norway.

The specifications that governed the development of both the *R.100* and the *R.101* were stringent. Both ships were to have a capacity of five million cubic feet, giving them a gross lift of 150 tons, and their structure had to meet certain definite stress factors. Maximum speed with 100 passengers on board was to be not less than 70 m.p.h., with a cruising speed of 63 m.p.h. Structural weight, including the power plants but excluding fuel, was not to exceed 90 tons, giving a useful lift of 60 tons. The engines and their fuel systems were to be capable of operating efficiently in tropical climates.

The Air Ministry designers of the *R.101* at Cardington had to start virtually from scratch; the only airship design they could take as a guide was that of the ill-fated *R.38*, and it appeared that no calculations on the stresses likely to be imposed on her structure during various manœuvres in flight had ever been made. The first task, therefore, was to carry out a thorough investigation into the aerodynamic forces acting on an airship in flight, and to compile data on the distribution of stresses in the structure of an airship caused by these aerodynamic forces and by static forces resulting from loading and other factors.

The basic research work was undertaken by the scientists of the National Physical Laboratory, who tested various models in wind tunnels to evolve a definitive shape that would cut down air resistance to the absolute minimum. To check out the data compiled with the aid of these models, the *R.33* and the *R.36* were re-commissioned and their hulls and control surfaces festooned with instruments for measuring stresses and strains. A complete hull section of the *R.101* was also built at Cardington and tested to destruction. The designers professed the results to be satisfactory, but there is no doubt that they stopped at a crucial point in the *R.101*'s development: the airship's construction was an almost complete breakaway from conventional methods from the gas-bag wiring and the relief valves right down to the steering gear and the type of engine to be used, but just when the *R.33* and the *R.36* could have been used profitably to test these new techniques under actual flight conditions the Government ordered the scrapping of both airships on grounds of economy.

So the first step was taken on the road that was to lead to disaster. Although many problems were solved by means of theoretical calculations made with the use of models, this was no substitute for full-scale flight testing. Although the information gathered by the Air Ministry team was made available to the Airship Guarantee Company, there was no real co-operation between the two, and approaches made by Barnes Wallis and his colleagues with a view to closer collaboration were ignored, despite the fact that relations remained quite friendly. Throughout the period of construction, the Cardington team received an enormous amount of publicity. This in itself was another contributory factor to the eventual tragedy, for as each new technique and refinement in the *R.101*'s design came along it received so much publicity that the designers had to incorporate it, even though it showed up poorly during trials.

One good example of this was the *R.101*'s specially developed diesel engines. The decision to use diesels had been influenced by safety considerations, diesel fuel burning less fiercely than petrol. The snag was that the engines were far too heavy, with a weight of eight pounds per horse-power instead of the estimated four. Moreover, no amount of experiment and improvement would coax the engines to develop more than 650 h.p. each—but the requirement had specified a minimum of 700 h.p.

Diesels of the *R.101* type had also been considered as a possible power source for the *R.100*, but the fact that they were too heavy was discovered in time and they were replaced by six Rolls-Royce Condor engines. The risk of fire from these motors was only marginally greater than if diesels were used, and the Condors had an overwhelming advantage in that they were already tried and proven. In general, the constructors of the *R.100* went about their task in a much more workmanlike fashion than did their rivals at Cardington, detecting snags and eliminating them in the early stages before much money had been wasted. Construction went ahead steadily with none of the fuss and publicity that surrounded the *R.101*, and in the middle of 1929 the ship's fourteen gasbags were inflated and she was floated in her shed, still without her outer envelope.

The *R.101* was completed first. On 12 October 1929 she was walked out of her shed and moored at the Cardington mast in readiness for her maiden flight, which was to take place on the 14th. During her first flight, which lasted 5½ hours, only two of her five troublesome engines were working for most of the time, but during the second trip—made on 18 October and lasting 9½ hours—four engines were in operation. Incredibly, no written reports were made on either of these flights. The third test flight was made on 1 November and lasted 7½ hours, and the following day the airship made her first night flight, taking off from Cardington at 8 p.m. and setting course towards the Isle of Wight. During this flight the ship was scheduled to make a speed trial, but one of her engines broke down and the attempt had to be abandoned. The *R.101* finally landed back at Cardington at 10 a.m. on 3 November.

A week later, on 11 November, a severe gale blew up while the *R.101* was at her mooring-mast. Throughout most of the afternoon the average wind speed was 55 m.p.h., and gusts of up to 83 m.p.h. were recorded. The ship rode out the gale successfully, withstanding a load of up to 15½ tons on her nose coupling, but she experienced a slow rolling motion during the stronger gusts of wind and her gas bags became chafed as a result. The airship's coxswain, G. W. Hunt, inspected the *R.101* during the storm and submitted the following report:

During storm routine, whilst looking round, it was observed that in the case of Nos. 3 to 14 bags inclusive, a very considerable movement from side to side was taking place on each flat end, as much as 3 ins. to 4 ins., and at times the surge of the bags in a forward direction was considerably more than that.

Owing to the combined two movements, where the bags were touching the radial struts around main frames, especially at C and D longitudinals, the plates on top of the radial struts rubbed and chafed the bags and in places, such as No. 8

starboard fore end, tore the bag 9 ins. in a jagged tear. No. 8 thus became deflated to 60 per cent, and on inspection taking place it was noticed that on every roll the valves opened to the extent of $\frac{1}{4}$ in. to $\frac{1}{2}$ in. The valves were lightly stopped back until the bag was gassed to 95 per cent. The holes on top of No. 14 bag were caused by the bag bearing hard on O girder where several nuts project, and, combined with the movements of the bag, caused punctures.

The damage was repaired, and on 17 November the *R.101* set off on an endurance flight that was to have lasted 48 hours. In fact the flight was abandoned because of various technical troubles after 30 hours 41 minutes, but during this time the airship covered a distance of 1,000 miles. It was the longest flight she was ever to make. Afterwards, the ship remained at her mooring-mast until 30 November, when she was taken into her shed. So far, she had made a total of seven flights and logged 70 hours in the air, but all the flights had been made in good weather and none of them had involved a lengthy full-speed trial.

Meanwhile, in November 1929, the *R.100* had also made her first flight, and in December she was flown down from Howden and moored at Cardington for the start of her trials. She soon showed herself to be much the better of the two ships, clocking a speed of 81 m.p.h. during her early trial flights and showing herself capable of operating in all weathers. Her design was somewhat unusual, with tubular longitudinal girders and a passenger coach built inside the hull instead of protruding beneath, as was more common.

Although the *R.100* suffered a number of technical troubles with her envelope and gas bags, her performance met the specification quite adequately and the success of her test flight programme did nothing to raise the morale of the *R.101* team, especially since the effects of the American depression were making themselves felt in Britain's economy and there was a strong rumour that the less successful of the two airships would be scrapped. A prestige flight to India was in the wind, but before there was even the remotest chance of this taking place something had to be done to increase the *R.101*'s useful lift, which—at only twenty-five tons—was less than half that of the *R.100*. After lengthy discussions, the designers decided to remove some of the ship's fittings, including some of the passenger sleeping-accommodation, and to enlarge the gas-bag wiring to allow greater expansion. This, it was estimated, would increase the useful lift by about six tons. Another nine tons could be obtained by creating an additional middle bay, allowing space for another gas bag by lengthening the ship.

Even with these modifications, the flight to India could still not be attempted until the airship had received a full Certificate of Airworthiness, and one of the requirements for this was an endurance flight of at least forty-eight hours. Accordingly, it was decided to complete the first set of modifications and then put the *R.101* through a further series of test flights before adding the new bay and gas bag.

When the airship was examined prior to the re-wiring of the gas bags, it was found that every one of the bags was holed—some of them badly. No. 11 bag, for example, had 103 holes and No. 5 had 57. These were repaired, and the projections thought to be responsible for the damage were carefully padded. The designers realized that enlarging the bags was going to add to the danger, but the plan went ahead—and the solution to the problem was simply to increase the amount of padding. The complex and weighty servo-controls governing elevators and rudder were also scrapped and replaced with a simpler and lighter control system similar to that installed in the *R.100*—a system that worked just as well.

It was six months before these modifications were completed, and it was not until 23 June 1930 that the *R.101* emerged from her shed once more. She had hardly been manœuvred into position at her mooring-mast when, without warning, a split 140 feet long appeared in the starboard side of her envelope. This was quickly repaired, but the next day a smaller split appeared in the top of the envelope. Both crew and designers knew that if the envelope ripped open in such a manner while the ship was airborne, the consequences could be catastrophic; nevertheless, the damage was repaired and the test programme went ahead with a $4\frac{1}{2}$-hour flight on 26 June. During this trip, the airship's eighth, the craft became dangerously heavy through loss of lift and over two tons of diesel fuel had to be jettisoned before a safe landing could be made.

As part of a renewed publicity programme the *R.101* was scheduled to take part in the RAF air display at Hendon, and on 27 June she took off on a rehearsal flight which lasted $12\frac{1}{2}$ hours. To keep her at an altitude of 1,000 feet the crew had to jettison no less than nine tons of water ballast. The airship flew over Hendon the following day and the trouble was repeated, the craft losing height steadily as she leaked large quantities of gas. The crowd that watched her as she cruised overhead and marvelled at her majesty never dreamed that she was virtually crippled, and that her crew had to use all their skill to bring her safely back to Cardington.

On 29 June the *R.101* was taken back into her shed so that work could begin on inserting the new bay. Once more, she was subjected to a thorough overhaul which revealed a number of horrifying faults. First of all, it was found that when the valves on the gas cells were tilted at an angle of four degrees or more from the vertical, they opened—which meant that gas was bound to escape at a fast rate if the ship rolled beyond the four-degree limit as she passed through areas of turbulence. Secondly, there was the discovery that the padding around the gas cells had proved inadequate and that the bags were now being fouled by literally thousands of projections. There were two possible solutions: either a drastic alteration of the structure, or more padding. Predictably, it was the latter alternative that was chosen.

Meanwhile, the *R.100* had completed seven test flights, most of them successful, and had logged a total of 150 hours in the air. She was now ready for the first of the 'Empire' flights which, it was hoped, she would eventually share with the *R.101*. At 2.50 a.m. on 29 July 1930 she left the mast at Cardington and set course for her destination—Montreal. Her commander was Captain R. S. Booth, with Captain G. F. Meager as his First Officer and Squadron Leader E. L. Johnston as navigator. Also on board were Sir Dennis Burney, Nevil Shute Norway,

Lieutenant Commander Prentice—the Admiralty observer—
Flight Lieutenant Wann, survivor of the *R.38* crash, and Major
G. H. Scott, officer in charge of flying operations at Cardington.
The flight across the Atlantic was uneventful and the crossing
was made in record time. Near Quebec, however, the airship
ran into a heavy storm which tore away large areas of fabric
from her fins. Riggers and engineers at once set about repairing
the damage, fifteen men working on the port fin alone. Within
two hours the trouble had been patched up and the ship was
able to continue on her way at increased speed.

At 7.30 p.m. on the 31st, while flying at 1,200 feet in darkness,
the *R.100* encountered a heavy thunderstorm. She was seized
by strong up-currents and continued to rise rapidly, even with
her nose pointing down at an angle of twenty degrees. She shot
up to 2,500 feet in fifteen seconds before she finally got clear of
the turbulence. Several hours later, at dawn on 1 August, she
landed at St Hubert Airfield, Montreal, after a flight of 78
hours 51 minutes. With forty-two crew and thirteen passengers
on board, she had covered 3,300 miles at an average speed of
42 m.p.h. The airship stayed at Montreal for the best part of a
fortnight, making one twenty-four-hour demonstration flight
before taking off on the return transatlantic flight at 9.28 p.m.
local time on 13 August. With the prevailing wind behind her,
the return journey was a good deal faster than the westbound
run, and Cardington was reached at 10 a.m. GMT on 16 August,
after a flight of 56 hours 30 minutes. Afterwards, she was taken
back to her shed and overhauled in readiness for more flights
abroad. But the *R.100* never flew again; the tragedy of the
R.101 saw to that.

Work on the *R.101* had, in the meantime, being going on by
day and night in a desperate attempt to get the ship ready for a
flight to India in September. Even so, the ship would not be
ready before the end of September at the earliest, and the
Cardington team were reluctant to take her on such a voyage
before she was fully certificated—which meant a flight of forty-
eight hours, one of twenty-four hours under adverse weather
conditions, and high-speed trials. The whole affair was complicated still further by the Air Minister, Lord Thomson, who

announced his intention to visit India in September to take part in a number of political engagements and who saw no reason why the airship should not be ready in time to get him there. He had aspirations to become the next Viceroy of India, and wished to create as big an impression as possible by arriving in dramatic fashion. His views were expressed in a minute to the director of the Airship Works at Cardington: 'I must insist', he wrote, 'on the programme for the Indian flight being adhered to as I have made my plans accordingly.' Those plans involved being back in England by not later than 19 October in order to participate in an Imperial Conference on the 20th.

When he learned that the ship would not be complete in time to make the flight in September, he was furious. Nevertheless, he revised his schedule to allow for a departure on 4 October —but not a day later. The Cardington team stifled their protests: argument would have meant the almost certain end of the whole $R.101$ project. Instead, they rushed the work on the new bay, leaving no time for real testing either on the ground or in flight. Hasty repairs were also carried out on the envelope, which was in a pitiful state—but there was no time to replace it entirely. Several parts were simply patched up with tape, attached to the doped fabric with a rubber solution—in complete ignorance of the fact that rubber solution and dope do not mix. The work was completed by 25 September, and over the next few days a number of lift and trim tests were carried out inside the $R.101$'s shed. It was found that the extra bay now gave the ship a useful lift of 49·3 tons. On 1 October she was taken out of her shed and took off on a flight lasting 16 hours 51 minutes. The flight took place in perfect weather conditions and it had been hoped to put the airship through her high-speed trials, but this plan was abandoned when one of the $R.101$'s engines broke down.

The following day, Sir Sefton Brancker, the Director of Civil Aviation, called on Lord Thomson and confided that he was far from happy about the $R.101$'s state of airworthiness. Wing Commander Colmore, the Director of Airship Development, also shared his views; both men wanted the $R.101$ put through more trials before she was taken on a journey of such magnitude, and particularly one during which she would be subjected to enormous variations in temperature as she passed over regions such as the Alps and the Sahara. Thomson refused to listen. The *R.101* was, he declared, as safe as a house—except for the millionth chance.

The ship still had no Certificate of Airworthiness, and without one the planned flight to India would not have been legal. But there was an answer for this, too, even though it involved a slight bending of the regulations: shortly before the airship took off, a temporary certificate was handed to her captain, Flight Lieutenant H. C. Irwin, and it was decided that the qualifying full-speed trials would be made during the voyage itself with all the passengers and crew on board.

At 6.36 p.m. on 4 October 1930 the *R.101*'s 777-foot length slipped away from the Cardington mast and the journey to India began. On board were fifty-four people—forty-two crew, six officials from the Airship Works, and six passengers—including Lord Thomson and Sir Sefton Brancker. The airship carried 25 tons of fuel and 9¼ tons of water, but four tons of this were dropped while the ship was still at her mast. The wind was blowing in gusts and its strength increasing all the time; the barometer had been falling all day. As the *R.101* cruised over Hitchin at 1,000 feet she encountered a rainstorm, and as she passed through it an alarming rolling and pitching motion developed. Soon afterwards, the aft engine broke down; two engineers were detailed to repair it, and the ship continued on her way.

At 9.35 p.m. the *R.101* crossed the Channel coast at Hastings and the Captain sent a signal to Cardington reporting that although the faulty engine was still out of action, the ship generally appeared to be responding well. The engine was finally restarted halfway across the Channel, but by this time her altitude was down to 700 feet and it was only with extreme difficulty that she was able to climb to 1,000 feet once more.

At 11.26 the airship crossed the French coast at Pointe-Saint-Quentin, north-east of Dieppe. She was now making slow progress against a headwind of 35 knots and experiencing severe buffeting as she ran through areas of turbulence. Despite this, Flight Lieutenant Irwin still seemed pleased with the ship's performance, as was indicated by another signal which he transmitted to Cardington: 'After an excellent supper our distinguished passengers smoked a final cigar and, having sighted the French coast, have now gone to rest after the excitement of the leave-taking.' With all the passengers and most of the crew in bed, the duty crew settled down on watch in the control cabin. It seems certain that they must have had a continual struggle to maintain height, for when the airship passed over Poix airfield just after 1 a.m. observers on the ground estimated her altitude as no more than 300 feet. At 1.52 a.m. the ship radioed Le Bourget and gave her position as five-eighths of a mile north of Poix, her altimeter indicating 1,000 feet above sea level. It was her last message.

At 2 a.m. the watch was changed. The ship was passing over Beauvais, and residents of the town who saw her later stated that she was rolling badly. She was very low. At 2.5 a.m., without warning, the *R.101* went into a steep dive, which was checked just in time by the release of water ballast. The coxswain fought to bring her nose up, but the elevators failed to respond; the ship was too heavy and too low. Seconds later she went into another, more shallow, dive, and at 2.8 a.m. she struck a hillside near Beauvais with a prolonged crunching noise. The airship skidded along on her keel for sixty yards; the impact was quite gentle, and those on board who were fully awake prepared to make an emergency exit as soon as the motion stopped. But there was no time. An instant later, five and a half million cubic feet of hydrogen erupted and the *R.101* became a blazing funeral pyre from stem to stern. Out of the fifty-four on board there were six survivors, all of whom had miraculous escapes. Lord Thomson and Sir Sefton Brancker were not among them.

An inquiry concluded that part of the fabric on the top of the airship's envelope had torn away during the buffeting she had received over the French coast. The gas-bags, already badly chafed, would then have been further damaged by exposure to the weather and sprung leaks—and more gas must have been lost through the continual opening of the valves as the ship rolled, for this fault had never been rectified. The result was that she became steadily heavier and more waterlogged, until she became powerless to recover from the sudden downdraughts that seized her: she crashed to her destruction on the rain-swept hillside near Beauvais—a burnt-out testimony to bungling, mismanagement and crass governmental stupidity which, fortunately, has had few parallels in the history of aviation.

The destruction of the *R.101*, and the death of many of the finest brains associated with airship development, marked the end of Britain's part in the story of the big rigids. The *R.100* never flew again; she was broken up and sold for £450 as scrap. An ignominious end to a good ship, and to the years of skill and devotion that had gone into her making.

10 Military Airships in the USA, 1918–38

As mentioned in Chapter Five, the first really successful military airship developed in the United States was the B Class non-rigid, designed by the Navy's Bureau of Construction and Repair and built in 1916 by Goodyear, the B. F. Goodrich Company and the Connecticut Aircraft Company. The latter company had in fact been awarded a Navy contract worth $45,636 to build an airship in 1915, but this craft, the *DN.1*, was not completed until 1917. With the US Navy designation *A-1*, she flew three times at Pensacola in Florida, but she was a failure and was scrapped.

Subsequent contracts to build non-rigids for the US Navy went to Goodyear, who in 1917 produced the C Class—a more advanced version of the B, with a speed of 60 m.p.h., a capacity of 77,000 cubic feet and considerably longer range. On 12 December 1918 the dirigible *C-1* commanded by G. Crompton carried a Curtiss JN-4 biplane to a height of 2,500 feet and released it, the first time this experiment had been undertaken in the United States. The aircraft, piloted by A. W. Redfield, glided safely to earth.

Another dirigible of this class, the *C-5*, was a contestant in the race to become the first to cross the Atlantic. Commanded by Lieutenant Commander E. W. Coil, she took off from Montauk at 8 a.m. on 14 May 1919 and landed safely at St John's, Newfoundland, 25 hours 50 minutes later, after a flight of 1,022 miles. Two days later, however, she was torn from her moorings by a westerly gale and was lost over the Atlantic, fortunately with no one on board.

On 9 August 1919 the Secretary of the Navy approved plans for the construction of a rigid airship based on the design of Zeppelin *L.49*, plans of which had been circulated among the Allied powers after she had been captured almost intact following a forced landing at Bourbonne-les-Bains, France, in October 1917. In the meantime, arrangements were made to train US Navy crews in rigid airship handling techniques in Britain, and to purchase the British rigid airship *R.38* (*ZR-2*) at a cost of £500,000. The destruction of the *R.38* in August 1921, however, with the loss of fifteen American lives, caused a delay in the building of the American ship and she was not completed until August 1923. On the 13th of that month inflation with helium was started inside the airship's hangar at Lakehurst, a process that took a week. She was the second airship to be inflated with this gas; experiments with helium as a lifting medium instead of the highly inflammable hydrogen had been carried out some eighteen months earlier with the non-rigid dirigible *C-7*.

On 4 September 1923 the airship—designated *ZR-1* and named *Shenandoah*, an Indian name meaning 'Daughter of the Stars'—took off on a maiden flight lasting an hour. She was captained by Commander F. R. McCrary, USN, who reported a successful flight. The first long-range flight took place on 1 October, when the airship flew from Lakehurst to St Louis with forty-two people on board in 24 hours 46 minutes. After a short stay of two hours, she returned to her home base in 20 hours 28 minutes.

During the autumn of 1923, she was used for experimental work in connexion with a new mooring-mast at Lakehurst. On 16 January 1924 she was moored at this mast when a severe winter storm blew up and she was buffeted by gusts of up to 63 m.p.h. Suddenly, at 6.44 p.m., an exceptionally violent gust of over 70 m.p.h. hit her at an angle and twisted her about her longitudinal axis. There was a horrible tearing noise as she ripped away from her mooring and began to drift astern towards a row of pine trees, losing height steadily. Fortunately, a skeleton crew was aboard and they dropped ballast, enabling the airship to clear the trees by a matter of feet. Her temporary commander, Lieutenant Commander M. R. Pierce, quickly assessed the damage: the ship was down by the bow, with her two forward gas bags ripped open, but her controls were still functioning. By careful re-distribution of fuel and ballast the

Shenandoah was brought to an even keel and her engines were started. Painfully slowly, she crept home and was brought in for a safe landing at 3.30 the following morning.

Repairs were completed by 22 May and the airship resumed her flying duties under the command of Commander Zachary Lansdowne, USN, an officer who had completed his airship training in Britain. Under his direction, she carried out a series of seaborne mooring trials at a mast erected on board the USS *Patoka* and also took part in naval manœuvres, logging one flight of forty hours' duration. On 7 October 1924 she left Lakehurst on a trans-continental flight across the United States via El Paso, southern New Mexico, Arizona and California. Her commander decided to take her through the mountain passes on her route instead of flying over the peaks, which would have meant the loss of a large quantity of helium; the passes were successfully negotiated in spite of bad weather and severe turbulence, and the *Shenandoah* arrived back at Lakehurst on the evening of 26 October after covering 9,317 miles in 19 days 19 hours.

During the following year the airship logged 750 hours in the air, covering a total distance of 28,000 miles. Then, on the afternoon of 2 September 1925, once again under the command of Zachary Lansdowne, she took off from Lakehurst on a flight to the Middle West. At four o'clock the following morning she ran into strong headwinds over Byesville, Ohio, at 2,100 feet, and could make little progress even with all five engines running. Minutes later, the coxswain reported that the ship was rising and that he was unable to check her. Her engines were opened up and her bow put down at an inclination of 18 degrees, but even with the elevators hard down and the rudder hard over she failed to respond and continued to shoot up rapidly through 4,000 feet. Gas was hastily valved off and at 6,200 feet the upward surge was finally checked, but the ship was now heavy and she began to fall. To check the descent tons of water ballast were jettisoned, but the *Shenandoah* continued to fall at 1,400 feet per minute for two minutes. Then, suddenly, she was caught in a vicious upcurrent, and this time—since all the water ballast was gone and two engines were out of action—the crew prepared to jettison fuel tanks, spare parts and other weighty equipment in an effort to bring the ship under control again.

To supervise this operation, the ship's executive officer, Lieutenant Commander Rosendahl, climbed up into the keel from the control car. Moments later, there was a sharp cracking sound and the car tore away, swinging on its control wires for a second before those too snapped and it went spinning down into space. Horrified, Rosendahl found himself staring into nothing as ahead of him the after section of the ship broke away. The 200-foot bow section, with Rosendahl and six other men inside, drifted clear and rose to a height of 10,000 feet. By valving gas and throwing heavy objects overboard, the seven men managed by a miracle to bring this section safely to earth. The after section with twenty-five men on board also drifted to earth like a free balloon, but when it was still some distance from the ground two of the engine cars broke away and three engineers crashed to their deaths.

In all, twenty-nine men survived the disaster. Apart from the three engineers, three more of the crew had been flung overboard when the ship broke up and eight had died in the control car. A Court of Inquiry was set up immediately, but its task was made difficult by the fact that hordes of souvenir hunters descended on the wreck and removed parts of the aluminium framework before a guard could be mounted. The Court's eventual conclusion was that 'the ship was lost by being broken in two by the aerodynamical stresses imposed upon her by the vertical currents of the storm in which she had been entrapped without warning'.

The loss of the *Shenandoah* left the US Navy with one rigid airship, the *ZR-3* (*LZ.126*), named *Los Angeles*, which had arrived in the United States in October 1924 after her flight from Germany (see Chapter Six). She had done comparatively little flying while the *Shenandoah* was in commission, since both ships had to share a rationed amount of helium, which at that time was still in short supply. Nevertheless, she had made a number of notable flights during 1925: the first of these was on 24 January, when she followed the path of a solar eclipse with twenty-five scientists on board. Her first really long voyage was on 20

30. The *R.33* at its mooring-mast, Pulham Airship Station, Norfolk, in 1921

31. The *R.33* and the *R.34* together in the large airship hangar at Pulham, Norfolk

32. The US Navy ZR-I, the *Shenandoah,* on its mooring-mast, soon after its launching in 1923. The *Shenandoah* was one of the first airships to be inflated with helium

33. The Italian airship *Norge,* which flew over the North Pole on 12 May 1926

34. The *Graf Zeppelin* on a visit to London in April 1930, passing over the Gaiety Theatre in the Strand

35. The *Graf Zeppelin* on its unexpected arrival at the RAF station, Cardington, Bedfordshire

36. The *Graf Zeppelin* passing over Basel on the first stage of the flight to America in October 1928

37. The *Graf Zeppelin* over Cairo during the flight to Egypt in 1931

38. & 39. The passenger accommodation aboard the *Graf Zeppelin,* affording comfort comparable with that of a luxury liner. *Right:* A passenger cabin at night, with the couch converted into a bed and a second bunk slung overhead. *Below:* The dining-room

40. The massive skeleton of the *R.100* under construction in 1929

41. A gas-bag being inflated in the partially built *R.101*

42. The *R.101* under construction

43. An engine-car of the *R.101*

44. The *R.101* in its hangar, seen from the tail

45. The *R.100* in flight in June 1931; note the biplane near its tail

46. Major G. H. Scott, commander of the *R.34*, looking out of the control car of the *R.101*

47. The *R.101* at its mooring-mast in 1930

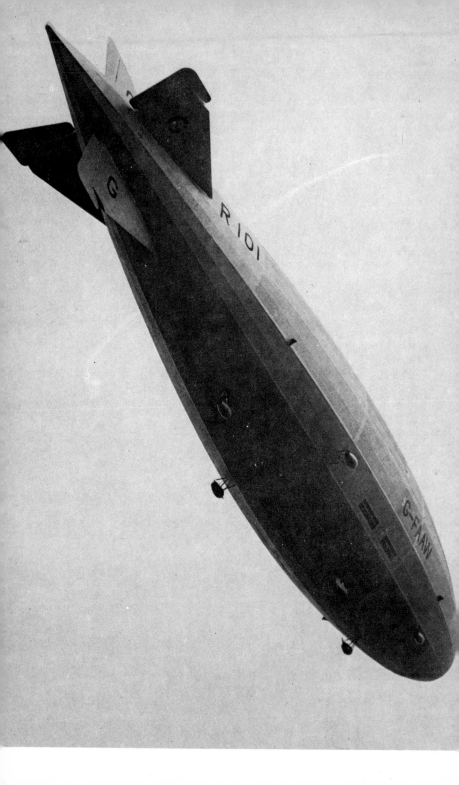

49. The *Hindenburg* on her first trial flight over Lake Constance, 23 March 1936

48. The *R.101* in flight

50. A US Navy blimp on convoy escort in June 1942. No ship guarded by these blimps was sunk by the enemy during the Second World War

51. US Navy blimp being winched up to a mooring-mast

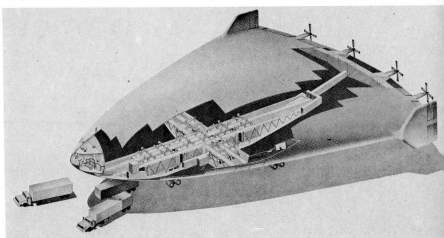

52. & 53. General view and cutaway of the Aereon Corporation's project for a four-engined 'lifting body' cargo airship (1967)

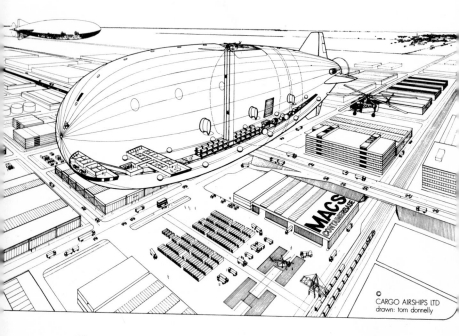

54. This drawing illustrates the layout and some features which could be incorporated into a modern airship as visualized by Cargo Airships Ltd. The main difference will be in the hull structure. Modern airships would have a stiff outer shell instead of the old 'Zeppelin' structure, which was essentially a metal skeleton framework covered with doped fabric.

Just below the nose of the ship is the bridge. Leading back from it is the computer room, and aft of that are the crew's quarters. Containers are picked up from a container base by a straddle helicopter and are fed into the airship from a helipad on top of it. This helipad has a retractable cover. The container is then lowered to the cargo deck on the keel by means of an elevator. Aft of the cargo deck is a diesel/electric combination which provides power for the main motor and propeller at the stern, also for the line of manoeuvring propellers on either side of the airship which are used to provide downthrust when the airship is standing still in the air. When the airship is underway the manoeuvring propellers swivel through 90° and provide assistance to the main propulsive unit at the rear

February, when she made the round trip from Lakehurst to Bermuda—a distance of 1,500 miles. The following May, she flew from Lakehurst to Puerto Rico and back in 31 hours.

The *Los Angeles* remained in service for seven years, carrying out many experimental missions. During one of these, in January 1928, she landed on the aircraft carrier *Saratoga* and took off again several hours later after being replenished. This was followed, on 26 February, by a flight from Lakehurst to France Field (Panama) during which she covered a distance of 2,300 miles in 39 hours 45 minutes; two days later she flew from Panama to Guacanaya Bay (Cuba), where she landed on the carrier *Patoka* before returning to Lakehurst in 21 hours. On 27 August 1929 she picked up an aircraft in flight over Lakehurst at 2,500 feet and released it again from a specially designed trapeze after the machine had taken aboard one of the airship's crew, Lieutenant C. M. Bolster. Several more successful experiments of this kind were carried out during 1930. During her seven years of useful life, the *Los Angeles* made 331 flights and logged a total flying time of more than 5,000 hours. She was finally retired from service on 30 June 1932, but she was not finally broken up until 1940.

In 1926, the United States Congress authorized the Navy to build two rigid airships with a capacity of 6,500,000 cubic feet—the largest ever—and asked for bids from various companies, issuing specifications governing performance and structural requirements. Altogether, thirty-seven different designs were submitted, and after a long study the contract finally went to Goodyear on 6 October 1928. Before work could be started, a special hangar had to be built, and the Goodyear technicians found this no easy task. Since an ordinary rectangular building might set up wind currents and eddies that would make handling on exit and entry extremely difficult, the hangar had to be aerodynamically designed; after extensive wind-tunnel experiments a semi-paraboloid or 'turtle-back' structure was evolved with semi-circular 'orange-peel' doors that folded back around the contour of the building when opened. The resulting hangar was 1,175 feet long, 325 feet wide and 211 feet high, with an area of 8½ acres.

Construction of the first giant airship, the *Akron*, was begun on 7 November 1929 and was completed on 8 August 1931. The airship, designated *ZRS-4*, was enormous: she had a length of 785 feet, a diameter of 132·9 feet and a capacity of 6,500,000 cubic feet. She was powered by eight engines developing a total of 4,480 h.p. and giving her a maximum speed of over 83 m.p.h. Gross lift was· 430,000 pounds, and useful lift 182,000 pounds. Her ribs were covered with more than 55,000 square yards of doped weather-proof fabric; another 55,000 square yards of gelatin-latex fabric were used in her gas cells. Her still-air range without refuelling was 10,500 miles. The *Akron* made her first flight on 23 September 1931, with 113 people on board. Her commander was Lieutenant Commander C. E. Rosendahl, one of the survivors of the *Shenandoah* disaster. On 3 November she made a ten-hour flight with 270 people on board, setting up a record for the number of passengers carried.

One of the airship's features was a built-in hangar, big enough to accommodate five pursuit aircraft. These could be launched and taken on board again during normal cruising flight by means of a trapeze lowered through a trap-door in the bottom of the hull. The pilots who were assigned to the *Akron*'s aircraft flight called this manœuvre 'belly bumping'. It was a success: on one occasion, six pilots made 104 take-offs and hook-ons in the space of three hours.

During her eighteen months of US Navy service, the *Akron* took part in several fleet manœuvres and showed the value of the airship–aircraft combination by launching air patrols over the surface forces at times when surface weather conditions made operations by carrier aircraft hazardous, if not impossible.

On 4 April 1933 she left Lakehurst to take part in another Fleet manœuvre in the Atlantic. She was captained by Commander F. C. McCord, USN, with Lieutenant Commander Wiley as his executive officer. She carried a crew of seventy-six and also Admiral William A. Moffett, Chief of the Bureau of Aeronautics. Over Philadelphia, lightning was sighted away to the south and McCord altered course to the east, heading directly for the coast. This was crossed at 10 p.m., the airship cruising out into the Atlantic at 1,600 feet. A few minutes later the storm caught up with her, and for one and a half hours she ran through heavy rain and violent winds. At 12.30 a.m., without warning, she was struck by severe turbulence and the helmsman reported that she was starting to drop rapidly. A large amount of ballast was dropped, but the fall continued steadily until the airship was at a height of 700 feet, when she checked and began to rise rapidly again. At 1,600 feet full control was regained and the flight was resumed.

A few minutes later, however, the turbulence struck again, more violently than before. Once again she began to fall at a speed of 14 feet per second, and there was a loud crack as her rudder controls parted. At 300 feet the white wave-crests were sighted through the darkness, but there was little the crew could do except hang on and wait for the inevitable impact. Twenty seconds later she struck in a tail-down attitude and broke up rapidly, pounded by the wind and waves. An hour later, three survivors, one of them Lieutenant Commander Wiley, were picked up by a steamer. The ship searched the area, but there was no other sign of life.

A subsequent Board of Inquiry blamed the relative inexperience of the ship's captain, Commander Frank McCord, for the disaster. The ship had been in perfect condition on take-off, so there was no question of her being mechanically imperfect. However, despite the fact that her commander had known of the existence and location of the storm, he had steered towards it on a collision course. Furthermore, no correction had been made to the altimeter to compensate for the drop in atmospheric pressure resulting from the storm; consequently, the airship's indicated altitude of 1,600 feet had been closer to 1,000 feet in reality. Most of the *Akron*'s wreckage was later brought to the surface by the salvage ship *Falcon*, and an examination showed beyond doubt that the airship had not suffered structural failure before the impact.

A reassurance of this kind was badly needed, for less than a month after the crash the *Akron*'s sister ship, the *ZRS-5 Macon*, made her first flight. During her maiden voyage on 21 April

1933 she reached a speed of 85 m.p.h. Like the *Akron*, she had a compartment for the housing of five fighter aircraft. She was commissioned at Lakehurst on 24 June, with Commander H. Dressel as her captain. From Lakehurst she was flown to her new base at Sunnyvale in California, from where she worked with the Pacific Fleet throughout 1933–4. By the autumn of 1934 she was badly in need of an overhaul, but because of her operational commitments this was put off several times. Her already overworked structure received an additional battering when, running at high speed with a full load of fuel on board during a flight from California to the West Indies, she hit severe turbulence over the south-west corner of the United States. Sharp rudder and elevator movements were necessary to keep her flying more or less straight and level, and these imposed great stresses on her structure over a period of several hours. When she was through the turbulence, it was found that some of the girders were damaged at the point where the fins joined the main structure.

Temporary repairs were carried out when the ship landed at Miami, and reinforced girders were ordered when the *Macon* returned to Sunnyvale. These were installed as they arrived—the ship remaining in operational service the whole time—and by the beginning of February 1935 only the girders at the point where the upper fin joined the fuselage were still in need of replacement. On 11 February the *Macon* left Sunnyvale to take part in naval manœuvres over the Pacific. The weather was bad, and for twenty-four hours the airship was buffeted by wind speeds of up to 60 m.p.h. While returning to her base on the night of 12–13 February, she ran into a solid bank of cloud that rose almost from ground level up to 2,000 feet near Point Sur. As she flew over the clouds she was struck by severe turbulence and dropped rapidly from 2,700 feet to 1,700 feet. At that moment, her top stabilizing fin broke away, taking part of the hull with it and puncturing three gas bags so badly that they deflated. The bow reared up and the crew hastily dropped ballast and fuel aft and amidships to correct the trim, but the badly damaged stern structure continued to disintegrate and the ship's captain, now Commander Wiley, one of the survivors of the *Akron* disaster, decided to stop all engines and make an emergency landing on the water.

The *Macon* alighted gently on the sea in a tail-down attitude at an angle of 25 degrees. For some unexplained reason, one crew member, a wireless operator, jumped clear when the ship was still at a height of 125 feet and was killed. The remainder fired distress flares to guide American warships to the scene as the *Macon* began to settle slowly. At the last minute, they clambered into twelve rubber life-rafts and paddled away from the wreck as the waves closed over it. A few minutes later a cruiser arrived and began to pick up the survivors. Out of the crew of eighty-three, only two men were missing: one was the unfortunate radio operator and the other was a Filipino mess steward, who had gone back into the wreck to fetch some belongings and who had presumably been trapped.

Out of the five rigid airships built on behalf of the United States Navy, only one—the splendid German-built *Los Angeles*—survived after the loss of the *Macon*. In America, opinion—both official and public—held that the day of the big rigid was over. It was an opinion that was to be underlined in tragic circumstances just over two years after the destruction of the *Macon*, when the giant *Hindenburg* fell in flames at Lakehurst.

By the end of 1935, the *Graf Zeppelin* had made some 500 voyages, more than a hundred of them ocean crossings. On 25 March of that year Hermann Göring had officially inaugurated the German Zeppelin Airline; from then on, the commercial Zeppelin enterprise enjoyed full State support. Under the able direction of Hugo Eckener, the capabilities of the commercial airship had been admirably demonstrated, and the success of the *Graf Zeppelin* had done much to raise the morale and prestige of the German people in the bitter years after the First World War.

Eckener, however, was already well aware in 1934 that the *Graf Zeppelin* had been pushed to the limits of her performance. If the advantage she had gained was to be exploited, a bigger ship would have to be built which offered an improved performance as well as higher standards of comfort and safety. One of the main requirements was for a higher cruising speed—about 84 m.p.h. compared with the *Graf Zeppelin*'s 72·5—and initial calculations showed that to meet this the new ship would have to have double the horse-power of the earlier Zeppelin. Safety requirements, too, demanded the use of heavy oil engines instead of petrol motors, and it was hoped that the safety factor would be increased still further by the use of helium instead of the inflammable hydrogen. Since helium was a heavier gas than hydrogen, this meant in turn that the capacity of the new ship would have to be about 7,000,000 cubic feet—almost double that of the *Graf Zeppelin*.

The new Zeppelin, the *LZ.129*, was laid down towards the end of 1934. Even before construction started, it was decided that she would be named the *Hindenburg* in honour of the great German statesman. The craft was designed from the start on the assumption that the United States would be willing to part with quantities of the costly helium—an assumption that proved dangerously false—and this was reflected in her dimensions. She was the biggest airship ever built, with a length of 800 feet, and was powered by four Daimler diesel engines of 1,100 h.p. each. There was accommodation for fifty passengers, and their quarters were as luxurious as those in any ocean liner. There was a fifty-foot promenade on either side of A Deck, from which the passengers could survey the scenery through slanting observation windows. There was a saloon, a reading- and writing-room, a magnificent dining-room with walls decorated with pictures showing the history of airships, 25 double bedrooms with their own bathroom and toilet, a fully electric galley and spacious luggage rooms.

And the *Hindenburg* was safe: the crude oil that fed her motors would not burn even if a lighted match was thrown into the tank. The catwalks were covered with rubber and the ladders were rubber-insulated: crew members who had to work or move between the huge gas cells wore asbestos suits; the ship's smoking-room was fully fireproofed and the atmosphere kept at fairly high pressure to prevent the entry of any leaking gas from outside; it was equipped with cigar and cigarette lighters, chained down so that a forgetful passenger could not take one away; and, finally, all matches and lighters were confiscated from the passengers as they came aboard. She was as safe as the technology of the time could make her—despite the fact that the repeated efforts of the German Government to obtain helium from the USA ended in failure, and that consequently the ship's cells had to be filled with hydrogen.

The *Hindenburg* made her maiden flight of one hour's duration over Lake Constance on 23 March 1936. Three days later, accompanied by the *Graf Zeppelin*, she made a publicity voyage over Germany—the first time since the end of the war that two airships had appeared together in German skies. On 31 March she took off on her first long flight: a crossing of the South Atlantic to Rio de Janeiro. During the return journey, with seventy-five people on board, two of her engines failed and her ground speed was reduced to only 32 m.p.h. over the eastern Atlantic; one of the motors was started again, however, and the ship finally reached home safely on 10 April after running for forty-two hours on the power of two engines.

The *Hindenburg* was withdrawn from service for a month while the Daimler Company carried out modifications to the engines. Then, on 6 May, she began a series of regular scheduled crossings of the North Atlantic with a record flight from Friedrichshafen to New York of 61 hours 53 minutes. On this voyage she was commanded by Captain Ernst Lehmann, who had succeeded Eckener as Director of Zeppelin Flight Operations—Eckener having been 'demoted' to the Chairmanship of the Board of Directors when the company became a State concern.

During ten round trips across the North Atlantic the *Hindenburg* carried over a thousand passengers. During the winter of 1936–7 plans were made for the addition of twenty more cabins, making it possible for the ship to carry a hundred passengers. While this modification was being carried out a 'German-American Zeppelin Transport Corporation' was founded; its eventual aim was to start a regular transatlantic service with four airships, two German and two American.

In addition to the North Atlantic run the *Hindenburg* made the crossing to Rio and back seven times during 1936; in all, she made 56 flights both long and short, logging 2,810 hours in the air and carrying 2,656 passengers over a total distance of 190,000 miles. Her 1937 schedule began in the middle of March with another flight to Rio, after which she was pulled out of service to permit the installation of the twenty new cabins. This work was completed late in April, and on 4 May 1937 the giant airship left Frankfurt-am-Main with ninety-seven people on board, bound for New York on the flight that was to be her last.

At 3.30 p.m. on 6 May she passed the Empire State Building and headed for Lakehurst. On this occasion, the *Hindenburg* was commanded by Captain Max Pruss; Ernst Lehmann was also on board as an observer, but Hugo Eckener was on a lecture tour in Austria.

At Lakehurst, a group of reporters, photographers and newsreel cameramen waited in the Press Room; most of them had been there since early morning—the arrival of the airship having been delayed several hours by bad weather—and they were bored. After all, the landing of an airship had become just a matter of routine by now; it was still a good story, but the event had ceased to arouse a great deal of excitement.

At 4 p.m., the *Hindenburg* was sighted and the spectators stirred themselves—but they were in for yet another disappointment. A thin layer of stratus had gradually crept across the sky until it covered the landing-ground, and a thin drizzle fell from it, cutting down visibility. As the airship cruised overhead, Pruss informed the Lakehurst Station Commandant that he proposed to delay the landing until weather conditions became more favourable. It was not until 7 p.m., however, that there was a break in the weather; even some of the passengers were beginning to voice their irritation at the continual delay, and they were greatly relieved when Pruss finally announced his intention of landing.

On the ground, the 248 men of the handling crew took up their positions around the mooring-mast. At 7.25 p.m. Pruss began the gradual descent and the cameras of the newsmen started to click. In a hut on the edge of the field, a radio commentator named Herb Morrison from Station WLS Chicago gave a signal to his engineers; in a few seconds' time they would begin recording the closing stages of the year's first transatlantic flight for a radio magazine programme. It would not be easy to string together a good story: the *Hindenburg* carried hardly anyone who could be called a celebrity, and there would be little of interest in the landing itself.

In the *Hindenburg*'s control gondola, Pruss ordered the crew to valve off hydrogen and dump water ballast to bring the ship into equilibrium. Seven hundred feet from the mast the pitch of the propellers was reversed and the ship lost headway rapidly. A moment later, two trail ropes were dropped; they were seized by the ground crew and made fast to two railway cars positioned on a small track that ran in a circle around the mooring-mast. The ship hung there at rest, 75 feet from the ground, her engines idling.

In his hut, Herb Morrison described the scene in a matter-of-fact voice. 'Passengers are looking out of the windows waving; the ship is standing still now. The vast motors are just holding it, just enough to keep it from . . .' And then, his voice filled with horror:

'It's broken into flames. It's flashing! Flashing! It's flashing terribly! It's bursting into flames and falling on the mooring-mast. This is terrible, this is one of the worst catastrophes in the world. Oh, the humanity and all the passengers . . . I told you . . . it's a mass of smoking wreckage. Honestly, I can hardly breathe . . . I'm going to step inside where I can't see it . . . it's terrible . . . I . . . I . . . folks, I'm going to have to stop for a moment because I've lost my voice. This is the worst thing I've ever witnessed . . .'

It had happened quickly, almost too quickly to comprehend. A sudden flash near the stern, then a brilliant glare as a great mushroom of flame billowed up above the stricken ship. Within seconds the flames shot along the entire hull and the *Hindenburg* was falling towards the ground, horribly slowly at first and then faster and faster as explosions racked her and her structure crumbled. In the forward control gondola, Captain Pruss made a split-second decision that was to save many lives: instead of dropping ballast in an attempt to keep the ship level, he allowed the blazing stern to sink quickly to the ground. The bow shot up to a height of 500 feet and then came down slowly, a mass of flames, striking the ground and bouncing before finally settling.

Out of the ninety-seven people on board, sixty-two escaped from the inferno with their lives. Many of these escapes were little short of miraculous—such as that of the fourteen-year-old cabin boy who, trapped in a circle of flames, was saved by a bursting water tank which drenched him completely. Several passengers had jumped clear of the burning wreck as it sank, only to be injured when they hit the ground. Of those who died, twenty-two were crew members—including Captain Lehmann, who succumbed to his terrible burns several hours later.

The world knew of the tragedy within hours. In Germany, the initial shock was followed by widespread bitterness stemming from the thought that the disaster would not have happened if the Americans had supplied helium in the first place. The first reaction—including that of Hugo Eckener—was that the destruction of the *Hindenburg* had been an act of sabotage, and this suspicion was strengthened when a Luger pistol was found in the charred wreckage with one bullet missing. In America, a Board of Inquiry was set up immediately: it included six German specialists, one of whom was Eckener. On this occasion he had to make the Atlantic crossing by sea, for all further flights by the *Graf Zeppelin* had been suspended until the Board's findings were made known.

For several days, the Board assessed all the available information on the crash. The final analysis was made by Hugo Eckener, and his theory was accepted by both Americans and Germans. Eckener said that it had been proved that the ship had been stern-heavy throughout the mooring operation, and that the release of ballast had failed to correct this tendency. During the landing manoeuvres, one of the stern cells had developed a leak— probably through a gash torn by a bracing-wire which had broken as the airship's commander made a sharp turn in order to bring the craft into wind. The escaping gas had risen and filled the space inside the upper fin, where it had been set alight by a discharge of static electricity. The gas would then burn slowly until it mixed with air, at which point an explosion would have taken place and produced a chain reaction, setting fire to the hydrogen within the damaged cell.

So, through a combination of circumstances that could not possibly have been foreseen, the *Hindenburg* died. Resolutely, Eckener and his small band of colleagues attempted to save the Zeppelin enterprise from extinction yet again. A new Zeppelin, the *LZ.130 Graf Zeppelin II*, was already under construction, and if helium could be obtained to fill her cells she might yet recapture the public enthusiasm that had been won by the original *Graf Zeppelin*, and lost when the *Hindenburg* fell in flames at Lakehurst.

At first, it seemed as though Eckener had succeeded. The United States Congress resolved that the helium law of 1927 be amended to permit the sale of the gas to Germany, subject to the appointment of a Helium Commission to ensure that the gas was not used for military purposes. By the end of 1937 a quantity of helium had already been delivered to

Friedrichshafen, and hopes ran high that there would be enough to fill the cells of the *LZ.130* by the end of 1938.

It was Hitler who killed the dream. On 12 March 1938 German troops marched into Austria. A matter of days later, the Americans refused to export any more helium to Germany; negotiations were opened again, but it was useless. This time, the decision would not be reversed.

The *Graf Zeppelin II* was completed in September 1938 and made her first flight—filled with hydrogen—on the 14th of that month. A few more short flights were made during 1939, but flights ceased on the outbreak of war and in 1940 she was broken up, her aluminium framework needed to build aeroplanes. The big airship hangar at Frankfurt, where she had been housed, was also destroyed.

So the era of the rigid airship came to an end. Not with a bang, but a whimper.

12 US Naval Airships
in the Second World War and After

By the end of 1924, the Goodyear Company had built over a hundred non-rigid and semi-rigid airships. Most of these had gone to the US Navy, but a few, mostly C-Class ships, had been turned over to the Army, which had a limited interest in lighter-than-air activity and possessed two bases, one at Langley Field in Virginia and the other at Scott Field, Illinois. The first ship designed specifically to Army requirements was the *RS-1*, a semi-rigid with a capacity of 719,000 cubic feet. Originally ordered from Goodyear in 1923, the *RS-1* was built at Akron the following year and assembled at Scott Field in 1925. It served for a number of years, but by this time the Army's aviation programme revolved almost entirely around heavier-than-air machines and no further dirigibles were ordered.

In 1925, in fact, with the big rigid airships for the US Navy on the horizon, American interest in the smaller non-rigid dirigible showed signs of waning. Goodyear, however, were not slow to realize the potentialities of the non-rigid in the commercial field—particularly for advertising purposes—and in 1925 they began to build a fleet of non-rigids for commercial, experimental and training work as a private venture. The first of these was the *Pilgrim*, a helium-inflated craft (as were all subsequent Goodyear ships) with a capacity of 51,000 cubic feet. It was the first non-rigid ship to feature a completely enclosed control car fitted flush with the envelope. The useful life of this craft extended well into the 1930s, and before it was eventually retired it made 465 flights and covered a total distance of 94,975 miles.

The *Pilgrim* was followed in 1928 by the *Puritan*, a twin-engined craft with a capacity of 112,000 cubic feet. In 1929 came three more ships of the same type, the *Volunteer, Mayflower* and *Vigilant,* and these were followed in turn by a still larger craft, the 180,000-cubic foot *Defender,* which was capable of carrying ten passengers and which became the flagship of the commercial fleet. The *Defender* was, in fact, the prototype of five more 180,000-c.f. ships, the *Reliance, Resolute, Columbia, Enterprise* and *Ranger.* The first two were built in 1931–2 and replaced the older *Vigilant* and *Mayflower* in service. Together, in twelve years of commercial operation, the Goodyear ships carried 400,000 passengers over a total distance of more than four million miles and enjoyed a spotless safety record throughout.

One of the ships, the *Defender,* was later purchased by the US Navy for training and experimental work and was fitted with a variety of engines, including 225-h.p. Packard diesels and 165-h.p. Wright Whirlwinds. She was known as the *G-1* in Navy Service.

When war broke out in Europe on 3 September 1939, the US Navy's Airship Service was practically non-existent. The airship station at Lakehurst was still in being, thanks to the determined efforts of a handful of men led by Admiral Rosendahl, but no more than ten ships remained on the inventory and most of these were obsolete. They included two J-Class and two C-Class craft, the latter handed back from the Army some years previously; the *G-1* (ex *Defender*); a training ship of 123,000 cubic feet designated *L-1*; the *ZMC-2*, an aluminium-covered ship dating back to 1929; the *K-1*, an experimental craft of 320,000 cubic feet which had been used to test different types of diesel engine; and the *K-2*, the 170,000-dollar prototype of a projected new class of Naval patrol dirigibles, which had flown for the first time on 16 December 1938.

The success of the Naval non-rigids during the First World War had not been forgotten, and in the spring and summer of 1940—with the victorious German Armies in possession of the French Atlantic ports, and the consequent threat of large-scale submarine activity against convoys to Britain—negotiations got under way for the creation of a force of modern airships for patrol duties. The first step was taken on 19 October 1940, when Goodyear received a contract to build an initial batch of four K-Class non-rigid airships. The new craft were almost twice as big as the C-Class of 1918, with a capacity of 416,000 cubic feet, an endurance of fifty hours and a range of 2,000 miles.

The name 'Blimp'—originally coined in 1917 as a corruption of the designation 'Dirigible, Type B, Limp'—had now become official nomenclature for the US Navy's non-rigid airships after over twenty years of use as a nickname only. The first four of the new Goodyear Blimps, *K-3* to *K-6*, were completed in the spring of 1941, but it was not until after the Japanese attack on Pearl Harbor on 7 December 1941 that production really got under way.

On 2 January 1942, Airship Patrol Group One was commissioned at Lakehurst, with the 12th Airship Squadron as the resident unit. During the last week of January another Airship Squadron, the 32nd, came into being at Sunnyvale in California. On 1 March another Naval Airship Station was commissioned, at South Weymouth, Massachusetts, and this was followed by another at Weeksville, North Carolina, in April. Also in April, the Navy assumed complete control of the Army base at Sunnyvale and renamed it Moffett Field, and Airship Patrol Group Three was formed there a few months later. Yet another Airship Station was commissioned at Santa Ana, California, during the Autumn of 1942, and this became the home base of the 31st Airship Squadron.

At the beginning of 1943, by which time the number of K-Class blimps produced by Goodyear was approaching the one-hundred mark, more Airship Stations were added to the chain that was being steadily built up along the Atlantic and Pacific coasts of the United States. As it had been during the 1914–18 war, the task of the blimp squadrons was to escort convoys in coastal waters. It was a task at which the blimps excelled: they enjoyed several big advantages over heavier-than-air machines. The greatest advantage of all was their speed range—from zero up to 70 m.p.h.—which meant that they could give constant protection to any ship that happened to be lagging behind the main convoy. Their low patrol speed also made it far easier for the crews to detect submarines visually; on occasions, submerged U-boats were spotted at depths of up to ninety feet in clear water.

Convoys with blimp escorts were seldom attacked by U-boats, and submarine sightings were infrequent. In fact, the Americans claimed that no ship in a convoy escorted by a blimp was lost through enemy action during the entire war, and so far as may be ascertained this claim holds good. Only on one occasion did a blimp and a submarine actually 'shoot it out'; it happened on 18 July 1943 when the *K-74*, patrolling off the coast of Florida, surprised a U-boat cruising on the surface. The blimp came in for a bombing run, its crew blazing away with machine-guns. The U-boat replied and its bullets struck home, tearing great gashes in the airship's envelope. Losing gas rapidly, the blimp made a forced landing in the water as the submarine dived and headed away from the scene. One of the airship's crew was killed by a shark before rescue came. Later, the survivors had the satisfaction of learning that the U-boat had been destroyed by surface forces.

In the summer of 1943 airship cover was extended to the Caribbean, a station being commissioned at Trinidad on 2 August and another at Amapa, Brazil, shortly afterwards. On 26 September 1943 the *K-84* became the first American airship to cross the Equator, when it flew from Amapa to Igarape-Assu. This craft belonged to the 41st Airship Squadron.

On 4 February 1944 the *K-29* landed on a US aircraft carrier off the Pacific coast and resumed her patrol after replenishment. It was the first time that a blimp had carried out this operation, which later became fairly routine practice. Four months later, on 28 May 1944, six blimps of the 14th Airship Squadron—the *K-101, K-112, K-123* and *K-130*, plus two unidentified—took off from Weeksville and flew to Port Lyautey in Morocco via the Azores, arriving on 1 June after covering the 3,145 miles in a total flight time of 58 hours. They were the first non-rigid airships ever to make a trans-oceanic flight. The first blimp patrol in the European Theatre of Operations was flown by the *K-123* on 6 June, over the Straits of Gibraltar.

Another notable record for a non-rigid was logged by the *K-111* on 20 August 1944: the airship stayed airborne for 72 hours 30 minutes, replenishing from an escort carrier. The craft carried two crews, each of which stood a watch of twelve hours in turns.

In May 1944, when the 14th Squadron's blimps went to Morocco, it had also been planned to station the 42nd Squadron in the United Kingdom for patrol duties over the Western Approaches. The success of the Allied invasion, however, and the rapid capture of several key ports on the French coast, resulted in a marked drop in U-boat activity in the Atlantic, and the plan was abandoned. The 14th Squadron's detachment, nevertheless, remained at Port Lyautey for several months, and was in fact relieved by six more airships of the same squadron, including the *K-89* and the *K-114*, on 1 May 1945, a week before the end of the war in Europe. These six blimps left Weeksville on 28 April and made the 3,532-mile crossing via Bermuda and the Azores in 62 hours' flight time. The leg between Bermuda and the Azores—1,881 miles—was the longest over-water crossing ever made by a non-rigid, and the blimps did it in 29½ hours.

In all, 135 K-Class dirigibles were built for the US Navy during the Second World War. While production of this standard type continued, Goodyear designers came up with several projects for much bigger long-range blimps. Only one such prototype was built during the war years: the *XM-1*, a craft with a capacity of 725,000 cubic feet, which flew for the first time on 27 October 1943. The *XM-1* was used as a research craft, employed mainly in testing new search and weapons systems destined for the Navy's operational blimps. On 27 October 1946 this airship, commanded by Lieutenant H. R. Walton, usn, took off from Lakehurst on a cruise that took it to the Bahamas, Florida and Cuba. When it finally landed at Glynco, Georgia, on 3 November, it had been airborne for 170 hours 18 minutes without refuelling—a record for any type of aircraft.

The US Navy's airship forces were greatly reduced in size immediately after the end of the Second World War, several Groups being disbanded and their bases de-commissioned. Lakehurst, however, continued as the centre of Naval lighter-than-air activity, albeit on a greatly reduced budget, and in the early 1950s a number of newer and more advanced Goodyear blimps came into service. The first of these were the ZP-3 and the ZP-4, which made their first flights on 28 September 1950 and 8 May 1951 respectively; they were followed by the ZPN-1, the prototype of a new series of Naval blimps with a capacity of a million cubic feet. The ZPN-1 flew for the first time on 18 June 1951 and, with a length of 324 feet, was the largest non-rigid ever built. It entered service at Lakehurst on 17 June 1952.

The next version was the ZP3-K, which flew for the first time on 12 November 1952. This type was designed for operations from aircraft carriers. Another important advance was made on 20 March 1953 with the maiden flight of the ZP2N-1, the first of the US Navy blimps capable of being refuelled in flight. Twelve of this type were built, and on more than one occasion they proved their worth when, operating in conjunction with task forces during exercises in the Atlantic, they were able to provide air cover in weather conditions that kept every other kind of aircraft grounded.

In 1953 the designations of some of the Navy's blimps were changed: the ZPN-1 type, for example, became the ZPG-1 and the ZP3-K became the ZSG-3. The ZPG-1 was followed by the ZPG-2, a variant with increased endurance, more powerful engines and advanced avionics; on 25 May 1954 a ship in the ZPG-2 class landed at Lakehurst after smashing the endurance record with a flight of 200 hours and 6 minutes, an exploit that earned for its captain, Commander M. H. Eppes, USN, the Harmon Trophy of 1955. The following year, this trophy was won by a colleague of Eppes's, Lieutenant Commander Charles A. Mills, who received it in recognition of a series of hazardous airship flights from South Weymouth in December 1955, made to investigate the effects of ice accumulation on an aircraft in bad weather.

On 29 November 1956 a new 'blimp' variant made its first flight: the ZSG-4. This craft was the first to have an envelope made of synthetic plastic material (Dacron) in place of the more usual rubberized fabric. Dacron was another Goodyear invention of vital importance to the lighter-than-air field, for it reduced gas leakage to an absolute minimum—an important consideration in view of the high cost of helium.

Towards the end of 1956 the US Navy's airships assumed a new role when they became part of the North American Air Defence system's early warning radar chain. Equipped with AEW radar and patrolling along fixed lines well out over the Atlantic, their job was to extend the range of radar coverage beyond the maximum range of existing radar stations along the eastern seaboard of the United States. A number of ZPG-Class ships were adapted to carry long-range radar equipment and given the designation ZW. Extensive trials were carried out, and in January 1957 relays of airships from South Weymouth maintained a continuous watch up to 200 miles out over the Atlantic in extremely adverse weather conditions over a period of a fortnight, furnishing cast-iron proof of their all-weather capability. One ship, the *ZW-1*, was in the air for ten days, creating yet another endurance record. It was not to stand for long, however: on 4 March 1957 the ZPG-2 airship *Snowbird*, captained by Commander J. R. Hunt, USN, left South Weymouth on a flight that was to take her across the Atlantic to Portugal, down the west coast of Africa and back across the ocean to Florida. When the airship landed on 15 March she had covered a distance of 8,216 nautical miles in 264 hours (11 days) 14 minutes and 18 seconds, a flight that—for the third time since the war—won the coveted Harmon Trophy for a US airship crew.

The first Goodyear ship to be completely fitted out for early warning work was the ZPG-2W, which made its maiden flight on 6 May 1957. However, this was essentially a stop-gap craft, and in 1957 Goodyear were hard at work on a new airship designed for the early warning role from the outset. The result was the ZPG-3W, which flew for the first time on 21 July 1958. The ZPG-3W was the biggest non-rigid yet built, with a capacity of 1,500,000 cubic feet, and four were ordered by the Navy Department at a cost of twelve million dollars each. The ships were 403 feet long, with a height of 118 feet at the top of the vertical fin, and were powered by two Curtiss–Wright engines developing 1,500 h.p. each. The ZPG-3W carried a crew of twenty-five, divided into two watches, and a forty-foot radar scanner was fitted inside the envelope, revolving in the helium.

On 12 August 1958, a few weeks after the maiden flight of the new ship, one of the older Navy blimps—a ZPG-2, of the same class as the ship that had made the double crossing of the Atlantic over a year earlier—returned to South Weymouth after a 9,000-mile round trip across Canada to Fletcher's Island deep inside the Arctic Circle, where she delivered supplies to a scientific team that was carrying out work in connexion with the International Geophysical Year.

At the beginning of 1960, the United States Navy had 27 non-rigid airships in service, the majority based on Lakehurst but with detachments scattered around the coasts of the United States depending on operational requirements. As well as their routine tasks of anti-submarine and early warning patrol, the airships were often called upon to undertake special duties: the most notable of these was in connexion with the first under-water firings of a Polaris missile from the submarine *George Washington* in April and July 1960, when one ZPG-2 airship acted as a camera platform and others maintained constant surveillance around the test area, watching for (and sometimes locating) Soviet trawlers whose array of aerials betrayed their true purpose.

These operations during 1960 were marred by tragedy when one of the four ZPG-3W airships crashed into the Atlantic after a long split developed in its envelope. Only a few of the twenty-man crew were saved; the rest were trapped in the gondola and drowned.

By 1962, it was apparent that the useful life of the US Navy's non-rigids was fast coming to an end. For years they had filled a dangerous gap in the defences of the United States; but now that gap had been effectively sealed by the completion of the last of the great radar stations in the Ballistic Missile Early Warning chain, and by the entry into service of fast new aircraft with an endurance of twenty hours and more, crammed with the latest equipment for hunting and killing enemy submarines.

There could only be one outcome. One by one, the valiant

blimps were decommissioned and deflated. In 1964, several 'extensions' of the Distant Early Warning Line, North America's outermost radar defence chain before BMEWs came into operation, were disbanded. They included a number of radar towers positioned in the Atlantic—and the last Airship Group of the United States Navy.

13 Airships Present—and Future

Since the end of the Second World War, airships have flown in five countries: the United States, Germany, Japan, the Soviet Union and Britain. The Goodyear Company is still the undisputed leader of the field; since the little *Pilgrim* first flew in 1925, Goodyear commercial airships have made almost 204,000 flights, carrying 592,000 passengers over a distance of 6,100,000 miles without accident or injury. The total number of airships built by the Company since 1917 is 300, 55 of them commercial craft.

In February 1968, Goodyear started a five-million-dollar programme for expanding and improving its existing airship operations, which at that time were being carried out by two commercial non-rigids: the *Mayflower III* and the *Columbia II*, based respectively on Los Angeles and Miami. Both craft owed their design to the Goodyear non-rigid 'L' Class, and their capacity was 147,000 cubic feet. The new programme involved the rebuilding of both these ships, together with the creation of a new base at Houston, Texas, and also the construction of a much larger craft, to be named the *America*.

The new airship was built at Wingfoot Lake and made its first flight on 25 April 1969, after which it was moved to its operational base at Houston. Like its two sister ships—also back in service by the end of 1969—the *America* is helium-filled. It is powered by two 210-h.p. six-cylinder engines, each driving a pusher propeller, which give it a maximum speed of 50 m.p.h. and a cruising speed of 35 m.p.h. The ship has a length of 192 feet 1¼ inches, a maximum width of 50 feet and a height of 59 feet 6 inches at the top of the fin. Capacity is 202,700 cubic feet, and the craft has a ceiling of 7,500 feet and an endurance of twenty hours. The gondola has accommodation for a pilot and six passengers. Primary function of the *America, Columbia* and

Mayflower is advertising and public relations; all three ships carry advertising slogans on their envelopes, and that on the *America* can be read at a distance of one mile when the ship is cruising at a height of 1,000 feet.

In 1965, another American company, the newly formed Aereon Corporation, entered the lighter-than-air field, designing and building a triple-hulled rigid airship named the *Aereon III*. The design of this craft was unique, consisting of three hulls joined together by aerofoil-shaped centre-sections. An elevon—a combination of elevator and aileron—was mounted on the trailing edge of each centre section, and a fin and rudder were mounted beneath each of the outer hulls. The centre hull featured a retractable nosewheel on an extending leg, enabling the ship's angle of attack to be varied on take-off.

The craft was designed to carry a crew of two, seated side by side at the front of the centre hull. The power plant—a 70-h.p. Solar Titan shaft turbine driving a two-bladed reversible-pitch propeller—was mounted at the rear of this hull. The length of the *Aereon III* was 85 feet, and the overall width was 56 feet. Each hull had a diameter of 18 feet, and total capacity was 40,000 cubic feet. Estimated performance included a maximum speed of 65 m.p.h., a ceiling of 8,500 feet and an endurance of four hours.

The *Aereon III*, which was completed in February 1965 but which never flew because the Corporation's funds dried up, was intended as a flying scale-model of a far larger projected airship 400 feet long, powered by four 1,000-h.p. diesel engines and capable of carrying a 90-ton payload at a cruising speed of 150 m.p.h.

In 1967 Aereon also began design study work on a revolutionary new concept: the Lifting Body Airship, a craft combining principles of both lighter-than-air and heavier-than-air technology. The project envisaged a huge delta-shaped airship powered by four turboprop engines, with helium used to lighten the airframe. Since the buoyancy of the helium would bear up the weight of the empty airframe, the aerodynamic lifting force would only need to be sufficient to support the weight of payload and fuel under flight conditions. Apart from power for

205

acceleration during takeoff and climb, the LBA would be able to cruise on half power during normal operations. Because of its light wing loading and other design features, it would be capable of operating from small fields, needing a runway length of no more than 5,000 feet even with maximum load. The LBA project was initiated with a view to reducing the costs of air freight. Aereon estimate that an LBA 340 feet long could carry 150 tons for 2,000 miles, cruising at 150 m.p.h., at a direct operating cost of 1·8 cents per ton-mile.

Powered by four Rolls-Royce Tyne turboprops, the Aereon LBA would be able to carry six 40-foot containers totalling 300,000 pounds over a 1,750-mile range at a total operating cost of 1·5 cents per ton-mile, or four 40-foot containers (200,000 pounds) over 4,000 miles at 2 cents per ton-mile. Maximum range with reduced payload would be an estimated 7,000 miles. As Aereon pointed out, a craft such as the LBA would serve to complete the land–sea–air concept of containerization by its ability to airlift the standard 8×8×40 foot container at competitive rates over intercontinental distances.

Aereon have estimated that some 30 million dollars would have to be spent on development of the LBA before a prototype could be flown—a figure far lower than that spent on development of advanced aircraft projects such as the SST or the Lockheed C-5A Galaxy. However, despite a considerable case for the development of the LBA being set before Congress, no official support has so far been forthcoming—although Aereon have hopes that the new wave of interest in lighter-than-air craft for cargo transportation may result in the resurrection of the project.

The only European country to make use of airships for advertising purposes at the present time is Western Germany. On 16 March 1956 the Goodyear *L-19*—a Goodyear non-rigid which had served as a training ship with the US Navy since 1947—was sold at Stuttgart and purchased by an advertising firm. Renamed the *Underberg*, she flew at intervals during the late 1950s until in 1959 she changed hands for a second time and became the *Guldenring*. A new envelope was made for her by BallonFabrik Augsburg—the oldest aeronautical firm in the world, which had built kite balloons for the German Army before the First World War and also envelopes for the Parseval dirigibles. In 1961, the airship was bought by Schwab, the big mail-order firm of Hanau.

The *Schwab*, as the ship was now called, was powered by two 145-h.p. Warner engines giving her a maximum speed of 57 m.p.h. Capacity was 158,895 cubic feet. The 160-foot ship had an endurance of 17 hours, a ceiling of 7,550 feet and a maximum range of 370 miles. She had accommodation for a crew of two and four passengers. Unlike the American non-rigids, she was filled with hydrogen—helium being considered too costly by her owners. The *Schwab*, registered D-LAVO and later D-LISA, logged some 10,000 flying hours in German service. Then, in 1967, she was bought by the Nippon Airship Company of Japan and at the time of writing (1971) is still flying in that country.

Another West German non-rigid, the *Trumpf*, flew for the first time on 17 August 1958 at Stuttgart and was originally owned by L. Monheim GmbH of Aachen, one of Germany's leading chocolate manufacturers. Her dimensions and performance were similar to those of the *Schwab*, as her design was also based on that of the Goodyear 'L' class. In 1969 she was bought by the Deutsche Luftschiffahrt GmbH, who inflated her with helium. Named the *Braun Sixtant*, she is, as I write, being used for publicity purposes on behalf of the Braun Electrical Company of Frankfurt–Kronberg. Her registration is D-LEMO.

One country which has shown more than a passing interest in airships in recent years is the Soviet Union, where several design bureaux are reported to be considering the large rigid airship as a possible vehicle for an airborne nuclear power plant. There have also been reports that a Soviet design team headed by the engineer David Bimbat is developing a twin-engined non-rigid airship 165 feet long and 49 feet 6 inches in diameter; known as the *Ural-1*, this craft is said to have a top speed of 62 m.p.h. and is designed for forest fire patrol duties. According to one Soviet press report, the airship is equipped with detachable gondolas, enabling it to be used for various purposes such as transporting timber and other materials, and airlifting supplies and equipment to scientific expeditions in remote areas.

It was a film that inspired Great Britain's only effort in the airship field in recent years. The film was *Chitty Chitty Bang Bang*, and for it a replica of the 1903 *Lebaudy I* semi-rigid dirigible was built at Cardington. Powered by a 30-h.p. Volkswagen engine and carrying a crew of two, the craft made eleven flights in connexion with the film. It was 112 feet long, had a capacity of 34,000 cubic feet and cruised at 8 m.p.h.

So much for the present. But what of the future? On 4 November 1970 the British shipping company Manchester Liners Ltd, a subsidiary of the Furness-Withy group, announced that they were setting up a subsidiary company, Cargo Airships Ltd, to study the potential of cargo-carrying airships; their initial concept is based on a craft some 1,200 feet long, capable of carrying a 500-ton payload, and having a speed of 100 m.p.h. If the proposition appears economically feasible in terms of cargo rates, Manchester Liners say that they would be prepared to finance the building of a flying prototype to carry out practical trials. Their container-carrying airship could have a semi-monocoque hull, in which the stressed outer skin carries most of the torsional and bending stresses, strengthened at key load-bearing points by ring structures, like cross-sections of the traditional Zeppelin design. Such a ship would be stronger and safer than a Zeppelin, and also cheaper to mass-produce. A nuclear-powered engine could eventually be employed, giving virtually unlimited range—the ability to stay airborne for six or seven years at a time without refuelling, if necessary—and also the fascinating prospect of a virtually *silent* aircraft.

A similar project is also being studied by another British company, Airfloat Transport Limited, who—like Manchester Liners—have reached the conclusion that the most profitable field of future airship operation would be in the movement of large indivisible loads over moderate distances. To meet this requirement, the company has proposed an airship with a gas capacity of 30 million cubic feet, capable of carrying up to 280 tons over 1,000 miles at 5,000 feet, or up to 400 tons over shorter distances at 2,000 feet. However, Airfloat are quick to point out the difficulties of cargo airship operation. To achieve optimum operational flexibility, for example, the cargo airship must carry its own hoisting gear, capable of raising the maximum payload through about 200 feet on site, and the structure must be stressed to resist large concentrated loads; both these factors would make appreciable inroads upon the disposable lift. Furthermore, it would be necessary to exchange ballast for payload at pickup and delivery—which would mean that a trained ground crew would probably have to be carried in the airship. Bearing these factors in mind, an airship with a 400-ton transatlantic capacity might require a gas volume of 60 million or more cubic feet with conventional propulsion, or 40 to 45 million with nuclear power.

Despite all the problems, however, the enthusiasm of the airship protagonists remains undiminished. A few months before Manchester Liners and Airfloat announced their proposals, a shipping company in Lübeck indicated tentative plans to build a nuclear-powered passenger airship designed by an Austrian engineer, Dr Erich von Veress; the ship, which would be of the rigid Zeppelin type, would have an envelope of fireproof plastic; it would carry 500 passengers and 50 tons of cargo at a speed of 220 m.p.h. The Russians are studying a design for a similar nuclear-powered craft, capable of carrying 100 passengers at speeds of up to 150 m.p.h., and technical research has now been going on for about two years.

Whether the airship will ever make a 'come-back' as a passenger carrier—except on a limited scale, in remote areas where the lack of airstrips makes it an ideal form of transport—is doubtful, for the cost of a transatlantic airship ticket would probably work out about the same as a Jumbo Jet fare, and not many people would be willing to sacrifice time for extra comfort when the price is the same. The use of airships as cargo carriers, however, is an entirely different matter. At present, aircraft carry only about 0·05 per cent of the world's total cargo tonnage, and the snag with building bigger cargo aircraft is that as an aircraft gets larger, its structural weight increases out of proportion to its carrying capacity. With an airship, the problem does not arise: the bigger a lighter-than-air craft is, the more efficient it becomes.

This is just one advantage enjoyed by the airship over heavier-than-air machines. Equally as important is the airship's ability to operate in weather conditions that keep aircraft grounded: an airship can adjust its speed in relation to the conditions prevailing, inching its way down through dense fog, for example, for a radar-controlled approach to its mooring-mast. If the approach is not satisfactory, there is no question of the airship having to overshoot: it can come to a stop in mid-air and, if necessary, reverse. Another important factor is that an airship can operate from the heart of a city, which means that on short-haul flights it can compete very favourably with heavier-than-air machines, taking into account travelling times between cities and airports. Also, an airship operating a city-to-city service would be far quieter than the VTOL airliners now being studied at the project stage.

A study of the major airship accidents in peacetime over the past half-century reveals several important points. Without exception, the accidents resulted from one of three causes: lack of knowledge about weather conditions, technical inefficiency, or the use of explosive hydrogen. Today, a worldwide network of meteorological stations (not to mention weather satellites) eliminates the first problem, while helium, which has now been discovered in North Sea gas as well as in natural gases in the USA, has done away with the use of hydrogen in airships for good. From the technological point of view, every one of the factors that contributed to the airship disasters of the past—such as the strength and resistance of envelopes, and metal fatigue—has now been mastered by modern science.

The main problem now appears one of economy. The economists have yet to be convinced that the use of giant commercial airships would be a viable proposition, and this is likely to prove a far greater obstacle than any technical consideration. Everything now depends on the figures which will emerge from the studies at present being conducted in several countries: if those figures are attractive enough, the airship may once again become a familiar sight in the skies of our planet.

Appendix I

An Airship Chronology, 1268–1914

1268

Roger Bacon (England) describes in his *Opus Majus* the possibilities of constructing a lighter-than-air flying machine.

1690

Fr Francesco de Lana (Italy) designs a 'flying ship' which, in theory, could be lifted off the ground by globes of thin copper from which all the air had been exhausted.

1709

John V of Portugal awards Fr Bartholomeo Lourenço de Gusmao a prize of 600,000 Reis for designing a lighter-than-air craft.

1782

Cavallo (Italy) presents a paper to the Royal Society on the possibility of building an envelope which would rise from the ground when filled with 'inflammable air' (hydrogen).

1783

5 Jun.   First captive ascension in public of a Montgolfier balloon at Annonay (France).

27 Aug.   First flight (unmanned) of Prof. Charles's hydrogen-filled balloon *Le Globe* from Paris to Gonesse (France).

19 Sep.   First flight of a Mongolfier balloon carrying passengers— a cock, a duck and a sheep.

15 Oct.   First captive ascension of a Montgolfier balloon with a man on board: Pilâtre de Rozier.

21 Nov.   Pilâtre de Rozier and the Marquis d'Arlandes fly over the suburbs of Paris in a Montgolfière.

1 Dec.   Prof. Charles and Ainé Robert make the first free flight in a hydrogen-filled balloon.

3 Dec.   Jean-Baptiste Marie Meusnier presents his paper *Mémoire sur l'Equilibre des Machines Aérostatiques* to the French Academy. In this paper, Meusnier resolves in theory the problems of directing a balloon in flight.

27 Dec. Lavoisier (F) submits to the Academy of Sciences a paper on the problems of constructing a dirigible balloon.

1784

2 Mar.   Jean-Pierre Blanchard (F) attempts, without success, to direct a balloon in flight using oars.

25 Apr. Blanchard's experiment with an oar-powered balloon is repeated by Guyton de Morveau at Lyon, also without success.

1789

Baron Scott (Great Britain) proposes a dirigible balloon similar in shape and dimensions to the Zeppelins of more than a century later.

1804

7 Sep.   The aeronauts Francesco Zambeccari, Grassetti and Andreoli (Italy) make an ascension from Bologna and attempt to direct their balloon in flight. They land in the Adriatic and are rescued the following day.

1812

21 Sep. After several attempts to direct a Montgolfière in flight using the reaction principle (expulsion of hot air), Zambeccari is killed when his balloon catches fire.

1816

S. J. Pauly and Durs Egg (Switzerland) build an elongated oar-powered balloon, the *Dolphin*, in a shed in Knightsbridge (London). The project is abandoned through lack of funds.

1832

Lennox (F) and Le Berrier (F) ascend from Paris in a 'dirigible' balloon, using oars in an attempt to change the direction of flight. A second balloon is built and exhibited in London, but never flown.

1834

Lennox and Edon (GB) form a 'European Aeronautical Society' in London, a company whose aim is to open a regular air service between London and Paris using dirigible balloons.

17 Aug. The European Aeronautical Society's balloon, *The Eagle*, designed to be powered by twenty oars, fails to ascend from the Champ de Mars and is badly damaged by an angry mob.

1839

Eulriot (F) makes an unsuccessful attempt to direct an elongated balloon in flight.

1843

Monck Mason (GB) builds a model airship powered by a clockwork motor. The model is reported to have reached a speed of 5 m.p.h.

1844

Le Berrier (F) reveals a model steam-powered dirigible in Paris.

1850

6 Nov. Pierre Jullien (F) demonstrates a model clockwork-powered dirigible at the Paris Hippodrome. The craft is 22 feet long, elongated and streamlined.

1851

20 Aug. Henri Giffard (F) takes out a patent for a steam-powered dirigible balloon.

1852

24 Sep. First flight over Paris of Giffard's steam-powered dirigible. Flies from Paris to Trappes ($16\frac{1}{2}$ miles) at a ground speed

213

of 4–5 m.p.h. Estimated max. speed, zero wind conditions: 9 m.p.h.

1854

Cornu (F) proposes a steam-powered dirigible for use on a London–Paris air service.

1855

19 Aug.   G. Fremin (F) makes first (powerless) flight test of a dirigible of his own design, to be powered by a steam engine. The inventor dies before the project is completed.

1859

E. Farcot (F) publishes a pamphlet describing a design for a steam-powered dirigible fitted with twin propellers.

1865

Unsuccessful attempt to fly a man-powered dirigible by E. Delamarne and Gabriel Yon (F).

1866

Richard Boyman (GB) takes out a patent for a dirigible of all-steel construction.

1870

10 Oct.   Dupuy de Lôme (F) presents a project for a man-powered, propeller-driven dirigible to the Academy of Sciences.

1872

2 Feb.   Built with the help of Gabriel Yon, Dupuy de Lôme's dirigible—with a crew of 15 men turning the propeller—makes an experimental flight. No directional control is achieved. The dirigible's envelope was made from rubberized fabric and incorporated a ballonet filled with air from a blower.

13 Dec.   Paul Haenlein (Austria) makes the first test flight of a dirigible powered by a gas engine (4 cylinders, 3·6 h.p.) driving a propeller at 90 r.p.m. A still-air speed of 9 m.p.h. claimed; project later abandoned through lack of funds.

1873

In a memoire addressed to the King of Württemberg, Count Ferdinand von Zeppelin (Germany) outlines a project for a dirigible employing a series of separate gas cells, and describes the uses of such a craft as a war machine.

1876

17 Feb.   Gauchot (F) takes out a patent for a steam-powered twin-propeller dirigible design.

1878

C. F. Ritchel (USA) builds a man-powered dirigible consisting of an envelope 25 feet long with a bicycle-type framework suspended underneath. Four-bladed propeller driven by pedals could be angled for directional control. The machine made at least one flight at Hartford, Conn., and reached a still-air speed of $3\frac{1}{2}$ m.p.h.

1881

Albert and Gaston Tissandier (F) demonstrate a model electric-powered dirigible at the Paris Electrical Exhibition.

1882

11 Feb.   First experiments at Charlottenburg by Baumgarten and Karl Woelfert (G) with an electric-powered dirigible. Experiments repeated, with limited success, on 2 March.

1883

8 Oct.   The Tissandier brothers make the first test-flight of their full-scale electric-powered dirigible design, flying from Auteuil to Croissy-sur-Seine in 1 hr 15 min.

26 Nov.   Second flight by the Tissandiers in their electric craft, covering a distance of $15\frac{1}{2}$ miles from Auteuil to Mareolles-en-Brie.

1884

9 Aug.   Charles Renard and Arthur Krebs (F) make the first true dirigible flight in their electric airship *La France*,

215

taking off from Chalais-Meudon and returning to their starting-point after a 23-minute flight.

8 Nov.   Renard and Krebs make the second and third closed-circuit flights aboard *La France*.

1888

12 Aug. First flight of a dirigible (designed by Woelfert) powered by a petrol engine. Flight takes place at Gottlieb Daimler's Seelberg factory. A 2-h.p. Daimler motor drives twin propellers. Capacity of hydrogen-filled airship 8,750 cubic feet. Craft, flown by a mechanic named Michael, lands 2½ miles from its starting point.

1896

28 Aug. First flight of Woelfert's petrol-engined dirigible *Deutschland*.

1897

12 Jun. Woelfert ascends from Berlin in his petrol-engined dirigible. The craft explodes and burns in mid-air, killing Woelfert and his companion, Robert Knabe.

3 Nov.   Attempt to fly a dirigible designed by Schwartz (Austria) ends in failure when the craft is accidentally destroyed as a result of mishandling.

1898

18 Sep. First flight in Paris of the petrol-engined *Dirigible No. 1* of Alberto Santos-Dumont (Brazil).

1899

11 May   First flight of Santos-Dumont's *Dirigible No. 2* in Paris.

13 Nov. Santos-Dumont's *Dirigible No. 3* reaches a speed of 15½ m.p.h.

1900

2 Jul.   First flight over Lake Constance of Zeppelin *LZ.1*, first of the long series of airships built by Count Zeppelin.

21 Oct. Third and last flight of Zeppelin *LZ.1*. The dirigible, a failure, is broken up soon afterwards.

1901

13 Jul.   Santos-Dumont takes off from St Cloud in an abortive attempt to fly round the Eiffel Tower in *Dirigible No. 5*. After 40 minutes, he makes an emergency landing in Rothschild Park.

8 Aug.   Santos-Dumont makes a second abortive attempt to fly round the Eiffel Tower in *Dirigible No. 5*, force-landing on the roof of a house at Chaillot.

6 Sep.   Santos-Dumont's *Dirigible No. 6* is damaged during a bad landing.

19 Oct.   Santos-Dumont flies around the Eiffel Tower and returns to his point of departure. Take-off from the Aero Club Park at St Cloud at 14.42; Eiffel Tower reached at 14.51; overhead St Cloud 15.11; landing at St Cloud 15.12.

1902

12 May   Augusto Severo (Brazil) and Sachet (F) take off from Vaugirard aboard the dirigible *Pax*. The craft crashes in flames on the Avenue de Maine, Paris, killing both occupants.

22 Sep.   Dirigible designed by Stanley Spencer (GB) makes a flight of 1 hr 40 min. over London, covering a total distance of 30 miles.

13 Oct.   Dirigible flown by Ottokar de Bradsky (G) and Paul Morin (F) flies from Vaugirard to Gonesse. The car breaks away and both occupants fall to their deaths.

13 Nov.   The dirigible *Lebaudy No. 1*, constructed by Henri Julliot (F), makes its first free flight after several captive ascents, manœuvring in the air and returning to its point of departure.

1903

8 May   *Lebaudy No. 1* makes a flight of 23 miles, piloted by Juchmès.

24 Jun.   Piloted by Juchmès, *Lebaudy No. 1* makes a closed-circuit flight of 61 miles.

27 Jun.   Melle d'Acosta becomes the first woman passenger to fly in a dirigible—Santos-Dumont's *No. 9*.

14 Jul.   Santos-Dumont flies along the length of a military parade at Longchamp in *Dirigible No. 9*.

19 Nov.   *Lebaudy No. 1* badly damaged when its envelope becomes entangled in the branches of a tree.

1904

During the course of this year, the dirigible *Lebaudy II* —the rebuilt *No. 1*—makes a total of forty flights. On one occasion, it breaks its moorings and lands safely after a flight of 43 miles with no one on board.

13 Jul.   The dirigible *Méditerranéan II*, flown by Henri de la Vaulx, Hervé, von Willer, Laignier and Duhanot, makes a flight over the Mediterranean off the south coast of France.

14 Jul.   On a second flight over the sea, the *Méditerranéan II* hits the water. Its crew escapes unharmed.

3 Aug.   T. S. Baldwin (USA) makes a flight at Oakland, Calif., in a small dirigible powered by a Curtiss engine.

1905

5 Feb.   T. S. Baldwin takes part in a 10-mile race between his dirigible and an automobile. The car is beaten by three minutes.

4 May   First flight of an Italian dirigible, constructed by Schio.

3 Jul.   With Juchmès and Rey on board, *Lebaudy II* makes a record closed-circuit flight of 126 miles. First stage (Moisson–Meaux): 57 miles in 2 hrs 37 min. Second stage (Meaux–Jouarre): 10 miles in 40 min. Third stage (Jouarre–Camp de Chalons): 59 miles in 3 hrs 21 min.

12 Oct.   With Juchmès, Rey and Voyer on board, *Lebaudy II* covers a distance of 32 miles in 2 hrs 14 min., returning to its starting-point and setting up a world record on the same day that the *Fédération Aéronautique Internationale* is founded.

17 Oct.   During a flight in *Lebaudy II*, Richard and Bois drop dummy bombs and take photos of various objectives.

19 Oct.   *Lebaudy II* flies over the military stronghold at Toul during a flight lasting 2 hrs 31 min. and covering 31 miles. The crew, Juchmès, Rey and Voyer, are accompanied by General Pamard.

24 Oct.   *Lebaudy II* makes a flight from Toul with the French War Minister, M. Berteaux on board.

10 Nov.   During its 79th flight (its 25th in 1905) *Lebaudy II*, crewed by Juchmès, Rey and Voyer, reaches a record altitude of 4,500 feet.

30 Nov.   First flight of Zeppelin *LZ.2*.

1906

17 Jan.   Zeppelin *LZ.2* destroyed in a storm after a forced landing.

13 Jun.   The dirigible built in France on the orders of Walter Wellman (USA) arrives at Virgo Bay (Spitzbergen) in readiness for a planned flight across the Pole. The attempt is postponed until the following year.

12 Jul.   W. R. Turnbull makes the first airship flight in Canada.

18 Jul.   Dirigible flown by H. de la Vaulx makes a ten-hour flight from Longchamp, Paris.

11 Aug.   First flight by a woman in a dirigible in Britain: Mrs C. J. S. Miller flies as a passenger in an airship piloted by her husband, Major Miller.

9 Oct.   First flight of Zeppelin *LZ.3*.

11 Nov.   First flight of the dirigible *Ville de Paris* (F).

16 Nov.   The dirigible *Patrie* (F), built by Julliot for Lebaudy, makes its maiden flight.

1907

14 Jul.   The dirigible *Patrie* flies over Longchamp as part of a military parade.

22 Jul.   The German airship *Gross-Basenach I* makes its maiden flight.

7 Aug.   The dirigible *Patrie* makes a demonstration flight before the French President at Rambouillet.

2 Sep.	Walter Wellman's dirigible *America* takes off from Virgo Bay (Spitzbergen) in an attempt to reach the North Pole. Crew: Wellman, Melvin Vaniman, Louis Loud and Nikolai Popov. The flight is called off after three hours.
10 Sep.	Abortive attempt to fly the British dirigible *Nulli Secundus* by Colonel John Capper and S. F. Cody.
3 Oct.	*Nulli Secundus* (Capper and Cody) makes a 60-min. flight, covering a distance of 18 miles.
10 Oct.	*Nulli Secundus* destroyed by a storm.
22 Oct.	Dirigible *Patrie* makes a 33-mile flight around Paris with 8 people on board.
30 Nov.	The *Patrie* is torn from its moorings at Verdun by a strong wind which carries it westwards across the English Channel. It hits the ground briefly in Ireland, leaving behind one of its propellers (today preserved in the *Musée de l'Air*, Paris) before being swept out to sea and lost in the Atlantic.

1908

22 May	Dirigible built by R. Knabenshue (USA) flies at Toledo, Ohio, crewed by C. K. Hamilton and G. Duesler.
Jun.	First flight of the British dirigible *Beta*.
20 Jun.	First flight of Zeppelin *LZ.4*.
24 Jun.	First flight of the dirigible *République* (F), flown by Juchmès.
1 Jul.	German dirigible *Gross-Basenach I* accidentally destroyed.
1 Jul.	Zeppelin *LZ.4* makes a 12-hour endurance flight, covering a distance of 185 miles.
5 Aug.	*LZ.4* escapes from its ground crew during handling after a 21-hour, 370-mile flight and crashes in flames at Echterdingen.
12 Sep.	Dirigible *Gross-Basenach II* makes a night flight in the course of a 13-hour ascension, during which it covers a distance of 180 miles.

6 Oct. The dirigible *Lebaudy* sets up a new altitude record for this type of craft of 4,980 feet.

29 Oct. First flight of the French dirigible *Clément-Bayard*.

29 Nov. First flight of the French dirigible *Zodiac*, piloted by H. de la Vaulx.

1909

23 Jan. *Gross-Basenach II* flies over Berlin with Prince Heinrich of Prussia as a passenger.

19 Mar. Zeppelin *LZ.3* makes a flight with 26 on board, being manœuvred into its hangar with engines running. This craft now carries the military designation *Z.1*.

26 May First flight of *LZ.5* (*Z.2*), destined for the German Army.

30 May *LZ.5* (*Z.2*) covers a distance of 603 miles on a flight lasting 37 hrs 40 min. It is badly damaged in an accident, but returns safely to base after temporary repairs in flight.

15 Aug. Second and last attempt by Wellman to overfly the polar icecap in the dirigible *America*. The flight is called off after one hour.

23 Aug. Dirigible *Clément-Bayard* makes a forced landing in the Seine after an attempt on the altitude record. Among the crew is Colonel Nash, a Russian officer evaluating the airship with a view to its purchase by the Russian Government.

25 Aug. First flight of Zeppelin *LZ.6*.

29 Aug. *LZ.6* lands in Berlin after a flight from Friedrichshafen and is visited by Kaiser Wilhelm II.

24 Sep. *LZ.5* (*Z.2*) covers a distance of 140 miles in 4 hrs 10 min.

25 Sep. The dirigible *République* disintegrates in mid-air, killing the four members of its crew: Marchal, Chauré, Vincenot and Réau.

10 Oct. Albert 1, King of the Belgians, flies as a passenger in the French dirigible *Zodiac* piloted by H. de la Vaulx.

30 Oct.   German airships *Z.2*, *Parseval I* and *Gross-Basenach II* make a simulated air attack on a fort near Koblenz.

30 Oct.   French dirigible *Zodiac III* makes a lengthy flight over Belgian territory.

20 Nov.   German airships *Parseval I* and *Gross-Basenach II* fly from Cologne to a new Army base at Metz, one of the first real military airship stations.

1910

12 Feb.   First flight of the British military airship *Gamma*.

25 Apr.   *LZ.5* (*Z.2*) destroyed in a forced landing at Weilburg.

3 Jun.   British military airship *Beta*, completely rebuilt, flies from Farnborough to London and back in 4 hrs 4 min.

19 Jun.   First flight of Zeppelin *LZ.7*, the *Deutschland*.

22 Jun.   *LZ.7* makes a flight of 2 hrs 30 min. with 32 people on board.

28 Jun.   *LZ.7* crashes in the Teutoberg Forest as a result of engine failure. No casualties.

8 Aug.   The Willows non-rigid airship No. 2 (GB) flies from Cardiff to London in 9 hrs.

29 Aug.   Zeppelin *LZ.6* makes a 3-hr demonstration flight over Berlin.

14 Sep.   *LZ.6* is totally destroyed in a hangar fire.

10 Oct.   Walter Wellman, Melvin Vaniman, Murray Simon, J. R. Irwin and two others set off on an attempt to cross the Atlantic in the dirigible *America*. 86 hrs and 30 min. after taking off from Atlantic City, they are rescued by the British steamer RMS *Trent*; the abandoned airship takes to the air again and is lost.

16 Oct.   The dirigible *Clément-Bayard II* becomes the first to cross the Channel during its delivery flight to England. With a crew of 7, it flies 246 miles from Compiègne to Wormwood Scrubs at an average speed of 41 m.p.h.

26 Oct.   A Lebaudy airship ordered by the British Government flies from Moisson to Aldershot with 7 on board, covering the 230 miles in 5 hrs 30 min.

4 Nov.   The Willows dirigible *City of Cardiff* takes off from London at 15.30 hrs and lands at Douai at 2.00 the following morning, becoming the first airship to cross the Channel from west to east.

1911

Feb.   For the first time in Britain, experimental radio equipment is installed aboard an aircraft: the dirigible *Beta*.

30 Mar.   First flight of Zeppelin *LZ.8*, the *Ersatz Deutschland*.

16 May   *LZ.8* is badly damaged in a handling accident.

22 May   Britain's first rigid airship, the Vickers *R.1* (the *Mayfly*), is brought from her hangar and moored in the open in readiness for trials. She is destined never to fly: in September, she breaks her back during handling and is scrapped.

5 Jul.   The French dirigible *Adjudant Vincenot* sets up a new closed-circuit record for airships by flying 400 miles in 16 hrs 15 mins.

20 Jul.   First flight of Zeppelin *LZ.10*, the *Schwaben*.

15 Aug.   The Italian dirigible *P.2* flies from Venice to Monferrato (165 miles).

17 Oct.   First flight of the German airship Schütte-Lanz *SL.1*.

20 Oct.   First flight of Zeppelin *LZ.9*.

4 Nov.   First flight of the American dirigible *Akron*, designed by Melvin Vaniman.

6 Dec.   The French dirigible *Adjudant Réau* established a new altitude record of 7,100 feet.

1912

14 Feb.   First flight of Zeppelin *LZ.11*, the *Viktoria Luise*. Between this date and 31 October 1913, this airship makes 384

flights and carries 8,135 passengers, logging 838 hours flying time in DELAG service.

10 Mar.   The Italian airships *P.2* and *P.3* (Forlanini) overfly Turkish positions in N. Africa and drop several bombs.

13 Mar.   The Schütte-Lanz *SL.1* narrowly escaped crashing in the Forest of Tup. Four persons are accidentally thrown overboard and ' the airship, relieved of their weight, continues its flight.

25 Mar.   First flight of Zeppelin *LZ.12*.

13 Apr.   The Italian dirigibles *P.1* and *P.2* each carry out a 13-hour mission over enemy positions in N. Africa.

20 Apr.   A new altitude record of 9,500 feet is established by the French dirigible *Clément-Bayard III*.

1 May   The dirigibles *P.2* and *P.3* successfully bomb enemy positions in N. Africa.

11 Jun.   The airship *Schwaben* inaugurates the first air-mail service in Germany by carrying 20,000 postcards from Friedrichshafen to Mainz.

18 Jun.   French dirigible *Éclaireur Conte* sets up a new altitude record of 10,150 feet.

28 Jun.   The airship *Schwaben* is totally destroyed in a hangar fire.

2 Jul.   Melvin Vaniman (USA) is killed when the airship *Akron* explodes over the sea off Atlantic City.

30 Jul.   First flight of *LZ.13*, the *Hansa*. Up to 31 October 1913 this craft makes 297 flights in DELAG service, carrying 6,217 passengers and logging 632 hours.

7 Oct.   Launching of Zeppelin *LZ.14* (*L.1*), the first airship destined for the Imperial German Navy.

1913

16 Jan.   First flight of Zeppelin *LZ.15*.

17 Jan.   Schütte-Lanz *SL.1* is damaged when it hits the roof of its revolving hangar at Biesdorf.

14 Mar.   First flight of Zeppelin *LZ.16* (*Z.4*).

19 Mar.   *LZ.15* is accidentally destroyed.

3 Apr.   *LZ.16* (*Z.4*) lands at Luneville, France, with a high-ranking military commission on board, as a result of a navigational error.

3 May   First flight of *LZ.17*, the *Sachsen*.

6 Jun.   Launching of Zeppelin *LZ.19*.

25 Jun.   Castracane and Castruccio set up a duration record for Italian dirigibles with a flight of 15 hrs in the Forlanini *P.5*.

8 Jul.   First flight of Zeppelin *LZ.20* (*Z.5*).

30 Jul.   Castracane and Castruccio set up new distance record (Italian) of 500 miles in the *P.5*.

18 Aug.   First flight of the British airship *Eta*.

9 Sep.   First flight of *LZ.18* (*L.2*), second airship for the German Navy. Also on this day, the *LZ.14* (*L.1.*) crashes in the North Sea with heavy loss of life (14 dead, 6 survivors).

17 Oct.   *LZ.18* (*L.2*) explodes and burns at 1,500 feet over Johannisthal. 28 dead, no survivors.

10 Nov.   First flight of Zeppelin *LZ.21* (*Z.6*)

1914

8 Jan.   First flight of Zeppelin *LZ.22* (*Z.7*).

21 Feb.   First flight of Zeppelin *LZ.23* (*Z.8*).

8 Apr.   The Italian airship *Città-di-Milano* explodes on the ground, injuring twenty people.

11 May   First flight of Zeppelin *LZ.24* (*L.3*).

16 May   Zeppelin *L.3* climbs to a record altitude of 10,200 feet.

25 May   Italian dirigible *N.3* accidentally destroyed.

13 Jun.   Accidental destruction of Zeppelin *LZ.19*.

29 Jul.   First flight of Zeppelin *LZ.25* (*Z.9*), the last Zeppelin completed for the German Army before the outbreak of war.

1914

6 Aug.　　German Army Zeppelin $Z.6$ ($LZ.21$) drops 500 pounds of bombs on Liège. The airship is hit by anti-aircraft fire and is destroyed on crash-landing near Bonn.

7 Aug.　　German Army Zeppelin $Z.5$ ($LZ.20$) carries out a reconnaissance flight along the Polish Front.

9 Aug.　　The French airship *Conté* is fired on by French machine-guns for ten minutes and returns safely to base with 1,300 bullet-holes in its envelope.

10 Aug.　　First British coastal war patrol flown by dirigibles (Astra-Torres and Parseval) of the Royal Naval Air Service.

11 Aug.　　First mission under war conditions by a German Navy Zeppelin; $L.3$ locates Dutch battleship and four destroyers off Terschelling during a reconnaissance flight from Fuhlsbüttel.

16 Aug.　　German Army airship sheds at Prescati (Metz) bombed by French airmen.

17 Aug.　　Zeppelin $L.3$ reconnoitres the Skagerrak on the Naval Airship Division's first long war flight (radius 300 miles).

20 Aug.　　French dirigible *Dupuy-de-Lôme* drops six bombs in the vicinity of Genappe and Louvain.

22 Aug.　　Schütte-Lanz $SL.2$ makes a reconnaissance flight on a line Khólm–Lublin–Krasnik in support of Austrian ground forces. The information brought back by the airship played a major part in ensuring an Austrian victory at the Battle of Krasnik the following day.

22 Aug.　　German Army airship $Z.8$ ($LZ.23$) is shot down by a French 75-mm. gun battery.

24 Aug.　　French dirigible *Dupuy-de-Lôme* crash-lands at Courcy

226

after being fired on in mistake by French troops. One crew member, Lt Jourdan, is killed.

25 Aug. German Army airship *Z.9* (*LZ.25*) drops 9 bombs on Anvers, killing or wounding 26 people and damaging the palace where the Belgian royal family is in residence.

28 Aug. Zeppelin *L.3* goes out from Fuhlsbüttel in support of German surface forces engaging British warships in the Heligoland Bight, but returns to base with technical trouble.

28 Aug. Zeppelin *Z.5* (*LZ.20*) is hit by Russian ground fire which puts her steering gear out of action. The airship lands near Mlava after dropping her bomb-load on the Russians; only one crew member—Captain Grüner—is killed.

28 Aug. First flight of German Naval airship *L.4* (*LZ.27*).

22 Sep. German airship sheds at Düsseldorf unsuccessfully attacked by Flt Lt. C. H. Collet.

22 Sep. First flight of Zeppelin *L.5* (*LZ.28*).

24 Sep. German Army airship *Z.4* (*LZ.16*) commanded by Hauptmann von Quatz drops 14 bombs on Warsaw from an altitude of 9,000 feet.

8 Oct. Lt. Marix, RNAS, bombs the airship shed at Düsseldorf, scoring direct hits and destroying Zeppelin *Z.9* (*LZ.25*).

13 Oct. First flight of Zeppelin *Z.10* (*LZ.29*).

19 Oct. Zeppelin *L.5* (Oberlt. zur See Hirsch) makes a reconnaissance flight over the North Sea to within 60 miles of Great Yarmouth as a preliminary to a raid on the British coast by surface forces.

3 Nov. First flight of Zeppelin *L.6* (*LZ.31*).

20 Nov. First flight of Zeppelin *L.7* (*LZ.32*).

21 Nov. Three RNAS pilots—Briggs, Babington and Sippe—make an unsuccessful attack on the German airship sheds at Friedrichshafen.

14 Dec. First flight of Zeppelin *LZ.26* (*Z.12*).

17 Dec.   First flight of Zeppelin *L.8* (*LZ. 33*).

23 Dec.   Zeppelins *L.4* and *L.5* make a reconnaissance flight over the German Bight, but are forced back to base by bad weather.

24 Dec.   RNAS aircraft launched by seaplane carriers in the German Bight to attack Nordholz; only one finds the target in bad weather and no damage is caused. Zeppelins *L.5* and *L.6* take off to attack the British surface forces. *L.6* (von Buttlar) drops one bomb on the carrier *Empress* but misses the target; *L.5* (Hirsch) drops two bombs on the submarine *E.11* off Norderney, also with no effect.

25 Dec.   Schütte-Lanz *SL.2* bombs Nancy.

1915

6 Jan.   First flight of Zeppelin *LZ.34*.

11 Jan.   First flight of Zeppelin *LZ.35*

19 Jan.   Zeppelin *L.5* sights warships of the Harwich Force during a reconnaissance flight over the German Bight.

19–20 Jan. First Zeppelin raid on the British Isles. A previous attempt on 13 Jan. was called off because of bad weather. Three airships—*L.3*, *L.4* and *L.6*—take off on the 19 Jan. raid, but *L.6* turns back with engine trouble. *L.3* (Fritz) and *L.4* (von Platen-Hallermund) drop their bombs on Great Yarmouth and King's Lynn.

23 Jan.   Zeppelin *L.5* (Hirsch) flies a reconnaissance mission in support of German surface units during the Dogger Bank Battle.

25 Jan.   Parseval *PL.19* (Oberlt Maier) is shot down in the Baltic by a Russian battery commanded by Lt. Pankratóv after a raid on Libau. Crew of 7 taken prisoner.

4 Feb.   First flight of Schütte-Lanz *SL.3*.

17 Feb.   Zeppelin *L.3* (Fritz) crash-lands on the Danish island of Fano and is destroyed by its crew. *L.4* (von Platen) also crash-lands on the Danish coast at Blaavands Huk after engine failure in gale conditions; four crew lost when the

ship rebounds into the air and drifts out over the North Sea.

21 Feb.   Zeppelin *Z.10* (*LZ.29*) drops 2,000 pounds of bombs on Calais.

28 Feb.   First flight of Zeppelin *LZ.37*.

4 Mar.   Zeppelin *L.8* (Kapt. Lt. Beelitz) takes off from Gontrode (Belgium) in an attempt to raid England. It is hit by machine-gun fire over Nieuport and crashes near Tirlemont in the early hours of 5 March. One crew member (Bense) is killed.

8 Mar.   First flight of Zeppelin *L.9* (*LZ. 36*).

10 Mar.   German Army airships *Z.11* ʼ(*LZ.30*) and *LZ.34* bomb Warsaw.

17 Mar.   Attempt by German Army airships to raid England fails in thick fog. *Z.12*, using a 'cloud car'—a small nacelle lowered through the clouds on a cable and carrying an observer—bombs Calais through the overcast.

18 Mar.   First flight of the British non-rigid naval airship *SS.1* (*Willows No. 4*).

20 Mar.   German Army Zeppelins *LZ.29* (*Z.10*) and *LZ.35* (Frichs and Corsby) bomb Paris. *Z.10* is hit by French anti-aircraft fire and crash-lands near St Quentin. Schütte-Lanz *SL.2* bombs Compiègne.

29 Mar.   Zeppelins *L.6*, *L.7* and *L.9* patrol over the German Fleet during a short excursion into the North Sea.

3 Apr.   First flight of Zeppelin *LZ.38*.

13 Apr.   Zeppelin *LZ.35* is hit by anti-aircraft fire and crash-lands near Maria Aeltre (Belgium). The airship is destroyed by gale-force winds.

14 Apr.   Zeppelin *L.9* (Mathy) drops bombs on mining villages north of the River Tyne, injuring two people.

15 Apr.   German Army airships *Z.9* (*LZ.25*) and *LZ.34* bomb Warsaw for a second time.

15–16 Apr.   Zeppelins *L.5* (Kapt. Lt. Böcker) and *L.6* (von Buttlar) bomb Lowestoft and Maldon. *L.7* (Peterson) flies over Norfolk but fails to find her target in the blackout. All three ships return safely, although *L.6* is damaged by rifle fire.

24 Apr.   First flight of Zeppelin *LZ.39*.

25 Apr.   First flight of Schütte-Lanz *SL.4*.

May   (actual date uncertain): British non-rigid *SS.1* hits telegraph wires on the Dover–Folkestone road, crashes and burns.

3 May   Zeppelin *L.9* (Mathy) sights four British submarines on the surface off Terschelling and attacks one of them, the *E.5*, unsuccessfully with four 110-pound bombs. The airship also drops five bombs on the submarine *D.4* half an hour later—also without success.

12 May   Zeppelin *L.5* (Böcker) fails in an attempt to raid targets along the River Humber; the ship is forced to turn back short of the British coast through severe icing and engine failure.

13 May   First flight of Zeppelin *L.10* (*LZ.40*).

20 May   Zeppelin *Z.11* (*LZ.30*) catches fire in its hangar at Posen and is totally destroyed.

21 May   Zeppelin *LZ.34*, hit by artillery fire near Interburg, crash-lands and catches fire while being deflated.

25 May   Italian non-rigid dirigible *P-5*, commanded by A. Berardi, bombs Trieste.

26 May   Zeppelin *L.5* bombs Helsingfors.

31 May   German Army airship *LZ.38* (Hauptmann Linnarz) bombs London for the first time, dropping 3,000 pounds of explosives and killing 7 people.

2 Jun.   Zeppelin *L.5* (Böcker) narrowly escapes being attacked by a Sopwith Schneider floatplane over the German Bight. The Seaplane's pilot mistakes a smoke-screen for a recall signal and returns to the cruiser *Arethusa*.

6 Jun.   Zeppelin *L.9* (Mathy) bombs Hull and causes £45,000 worth of damage.

7 June.   First flight of Zeppelin *L.11 (LZ.41)*.

7 Jun.   German Army Zeppelin *LZ.37* (Von der Haegen) is attacked by Flt Sub-Lt Warneford, RNAS, flying a Morane Parasol. Warneford drops 6 bombs on the airship, which explodes and falls in flames on the convent of Grand Béguinage de Sainte-Elisabeth at Mont-St-Amand. In addition to the entire crew of the Zeppelin, two nuns and two children are killed.

7 Jun.   Two RNAS pilots from Dunkirk (Mills and Wilson) bomb the airship sheds at Evère (Brussels), destroying Zeppelin *LZ.38*.

8 Jun.   Returning from a bombing mission, the Italian dirigible *M-2* (Felice di Pisa) is shot down in flames by an Austrian aircraft flown by G. Kissing and H. R. F. von Gronenwald.

15 Jun.   First flight of Zeppelin *LZ.42 (LZ.72* in Army service— — see p. 248).

15 Jun.   Zeppelin *L.10* (Hirsch) bombs Wallsend, South Shields and Jarrow, killing 17 people and injuring 72.

21 Jun.   First flight of Zeppelin *LZ.43 (L.12)*.

27 Jun.   Capt. E. Gilbert (F) makes an unsuccessful attempt to bomb the Zeppelin works at Friedrichshafen. He lands in Switzerland and is interned, but escapes in 1916.

3 Jul.   Zeppelins *L.6, L.7, L.9, L.10, L.11* and Schütte-Lanz *SL.3* shadow the Harwich Force in the German Bight. A British plan to intercept the airships fails when the sea proves too rough for the RNAS floatplanes to take off.

8 Jul.   First flight of Zeppelin *LZ.44 (LZ.74* in Army service).

23 Jul.   First flight of Zeppelin *LZ.45 (L.13)*.

2 Aug.   First flight of Zeppelin *LZ.49 (LZ.79* in Army service)

2 Aug.	Zeppelin *Z.12* is hit by anti-aircraft fire over Osowiec and lands on the water at the port of Allenstein with three engines out of action. Both airship and crew are saved.
5 Aug.	The Italian airship *V-1 Città-di-Jesi* crashes in the Adriatic.
6 Aug.	Zeppelin *L.5.* is hit by gunfire over Dünamünde and is damaged beyond repair.
6 Aug.	Schütte-Lanz *SL.3* badly damaged on landing at Nordholz after flying through a rainstorm.
9 Aug.	First flight of Zeppelin *LZ.46* (*L.14*).
9 Aug.	Zeppelin *L.7* (Kapt. Lt Dietrich) and Parseval *PL.25* (Hauptmann Manger) attempt to warn crew of German minelayer *Meteor* of approach of British warships in German Bight. They fail, and the *Meteor* is scuttled by her crew to avoid capture.
9–10 Aug.	Zeppelins *L.9*, *L.10*, *L.11*, *L.12* and *L.13* set out to attack London and the Humber. *L.9* (Loewe) bombs Goole, Yorkshire, killing 16 people; *L.10* (Wenke) bombs Eastchurch; *L.11* (von Buttlar) jettisons its bombs in the sea off Lowestoft; *L.12* (Peterson) bombs Dover; and *L.13* (Mathy) turns back short of the British coast with engine trouble. *L.12* is hit by the Dover guns and makes a forced landing in the Channel. It is towed to Ostend by a torpedo-boat, surviving attacks by RNAS aircraft. The airship's forward section explodes and burns during the dismantling operation, but the after section is salvaged.
12–13 Aug.	Zeppelin *L.10* (Wenke) bombs Harwich, causing insignificant damage. *L.11* (von Buttlar) reaches the British coast, but returns to base without dropping any bombs, flying through a violent thunderstorm *en route*.
17 Aug.	Zeppelin *L.10* (Wenke) bombs the north-east London suburbs of Leyton and Wanstead Flats, killing 10 people and injuring 48. *L.11* (von Buttlar) drops 62 bombs on Ashford and Faversham.
3 Sep.	Zeppelin *L.10* (Hirsch) explodes and burns in mid-air

near Neuwerk Island during a training flight from Nordholz. 19 crew killed; no survivors.

7 Sep. London raided by German Army airships *LZ.74* and *SL.2*. *LZ.74* bombs Cheshunt and drops one incendiary on the City of London; *SL.2* drops its bombs on the docks of Millwall, Deptford, Greenwich and Woolwich. On its way back to base the latter airship makes a forced landing near Berchem Ste Agathe and is badly damaged.

8–9 Sep. Zeppelins *L.9* and *L.13* raid the British Isles. *L.9* (Loewe) bombs Skinningrove on the North Yorkshire coast; *L.13* (Mathy) causes damage amounting to over half a million pounds in London. One of the bombs weighed 660 lb.—the biggest dropped on Britain so far.

9 Sep. First flight of Zeppelin *LZ.48* (*L.15*).

12 Sep. First flight of Zeppelin *LZ.55* (*LZ.85* in Army service).

19 Sep. First flight of Schütte-Lanz *SL.6*.

22 Sep. French non-rigid dirigible *Commandant Coutelle* is destroyed by German artillery, but the crew is saved.

23 Sep. First flight of Zeppelin *LZ.50* (*L.16*).

2 Oct. French non-rigid dirigible *Alsace* is shot down over the German lines. One crew member (Druming) jumps clear and is killed; the other six are taken prisoner.

7 Oct. First flight of Zeppelin *LZ.51* (*LZ.81* in Army service).

8 Oct. Germany Army Zeppelin *LZ.74*, lost in fog, strikes the ground and two engine nacelles are torn away. The airship rebounds out of control to 12,000 feet. A safe landing is made at Orthe, but the airship has to be dismantled.

10 Oct. First flight of Zeppelin *LZ.56* (*LZ.86* in Army service).

13–14 Oct. London raided by five Naval Zeppelins: *L.11*, *L.13*, *L.14*, *L.15* and *L.16*. *L.11* (von Buttlar) drops its bombs on villages in Norfolk; *L.15* (Breithaupt) bombs the area north of the Strand; *L.13* (Mathy) bombs the village of Shalford and Woolwich Arsenal; *L.14* (Böcker) bombs the suburbs of Croydon and *L.16* (Peterson) attacks the town of Hertford. Despite heavy anti-aircraft fire and attempts at interception by British fighters, all the airships return safely to base.

20 Oct.   First flight of Zeppelin *LZ.53* (*L.17*).

3 Nov.   First flight of Zeppelin *LZ.52* (*L.18*).

14 Nov.   First flight of Zeppelin *LZ.58* (*LZ.88* in Army service).

17 Nov.   Zeppelin *L.18* is destroyed by explosion and fire while being inflated in the 'Toska' shed at Tondern.

27 Nov.   First flight of Zeppelin *LZ.54* (*L.19*).

6 Dec.   First flight of Zeppelin *LZ.57* (*LZ.87* in Army service).

7 Dec.   German Army Zeppelin *LZ.39* loses two engines through structural failure while returning from a raid on Kovno. It regains its base at Luck, but has to be dismantled.

20 Dec.   German Naval Zeppelins *L.35* and *L.38* arrive at Wainoden in Kurland in readiness for a raid on St Petersburg.

21 Dec.   First flight of Zeppelin *LZ.59* (*L.20*).

27 Dec.   Zeppelins *L.35* and *L.38* take off from Wainoden to attack Reval, Helsingfors, Oesel, Dagö and western Estonia. Both ships are forced to abandon the mission because of severe icing and engine trouble. *L.38* makes a forced landing in German-held territory at Seemuppen and is dismantled.

1916

1 Jan.   First flight of Zeppelin *LZ.60* (*LZ.90* in Army service).

10 Jan.   First flight of Zeppelin *LZ.61* (*L.21*).

29 Jan.   German Army Zeppelins *LZ.77* and *LZ.79* bomb Paris. French airmen make 42 sorties, but fail to intercept.

30 Jan.   Paris bombed by Zeppelin *LZ.79*. Soon after the attack, the airship is shot down at Mainveaux (Belgium) by the French pilot J. de Lesseps.

31 Jan.   First flight of Zeppelin *LZ.65* (*LZ.95* in Army service).

31 Jan.   German Army Zeppelin *LZ.85* (Hauptmann Scherzer) bombs Salonika and returns to its base at Temesvar

after an 18-hour flight. The raid causes considerable damage to a group of warehouses—owned by a German company!

31 Jan.– 1 Feb.

Nine Zeppelins—*L.11, L.13, L.14, L.15, L.16, L.17, L.19, L.20* and *L.21*—attack Liverpool and targets in the Midlands, killing 70 people and injuring 113. On the way home *L.19*, with three engines out of action, comes down in the North Sea and the British trawler *King Stephen* refuses to pick up the crew. Kapt. Lt Odo Loewe and the other 15 crew members are drowned.

21 Feb.

German Army Zeppelins *LZ.77* and *LZ.95* set out with two others to bomb railroad junctions near Verdun. *LZ.77* (Hauptmann Horn) is hit by French gunners and crashes in flames at Revigny: no survivors. *LZ.95* is also hit and crashes near Namur.

23 Feb.

First flight of Zeppelin *LZ.63* (*LZ.93* in Army service).

2 Mar.

First flight of Zeppelin *LZ.64* (*L.22*).

5–6 Mar.

Zeppelins *L.11* and *L.14* attack targets on the Humber. *L.13* (Mathy) abandons the attack through engine trouble.

18 Mar.

German Army Zeppelin *LZ.85* (Scherzer) attacks Salonika for a second time, landing at Sofia after a flight of 27 hrs.

30 Mar.

First flight of Schütte-Lanz *SL.8*.

31 Mar.

Zeppelins *L.13, L.14, L.15, L.16* and *L.22* attack London, Stowmarket, Thameshaven, Brentwood and Cleethorpes. *L.15* (Breithaupt) is attacked by a B.E. 2C flown by 2nd Lt A. de B. Brandon, RFC; severely damaged by Ranken darts and anti-aircraft fire, the airship comes down in the Thames Estuary at Knock Deep. 17 of the crew are taken prisoner; one drowned.

4 Apr.

First flight of Zeppelin *LZ.67* (*LZ.97* in Army service).

8 Apr.

First flight of Zeppelin *LZ.66* (*L.23*).

17 Apr.

Zeppelin *L.22* is badly damaged while being manœuvred into the Toska shed at Tondern.

24 Apr.   Eight Zeppelins (led by Peter Strasser in *L.21*) take off to attack southern England. The raid is foiled by dense fog and rain and most of the ships return to base with their bombs still on board.

25 Apr.   Zeppelin *L.9*, scouting for German warships shelling towns on the British east coast, narrowly escapes destruction by two British B.E. aircraft (Flt Cdr Nicholl and Flt Lt Hards, RNAS).

29 Apr.   First flight of Zeppelin *LZ.68* (*LZ.98* in Army service).

2–3 May   Eight Zeppelins attack targets in Britain; most of the bombs fall in open country. *L.20* (Stabbert), badly off course and over the Scottish highlands, heads for Norway and lands in a fjord south of Stavanger. 10 of the crew are interned, 6 repatriated.

4 May   The Italian dirigible *M-4* (G. Pastine), returning from a raid on Austrian positions, is shot down in flames near Gorizia by two Brandenburg C.1s and a Fokker E.III.

4 May   Zeppelin *L.7* shot down in flames by British cruisers off Horns Reef. 11 dead, 7 prisoners.

5 May   Army Zeppelin *LZ.85* (Scherzer) makes a forced landing near Salonika after being hit by anti-aircraft fire. The crew are taken prisoner after setting fire to the airship.

20 May   First flight of Zeppelin *LZ.69* (*L.24*).

21 May   French non-rigid *Champagne* is hit by gunfire and lands in a wood near Souilly. One crew member, a machine-gunner, escapes by parachute; the remainder stay on board and are unhurt.

24 May   First flight of Schütte-Lanz *SL.9*.

28 May   First flight of Zeppelin *LZ.62* (*L.30*).

31 May   German Naval Zeppelins take part in the Battle of Jutland, scouting for the German Fleet. Operations are hampered by poor visibility. One ship, *L.11*, comes under heavy fire from British warships but escapes unharmed.

2–3 Jun.   French dirigible *Adjudant Vincenot* put out of action by ground fire.

3 Jun.	A Caudron aircraft piloted by Girardi collides with the Italian dirigible *M-5*, which explodes killing its five crew. The pilot of the aircraft is also killed.
12 Jul.	First flight of Zeppelin *LZ.72 (L.31)*.
27 Jul.	German Army airship Schütte-Lanz *SL.10* leaves her base at Jamboli to bomb Sevastopol, commanded by Hauptmann von Wobeser. The craft disappears without trace.
31 Jul.– 1 Aug.	Small-scale raid by German Naval Zeppelins on Britain does little damage, almost all the bombs falling in open country. The same is true of a second raid on the night of August 2/3.
2 Aug.	First flight of Schütte-Lanz *SL.11*.
6 Aug.	First flight of Zeppelin *LZ.74 (L.32)*.
8–9 Aug.	Zeppelin *L.24* bombs Hull, causing some damage and killing 10 people. *L.17* and *L.23*, attempting to raid the Northumberland coast, are driven off by accurate gunfire from the trawler *Itonian* and jettison their bombs in the sea.
16 Aug.	Italian dirigible *M-7* breaks its moorings and is lost in the Adriatic.
19 Aug.	Naval Zeppelins fly in support of German warships operating in the North Sea, carrying out long-range reconnaissance over an arc stretching from the Norwegian coast to Scotland, Tynemouth and the Humber. *L.30* (von Buttlar) is hit and slightly damaged by shellfire from the trawler *Ramexo*. During this operation, the *L.31* (Mathy) works in conjunction with the submarine *U-53*—a foretaste of the co-operation between aircraft and U-boats that was to become established practice during the Second World War.
23 Aug.	First flight of Schütte-Lanz *SL.14*.
24 Aug.	Thirteen German Naval airships—including the Schütte-Lanz *SL.8* and *SL.9*—take off to raid south-east England. Six of the ships are fired on by British Naval forces over the sea; *L.13* (Proelss) is hit and returns to base, as do

four others, dropping their bombs in the sea. *SL.8* and *SL.9* also turn back after failing to reach the coast. The remainder bomb coastal targets with the exception of *L.31* (Mathy), which bombs London.

28–9 Aug. British Naval non-rigid *SS.40* makes a night reconnaissance flight over the Somme Front at the request of the Army.

30 Aug. First flight of Zeppelin *LZ.76* (*L.33*).

2 Sep. Schütte-Lanz *SL.11* shot down in flames at Cuffley by Lt W. Leefe Robinson, RFC. 16 crew killed; no survivors. *SL.11* was part of a force of 16 Army and Navy airships which set out to raid England; it was the last time that Army airships appeared over the British Isles. The other airships taking part in this raid were: (Army) *SL.8, LZ.90, LZ.97* and *LZ.98;* (Navy) *L.11, L.13, L.14, L.16, L.17, L.21, L.22, L.23, L.24, L.30* and *L.32.*

5 Sep. German Army airship *LZ.86* is badly damaged on landing after a bombing mission over Ploesti (Rumania). Eight crew members are killed, including three officers: Kramer, Benner and Köstlich.

15 Sep. British Naval non-rigid *SS.42* accidentally destroyed on landing after a three-hour runaway flight in a gale over the Bristol Channel. The occupant, Flt Lt Monk, escapes with slight injuries.

16 Sep. Zeppelins *L.6* and *L.9* destroyed by fire in their shed at Fuhlsbüttel.

22 Sep. First flight of Zeppelin *LZ.78* (*L.34*).

22–3 Sep. Twelve German Naval Zeppelins (the same as for the raid on 2 September, with the addition of *L.31* and *L.33*) attack London and the Midlands. *L.33* (Böcker), severely damaged by Lt A. de B. Brandon, crash-lands in a field at Little Wigborough and is set on fire by its crew, all 22 of whom are taken prisoner. *L.32* (Peterson) is shot down in flames near Billericay by 2nd Lt Frederick Sowrey, RFC. 22 dead; no survivors.

24 Sep. German Army Zeppelin *LZ.81* bombs Bucharest. Returning from a similar raid the following night, it is badly

hit by anti-aircraft fire and crash-lands at Tirnova in Bulgaria.

25 Sep.   Nine German Naval Zeppelins attack London and the Midlands.

1–2 Oct. Eleven German Naval airships set out to raid England; three turn back in bad weather. *L.31* (Mathy) is attacked over London by 2nd Lt W. J. Tempest, RFC, and falls in flames at Potters Bar. 19 dead, no survivors.

12 Oct.   First flight of Zeppelin *LZ.80* (*L.35*).

16 Oct.   First flight of Zeppelin *LZ.77* (*LZ.107* in Army service).

19 Oct.   Eight German Naval Zeppelins scout ahead of the High Seas Fleet during a brief sortie into the North Sea.

1 Nov.   First flight of Zeppelin *LZ.82* (*L.36*).

7 Nov.   German Army Zeppelin *LZ.90* (*LZ.60*) makes an emergency landing in a storm at Wittmund. It escapes from its ground crew and is lost over the North Sea; no casualties.

9 Nov.   First flight of Zeppelin *LZ.75* (*L.37*).

9 Nov.   First flight of Schütte-Lanz *SL.12*.

22 Nov.   First flight of Zeppelin *LZ.84* (*L.38*).

27 Nov.   First flight of British rigid airship Vickers *R.9*.

28–9
Nov.   German Naval Zeppelins attack targets in north-east England. *L.34* (Max Dietrich) is shot down by 2nd Lt I. V. Pyott of No. 36 Sqn, RFC, soon after bombing West Hartlepool; all 20 crew members are killed. *L.21* (Frankenberg) is also destroyed by three RNAS pilots (Cadbury, Pulling and Fane) from Great Yarmouth.

13 Dec.   First flight of Zeppelin *LZ.86* (*L.39*).

20 Dec.   First flight of Zeppelin *LZ.81* (*LZ.111* in Army service).

27 Dec.   French dirigible *Champagne* (repaired after its crash of 21 May) carries out a bombing mission near Verdun.

It is its last, the ship being withdrawn from service the following February.

28 Dec. Six German Naval airships take off to attack southern England but are recalled in the face of a rising gale. One of them, the Schütte-Lanz *SL.12* (Kölle) crash-lands at Aalhorn and is destroyed during the night by a storm.

28 Dec. Zeppelin *L.24*, being walked into its shed at Tondern after a patrol over the German Bight, breaks its back and catches fire. The flames spread to *L.17*; both ships are a total loss.

1917

5 Jan. First flight of Zeppelin *LZ.88* (*L.40*).

15 Jan. First flight of Zeppelin *LZ.79* (*L.41*).

31 Jan. First flight of Zeppelin *LZ.90* (*LZ.120* in Army service).

6 Feb. Zeppelin *L.36* (Kapt. Lt Eichler) hits the ice-covered estuary of the River Weser, takes to the air again after suffering substantial damage. Some time later it crashes on the ice of the River Aller and breaks up; there are no casualties.

16 Feb. Zeppelins *L.30* and *L.37* make a long-range scouting flight over the U-boat blockade area of the North Sea. *L.37* is fired on by a destroyer, but escapes unharmed.

16 Feb. German Army Zeppelin *LZ.107* (*LZ.77*) bombs Boulogne through cloud. The cloud-car observer, E. Zigan, is forced to spend 7 hours suspended at the end of his 900-foot cable when the winch breaks down.

22 Feb. First flight of Zeppelin *LZ.83* (*LZ.113* in Army service) and *LZ.91* (*L.42*).

23 Feb. The French non-rigid *Pilâtre de Rozier* (L. Prêcheur) is shot down and its crew killed.

24 Feb. Following the loss of the *Pilâtre de Rozier*, the French Military Command decides to withdraw all dirigibles from service at the Front. The surviving craft are turned over to the French Navy for anti-submarine and convoy protection duties.

6 Mar.   First flight of Zeppelin *LZ.92* (*L.43*).

16–17
Mar.   Southern England raided by German Naval Zeppelins
          L.35, *L.39*, *L.40*, *L.41* and *L.42*. After dropping its
          bombs on Kent, *L.39* (Kapt. Lt Koch) is carried as far
          as Compiègne by a gale. Shortly after dawn it is subjected
          to a fifteen-minute anti-aircraft barrage and is finally
          shot down in flames by a battery commanded by Capt.
          Galibert. 17 dead, no survivors. The other Zeppelins
          taking part in the raid bomb open country and cause no
          casualties; one of them, *L.35*, breaks its back on landing
          at Dresden and is out of action until June 14.

1 Apr.   First flight of Zeppelin *LZ.93* (*L.44*).

2 Apr.   First flight of Zeppelin *LZ.85* (*L.45*).

20 Apr.   First flight of the *DN-1*, a dirigible built to a US Navy
          contract by the Connecticut Aircraft Company. The craft
          is not a success and makes only two more flights before
          being scrapped.

21 Apr.   British Naval airship *C.17* is shot down in flames by two
          Brandenburg floatplanes (Kastner and Meyer) operating
          out of Zeebrugge.

23 Apr.   Norwegian bark *Royal*, bound for West Hartlepool with
          a cargo of timber, is arrested off the Danish coast by the
          German *L.23* (Kapt. Lt Bockholt) which lands on the
          water beside her and puts a prize crew on board.

24 Apr.   First flight of Zeppelin *LZ.94* (*L.46*).

1 May   First flight of Zeppelin *LZ.87* (*L.47*).

4 May   Zeppelins *L.23*, *L.42* and *L.43* scout over the North Sea;
          L.43 (Kraushaar) encounters British warships off Ters-
          chelling and bombs them, near-missing the light cruiser
          Dublin.

12 May   French dirigible *T.1* (Commdt Caussin) explodes over the
          sea and falls in flames off Sardinia during a flight from St
          Raphael to Bizerta.

14 May   Naval Zeppelin *L.22* (Lehmann) shot down in flames off
          Texel by a Curtiss *H-12* 'Large America' flying-boat

(Flt Lt Galpin and Flt Sub-Lt Leckie) from Great Yarmouth. 21 dead, no survivors.

22 May   First flight of Zeppelin *LZ.95* (*L.48*).

22 May   Italian dirigible *M-12* is hit by anti-aircraft fire and falls in the Adriatic.

23 May   Italian dirigible *M-3 Città-di-Ferrara* is shot down by Austrian artillery fire.

23–4 May   Southern England raided by Zeppelins *L.40*, *L.41*, *L.42*, *L.43*, *L.44* and *L.45*. *L.44* (Stabbert) drifts over enemy territory for nearly an hour after complete engine failure, but eventually returns safely to base. The raid, which takes place at high altitude (over 18,000 feet), does little damage. Returning from the raid, *L.40* (Sommerfeldt) is attacked by a Curtiss H-12 from Great Yarmouth (Galpin) and several hits are scored, but the Zeppelin escapes.

30 May   First flight of the US Navy non-rigid Goodyear *B-1*, commanded by R. H. Upson.

5 Jun.   For a second time, Zeppelin *L.40* (Sommerfeldt) is attacked by Flt Lt Galpin in a Curtiss H-12 and several thousand rounds of ammunition are fired at the airship over a period of 20 minutes, but with no effect. *L.40* returns the fire and escapes.

9 Jun.   First flight of Zeppelin *LZ.89* (*L.50*).

13 Jun.   First flight of Zeppelin *LZ.96* (*L.49*). The ship is severely damaged when its envelope tears during its delivery flight, but it reaches its base after a flight of 9 hours.

14 Jun.   Zeppelin *L.43* (Kapt. Lt. Kraushaar) is shot down off Ameland by a Curtiss H-12 (Flt Sub-Lts Hobbs and Dickey) from Felixstowe. 24 dead, no survivors.

16–17 Jun.   High altitude raid on southern England by Zeppelins *L.41*, *L.42*, *L.44* and *L.48*. The latter is attacked by Lt L. P. Watkins of No. 37 Sqn, RFC, and shot down in flames over Holly Tree Farm, near Theberton. 14 dead, including Kapt. Lt. Eichler; three survivors. Three aircraft also attempt to intercept *L.42* (Dietrich) on its way home, but the Zeppelin escapes.

6 Jul. First flight of Zeppelin *LZ.97* (*L.51*).

14 Jul. First flight of Zeppelin *LZ.98* (*L.52*).

26 Jul. Two Curtiss H-12 from Great Yarmouth (Galpin and Leckie) unsuccessfully attack Zeppelin *L.46* (Kapt. Lt Hollender) and attempt to intercept *L.44*. Both airships escape by climbing.

26 Jul. Zeppelin *LZ.120* (Lehmann) makes a record endurance flight of 101 hrs over the Baltic.

1 Aug. Process of disbanding the German Army Airship Service begins. Most of the surviving airships are dismantled; *LZ.113* and *LZ.120*, the Army's two six-engined 'height climbers', are turned over to the Navy.

13 Aug. First flight of Zeppelin *LZ.99* (*L.54*).

18 Aug. First flight of Zeppelin *LZ.100* (*L.53*).

21 Aug. Eight Zeppelins make a high-altitude raid (20,000 feet) on Hull and East Anglia, causing insignificant damage. Because of their extreme height, the raiders are almost completely undetected by the British defences.

21 Apr. Zeppelin *L.23* (Oberlt zur See Dinter) is shot down off the Jutland coast by a Sopwith Pup launched from a turret platform on HMS *Yarmouth* and flown by Flt Sub-Lt B. A. Smart. 18 dead, no survivors.

Sep. (date uncertain): The Austrian airman Fischa bombs the Italian airship sheds at Campalto, destroying the dirigibles *M-8* and *M-13*.

1 Sep. First flight of Zeppelin *LZ.101* (*L.55*).

5 Sep. Zeppelins *L.44* and *L.46* are attacked by a DH.4 (Flt Lt Gilligan and Obs. Lt Trewin) and a Curtiss H-12 (Flt Lt Leckie and Sqn Ldr Nicholl) over the German Bight. Both Zeppelins escape; both aircraft damaged by fire from German surface forces.

10 Sep. First flight of Schütte-Lanz *SL.20*.

22 Sep. Italian dirigible *P-10* is hit by Austrian gunfire and crashes at Latisana.

24 Sep.	Zeppelins *LZ.113* and *LZ.120*, now with Navy crews, bomb gun batteries at Zerel and Sworbe on the Island of Oesel.
24 Sep.	First flight of Zeppelin *LZ.103* (*L.56*).
24–5 Sep.	Nine Zeppelins make an ineffective raid on northern England. *L.35* (Ehrlich) bombs Rotherham but misses his target—a colliery and a steelworks.
26 Sep.	First flight of Zeppelin *LZ.102* (*L.57*).
1 Oct.	Zeppelins *L.30*, *L.37* and *LZ.120* bomb the ports of Salismünde and Sophienruhe.
3 Oct.	British coastal airship *C.9* bombs a U-boat which had just attacked an Italian merchant ship off the Cornish coast. No result observed.
8 Oct.	Zeppelin *L.57* explodes and burns while being manœuvred into her hangar at Jüterbog.
9 Oct.	Zeppelins *L.30*, *LZ.113* and *SL.20* patrol the Gulf of Finland in preparation for a landing by German forces on Oesel. Bad weather forces the airships back to base and they are unable to cover the actual landing.
19–20 Oct.	Thirteen Zeppelins are prepared for the last great airship raid over the British Isles: *L.41*, *L.42*, *L.44*, *L.45*, *L.46*, *L.47*, *L.49*, *L.50*, *L.51*, *L.52*, *L.53*, *L.54* and *L.55*. A crosswind prevents two of them, *L.42* and *L.51*, from leaving their hangar; the others, led by Peter Strasser, set course for targets in the Midlands. *L.44* (Stabbert) is shot down by French guns over Chennevières; 18 dead, no survivors. *L.45* (Kolle) makes a forced landing at Sisteron and is set on fire by its crew; 17 prisoners. *L.49* (Gayer) is brought down at Bourbonne-les-Bains under repeated attacks by pilots of the French Flying Corps's No. 152 'Crocodiles' Escadrille (Lafargue, de la Marque, Denis, Gresset and Lefevre); 19 prisoners. *L.50* (Schwonder) hits the ground during a rapid descent at Montigny-le-Roy; part of the ship, with four men still inside, takes to the air again and is lost over the Mediterranean. 16 other crew members taken prisoner. *L.55*

(Flemming) is destroyed on returning from the raid at Tiefenort, Germany. Because of the great height at which the Zeppelins flew over England, and because the defences were ordered to remain 'covered' in case gun-flashes and searchlights gave away the positions of targets, the attack was remembered as the 'Silent Raid'.

25 Oct. First flight of Zeppelin *LZ.104* (*L.59*).

29 Oct. First flight of Zeppelin *LZ.105* (*L.58*).

17 Nov. First successful crossing of the Mediterranean by a dirigible: the Astra-Torres *AT-6* (Denoix and Roustand).

21 Nov. Zeppelin *L.59* (Bockholt) leaves Jamboli in Bulgaria with a crew of 22 to ferry supplies and ammunition to German forces in East Africa. On 22 Nov., beyond Khartoum, the airship is recalled and returns to Jamboli after 95 hrs 35 min. in the air, having covered a distance of 4,200 miles.

11 Dec. The British coastal airship *C.27* (based on Pulham) is attacked by three Brandenburg W.12 floatplanes from Zeebrugge and is shot down in flames into the North Sea in less than two minutes. Its final destruction was credited to Oberlt Friedrich Christiansen; after its loss, no further British dirigible flights were made in areas which could be reached by German aircraft.

12 Dec. First flight of Zeppelin *LZ.106* (*L.61*).

13 Dec. British coastal airship *C.26* makes a forced landing in Holland. The craft is impounded and the crew interned.

18 Dec. First flight of Zeppelin *LZ.108* (*L.60*).

1918

5 Jan. Zeppelins *L.46*, *L.47*, *L.51*, *L.58* and the Schütte-Lanz *SL.20* are destroyed by a series of explosions and fire in their hangars at Aalhorn. The accident probably resulted from a petrol fire under the after gondola of *L.51*, although there was a possibility of sabotage. 15 dead.

19 Jan. First flight of Zeppelin *LZ.107* (*L.62*).

26 Jan.	A German Albatros D.III fighter is successfully released from *L.35* at a height of 4,600 ft.
3 Feb.	The Italian dirigible *M-17* crashes near Venice.
20 Feb.	French Zodiac Vedette *VZ.3* (Commdt Fleury) collides with the cliffs at La Heve and catches fire. One crew member survives. A few minutes later the fire causes the craft's bomb-load to explode, injuring 28 onlookers.
3 Mar.	French dirigible Astra-Torres *AT-1* makes its first flight in American service.
4 Mar.	First flight of Zeppelin *LZ.110 (L.63)*.
10 Mar.	Zeppelin *L.59* (Bockholt) drops 14,000 pounds of bombs on Naples, returning to Jamboli after a flight of 37 hrs 12 min.
11 Mar.	First flight of Zeppelin *LZ.109 (L.64)*.
12–13 Mar.	Five Zeppelins—*L.53, L.54, L.61, L.62* and *L.63*—attack targets in Britain. The raid is ineffective, most of the bombs falling in open country or the sea. Two crew members of *L.53* die from carbon monoxide poisoning on the return flight.
13 Mar.	Zeppelins *L.42, L.52* and *L.56* take off to raid the Midlands, but are recalled. *L.42* (Dietrich) ignores the order and bombs West Hartlepool.
20 Mar.	Zeppelin *L.59* (Bockholt) leaves Jamboli to attack Port Said, but abandons the mission in the face of strong headwinds and returns after a flight of 52 hrs 23 min.
7 Apr.	Zeppelin *L.59* explodes and burns over the Straits of Otranto. Cause of accident possibly a petrol fire. 23 dead, no survivors.
12 Apr.	Zeppelins *L.60, L.61, L.62, L.63* and *L.64* raid the British Isles. *L.62*, raiding the Midlands, is attacked by an FE.2b of No. 38 Sqn, RFC, but escapes after the Zeppelin's gunners wound the pilot, Lt C. H. Noble-Campbell, in the head.
17 Apr.	First flight of Zeppelin *LZ.111 (L.65)*.

27 Apr.   French dirigible *AT-1* (Commdt Culbert) logs 25 hrs 43 min. on one escort flight—a record for this type of craft.

2 May   British SS 'Zero' Class dirigible *Z-29* spots a periscope off Folkestone and directs surface forces to the scene, resulting in the destruction of *UB-31*.

10 May   Zeppelin *L.62* explodes and burns off Heligoland with no survivors. Possible cause: sabotaged bomb-load.

5 Jun.   First flight of Schütte-Lanz *SL.2*—the last of its type.

1 Jul.   First flight of Zeppelin *LZ.112* (*L.70*).

29 Jul.   First flight of Zeppelin *LZ.113* (*L.71*).

31 Jul.   Zeppelins *L.61*, *L.63* and *L.65* fly a scouting mission in support of minesweepers in the German Bight. *L.63* (von Freudenreich) bombs an unidentified submarine, claiming one hit.

1 Aug.   Zeppelin *L.70* (von Lossnitzer) drops ten 220-pound bombs on destroyers of the Harwich Force off the Dogger Bank. Results unobserved.

2 Aug.   British Naval aircraft fire on *L.64* off Terschelling, but with no result.

5–6 Aug. Zeppelins *L.53*, *L.56*, *L.63*, *L.65* and *L.70* carry out the last raid of the war on Britain. *L.70* (von Lossnitzer) is shot down in flames by Major Egbert Cadbury and Captain Robert Leckie in a DH.4 and falls in the sea near King's Lynn. 22 dead (including Peter Strasser); no survivors.

11 Aug.   Zeppelin *L.53* (Proelss) is shot down off Ameland by Lt Stuart Culley, flying a Sopwith Camel launched from a lighter towed behind the destroyer *Redoubt*. 19 dead, no survivors.

16 Aug.   The Italian dirigible *A–1* is lost on a patrol mission over the Adriatic.

Sep.   (date uncertain): First flight of the Goodyear *C.1* dirigible for the US Navy.

16 Sep.   German submarine *UB-103* (already damaged) is shadowed for seven miles off Cap Gris Nez by the British SS 'Zero' Class dirigible *Z-1*, which summons surface forces. The U-boat is destroyed.

29 Sep.   British rigid airship *R.29* locates the German submarine *UB-115* off Sunderland and drops a smoke float to mark its position; U-boat finally destroyed by surface forces.

12 Oct.   Zeppelins *L.63* and *L.65* carry out a short reconnaissance over the German Bight: the last flight under war conditions by rigid airships.

9 Nov.   Surviving Zeppelins of the German Navy hung up in their sheds and deflated. Armistice signed two days later.

Note on German airship designations

German Army Zeppelins were designated by the letter *Z* followed by a numeral—for example, *Z.1*. These numbers were not necessarily consecutive; when a ship was lost or withdrawn from service, it was replaced by another bearing an 'ersatz' or 'replacement' number, for example *EZ.1—Ersatz Z.1*. This practice continued up to December 1914, when it was abandoned with *Z.12* to avoid the possibility of having an 'unlucky' *Z.13*. After that, the Army simply used the Zeppelin builder's number to designate their ships, starting with *LZ.34*. In 1915, however, the Army began to add thirty to the builder's number—so Zeppelin *LZ.42* became *LZ.72*, and so on.

The Navy's system was far less complicated, beginning with *L.1* and continuing consecutively throughout the series up to *L.71*.

Appendix III

An Airship Chronology, 1918–38

1918

Dec. British dirigible *NS.11* logs 61 hrs 30 min. in the air during a minesweeping patrol.

4 Dec. Italian dirigible *O–5* hits an obstruction during a storm near Taranto. Two crew members jump clear; two more remain on board and are lost when the craft is carried out over the Mediterranean.

12 Dec. American dirigible *C-1* (G. Crompton) successfully releases a Curtiss JN-4 biplane (A. W. Redfield) at 2,500 ft.

1919

29 Jan. Italian dirigible *O–7* breaks its moorings in a gale and is lost.

14 May American dirigible *C-5* flies from Montauk to St John's (Newfoundland), a distance of 1,022 miles, in 25 hrs 50 min. The craft is ripped from its moorings by a gale two days later and lost.

23 Jun. Zeppelins *L.14*, *L.41*, *L.42*, *L.52*, *L.56*, *L.63* and *L.65* are destroyed by their crews.

26 Jun. Two Italian dirigibles, the *F.6* and *N.14*, open a passenger service between Milan and Venice.

2 Jul. First crossing of the North Atlantic by an airship: the British *R.34*.

17 Jul. British dirigible *NS.11* is struck by lightning and falls into the North Sea in flames.

24 Aug. First flight of Zeppelin *LZ.120 Bodensee*.

3 Sep. Commissioning of British rigid airship *R.32*.

24 Sep. *LZ.120 Bodensee* begins a regular service between Friedrichshafen and Berlin.

1920

21 Jun.   Zeppelin *L.64* is delivered to Great Britain.

30 Jun.   Zeppelin *L.71* is delivered to Great Britain.

9 Jul.   First flight of Zeppelin *LZ.114 (L.72)*. On 11 July, this craft is handed over to France as the *Dixmude*.

10 Aug.   The *Dixmude* (du Plessis de Grenedan) flies from Maubeuge to Cuers in 24 hrs 25 min.

28 Aug.   Zeppelin *L.61* is handed over to Italy.

8 Sep.   Zeppelin *LZ.113* is handed over to France.

1921

29 Jan.   The British *R.34* is severely damaged when she flies into a hillside in Yorkshire.

23 Apr.   The British *R.32* is tested to destruction at Howden, Yorkshire.

8 Jun.   First flight of Zeppelin *LZ.121 Nordstern*—later turned over to the French and renamed *Méditerranée*.

23 Jun.   First flight of the British rigid airship *R.38*.

3 Jul.   Zeppelin *LZ.120 Bodensee* is handed over to Italy and renamed *Esperia*.

24 Aug.   The British *R.38* breaks up over Hull and falls in the River Humber. 44 dead, 5 survivors.

15 Nov.   First flight in the USA of the Italian dirigible *Roma*, purchased from Usuelli.

Dec.   First flight of the world's first helium-filled dirigible, the American *C-7*.

1922

21 Feb.   The *Roma* is destroyed at Hampton Roads, USA. 34 dead, 11 survivors.

14 Sep.   The non-rigid US dirigible *C-2* (H. A. Strauss) makes the first non-stop air crossing of the N. American continent, from Langley Field (Va.) to Arcadia (Calif.).

1923

4 Sep.   First flight of the US airship *ZR-1 Shenandoah*.

25 Sep.   The French dirigible *Dixmude* (ex Zeppelin *L.72*) flies from France to Tunisia and back in 118 hours 41 min.

1 Oct.   The *Shenandoah* flies from Lakehurst to St Louis in 24 hrs 46 min. and returns the following day in 20 hrs 28 min. with 42 people on board.

18 Dec.   The *Dixmude* (de Grenedan) takes off from Cuers on a voyage to the Sahara. It is lost with all hands over the Mediterranean.

1924

8 Mar.   First flight of the Astra-Torres *AT-19*.

25 Sep.   First flight of Zeppelin *LZ.126*. Commanded by Hugo Eckener, it flies from Friedrichshafen to Malmö and back (2,150 miles) in 32 hrs 30 min. with 73 on board.

7–26 Oct.   The *Shenandoah* makes a two-way crossing of the N. American continent (Lakehurst–San Diego–Seattle–Lakehurst) in 19 days 19 hrs, covering a distance of 9,317 miles.

13 Oct.   Zeppelin *LZ.126* leaves Friedrichshafen on a transatlantic flight to Lakehurst for delivery to the US Navy as the *ZR-3 Los Angeles*.

1925

24–5 Jan.   The *Los Angeles* follows the path of a solar eclipse across the USA with 25 scientists on board.

20 Feb.   The *Los Angeles* flies from Lakehurst to Bermuda and back, a distance of 1,500 miles.

16 Apr.   The British rigid airship *R.33* is torn from its mast by a severe gale and drifts as far as Holland, but is brought back to base (Pulham) by a 20-man skeleton crew after 27 hrs over the North Sea.

4 May   The *Los Angeles* flies from Lakehurst to Puerto Rico and back in 31 hrs.

30 May   The Italian airships *N.1* (Nobile) and *Esperia* (ex-*Bodensee*) make a Mediterranean cruise to Spain and are visited by King Alfonso XIII at Barcelona.

2–3 Sep.   The *Shenandoah* (Cdr Zachary Lansdowne) breaks up over Ohio. 14 dead, 29 survivors.

15 Sep.   First flight of the American non-rigid dirigible *RS-1*.

15 Oct.   A D.H. 53 Humming Bird is successfully released in flight from the British airship *R.33*.

1926

10 Apr.   The dirigible *Norge* (Nobile *N.1*) leaves Italy for Spitzbergen via Pulham, Oslo, Leningrad and Vadsö on the first stage of Amundsen's Arctic expedition.

11 May   The *Norge* leaves King's Bay, Spitzbergen, on a flight over the North Pole. It lands at Teller, Alaska, on 14 May, after covering 3,000 miles non-stop across the Arctic ice-cap.

21 Oct.   Two Gloster Grebe fighters, piloted by Mackenzie-Richards and Ragg, are successfully released at 2,000 ft from a trapeze slung under the *R.33* and recovered in flight some minutes later.

1928

27 Jan.   The *ZR-3 Los Angeles* lands on the aircraft carrier *Saratoga* during a fleet exercise and resumes her patrol after replenishment.

26 Feb.   The *Los Angeles* leaves Lakehurst to carry out manœuvres with the Fleet in the Caribbean, returning to its base on 2 March.

15 Apr.   The Italian dirigible *Italia* leaves Milan for Spitzbergen via Seddin and Vadsö on the first stage of Umberto Nobile's Arctic expedition.

15 May   The *Italia* makes a 60-hr flight over Franz Josef Land and Novaya Zemlya before returning to King's Bay.

23 May   The *Italia* leaves King's Bay on the flight to the North Pole. Its log is as follows—23 May: 04.28 depart King's

Bay. 24 May: 12.20 hrs. North Pole reached. 25 May: distress message transmitted 200 miles from base. 9 June: first distress message since 25 May picked up at King's Bay; survivor's position 80° 30′ N, 28° 00′ E. 15 June: Professor Malmgren is left, dying, by Mariano and Zappi. 24 June: Lundborg (Sweden) lands and picks up Nobile in a D.H. Moth fitted with skis. Lundborg returns, suffers engine failure, and lives with other survivors until picked up on 5 July by Schyberg (Sweden). 12 July: Mariano and Zappi rescued by Soviet icebreaker *Krassin;* remaining survivors flown out.

18 Sep.   First flight of German *LZ.127 Graf Zeppelin.*

11–15
Oct.   *Graf Zeppelin* crosses the Atlantic from Friedrichshafen to Lakehurst in 111 hrs 43 min., carrying 62,000 letters. On board: 37 crew (commanded by Hugo Eckener) and 20 passengers.

29 Oct.–
1 Nov.   *Graf Zeppelin* crosses the Atlantic from west to east in 71 hrs 7 min., carrying 101,683 letters and postcards.

1929

16 May   *Graf Zeppelin* lands at Cuers in a gale, returning to Friedrichshafen on 23 May.

1 Aug.   *Graf Zeppelin* flies to Lakehurst in preparation for a flight around the world.

8 Aug.   Start of round-the-world flight by the *Graf Zeppelin.* Stage 1: Dep. Lakehurst 8 Aug., arr. Friedrichshafen 10 Aug.; Atlantic crossing made in 55 hrs 22 min. Stage 2: 15–19 Aug., Friedrichshafen–Tokyo in 101 hrs 44 min. Stage 3: 23–6 Aug., Tokyo–Los Angeles in 79 hrs 54 min. Stage 4: 27–9 Aug., Los Angeles–Lakehurst in 51 hrs 13 min. Total time for round-the-world flight: 21 days, 7 hrs, 34 min. Passengers carried: Seilkop, von Eschwege–Lichberg, von Perck, Hammer, Kander, R. Hartmann, M. Geisenheymer (German); Rosendahl, Richardson, Leeds (American); Lady Drummond Hay, Hubert Wilkins

(British); Megias (Spanish); L. Gerville-Reache (French); Iselin (Swiss); Karlin (Russian); Fuiyoshi, Kitano, Enti, Kusaka, Shibato and Shirai (Japanese).
Commander: Hugo Eckener. Executive officers: Ernst Lehmann, H. C. Flemming, H. von Schiller. Helmsmen: Knut Eckener, R. Muller, K. Schonhen, F. Bartschat, H. Bauer.

27 Aug.   Successful launch of an aircraft in flight from the airship *Los Angeles*.

1 Sep.   *Graf Zeppelin* returns from Lakehurst to Friedrichshafen in 67 hrs 20 min.

14 Oct.   First flight of British rigid airship *R.101*.

1930
31 Jan.   Second release of an aircraft (pilot R. S. Barnaby) from the *Los Angeles*.

18 May–
6 Jun.   Double crossing of the Atlantic (south and north) by the *Graf Zeppelin*, commanded by Hugo Eckener. Schedule: Dep. Friedrichshafen 18 May; Arr. Seville 19 May; Dep. Seville 20 May; Arr. Pernambuco 24 May; Dep. Pernambuco 28 May; Arr. Lakehurst 31 May; Dep. Lakehurst 3 June; Arr. Seville 5 June; Arr. Friedrichshafen 7 June. Cargo: mail. Total distance covered: 18,100 miles.

29 Jul–
16 Aug.   British airship *R.100* makes two-way crossing of the North Atlantic.

5 Oct.   British airship *R.101* crashes into a hillside near Beauvais and burns. 38 dead, 6 survivors.

1931
24 Jul.   The *Graf Zeppelin* flies from Friedrichshafen to Leningrad, which is reached the following day. On 26 July the airship leaves Leningrad and on 27 July it touches down off an island in Franz Josef Land, exchanging mail with the Soviet icebreaker *Malygin*. The *Graf Zeppelin* takes off again after 37 min. and makes a survey flight

over Franz Josef Land and Severnaya Zemlya, returning to Leningrad on 30 July and to Berlin the same day.

23 Sep.   First flight of the US Navy *ZRS-4 Akron*.

Statistical note on the *Graf Zeppelin*'s operations during 1931—Number of flights: 73. Total distance flown: 73,173 statute miles. Passengers carried: 2,056. Cargo: 27,615 kg. (freight) and 2,917 kg. (mail). Total number of flights since the start of operations in 1928 up to 31 Nov. 1931: 232. Total distance flown: 217,132 statute miles. Total flying time: 3,947 hrs 52 min. Passengers carried: 8,778. Cargo: 38,147 kg. (freight) and 11,899 kg. (mail—a total of 297,750 letters and cards).

1932

5 Apr.   *Graf Zeppelin* makes a record crossing from Friedrichshafen to Pernambuco in 61 hours.

30 Jun.   The American *ZR-3 Los Angeles* is withdrawn from service after 8 years, during which it has made 331 flights and logged more than 5,000 hours' flying time.

12 Sep.   *Graf Zeppelin* flies from Friedrichshafen to Rio de Janeiro via Pernambuco (6,341 miles) in 94 hrs 50 min.

1933

4 Apr.   The American *ZRS-4 Akron* hits the sea during a training flight off the east coast of America and breaks up. 3 survivors picked up by the German steamer *Phoebus*; 74 dead. During the subsequent search operation, the US Navy non-rigid dirigible *J.3* crashes in the sea the following day; 6 out of the 7 crew are picked up by a seaplane.

21 Apr.   First flight of the US Navy *ZRS-5 Macon*.

Statistical note on the *Graf Zeppelin* at 31 Dec. 1933—Total flights to date: 380. Total distance covered: 506,202 statute miles. Passengers carried: 9,543. Cargo: 38,561 kg. (freight) and 21,863 kg. (mail). Atlantic crossings: 51. Pacific crossings: 1.

1935

12 Feb.   The American *ZRS-5 Macon* comes down in the sea off Point Sur and is a total loss. Two dead, 81 survivors.

6 Apr.   First flight of the year to South America by the *Graf Zeppelin*. Flight time: 71 hrs.

22 Nov.   The *Graf Zeppelin* makes its 500th flight.

27 Nov.   The *Graf Zeppelin* is prevented from landing at Recife by a revolution; demonstrating one advantage over a heavier-than-air machine, its commander stands off and waits for the shooting to stop before landing. This brings the airship's total flight time for this voyage to 119 hours—a record.

    Statistical note on the *Graf Zeppelin* at 31 Dec. 1935— Total number of flights since September 1928: 505. Total distance covered: 844,385 statute miles. Passengers carried: 11,929. Total flight time: 13,413 hrs 35 min. Cargo: 23,875 kg. (freight) and 31,888 kg. (mail). Atlantic crossings: 115 (7 N. Atlantic, 108 S. Atlantic).

1936

23 Mar.   First flight of Zeppelin *LZ.129 Hindenburg*.

26 Mar.   The *Hindenburg* and *Graf Zeppelin* make a publicity tour of Germany—the first time that two airships have flown over German territory together since the end of the First World War.

31 Mar.   First crossing of the Atlantic (Friedrichshafen–Rio) by the *Hindenburg*, commanded by Ernst Lehmann.

6 Apr.   The *Hindenburg* leaves Rio for the return flight to Germany. Over the eastern Atlantic two of its engines break down and, after flying for 42 hours on the power of the remaining two, it lands safely on 10 April.

6 May   The *Hindenburg*, commanded by Lehmann and carrying 51 passengers, crosses the north Atlantic for the first time and sets up a new record of 61 hrs 53 min. for the Friedrichshafen–New York run.

12 May   The *Hindenburg* crosses the north Atlantic (west to east) in 42 hrs 53 min.

    Statistical note on the *Graf Zeppelin* at 31 Dec. 1936— Total number of flights since September 1928: 578. Total distance covered: 1,025,693 miles. Flying time: 16,322 hrs 32 min. Passengers carried: 12,782.

Statistical note on the *Hindenburg*—Between 23 March and 31 Dec. 1936, the *LZ.129 Hindenburg* made 56 flights, carrying 2,656 passengers over a total distance of 191,519 miles and logging 2,810 hours' flying time.

1937

6 May   *LZ.129 Hindenburg* explodes and burns at her mooring-mast at Lakehurst. 35 dead, 62 survivors.

1938

14 Sep.   First flight of *LZ.130 Graf Zeppelin II*.

16 Dec.   First flight of the Goodyear non-rigid dirigible *K-2*, prototype of the 135 US Navy 'blimps' constructed before the end of the Second World War.

Appendix IV

An Airship Chronology, 1940–5

1940

19 Oct. Contract awarded to the Goodyear Aircraft Corporation, for 4 model ZNP-K airships, *K-3* to *K-6* inclusive, at $261,499.00 each. The first class of aviation cadets begins airship training at US Naval Air Station, Lakehurst, New Jersey.

1942

2 Jan. Airship Patrol Group 1 commissioned at US Naval Air Station, Lakehurst. Airship Squadron 12 commissioned at US Naval Air Station, Lakehurst.

31 Jan. Airship Squadron 32 commissioned at US Army Air Base, Sunnyvale, California.

1 Mar. US Naval Air Station, South Weymouth, Massachusetts, placed in commission.

1 Apr. US Naval Air Station (Lighter than Air), Weeksville (Elizabeth City), North Carolina, placed in commission.

16 Apr. US Naval Air Station, Sunnyvale, recommissioned and taken over from US Army.

20 Apr. US Naval Air Station, Sunnyvale, redesignated US Naval Air Station, Moffett Field, California.

1 Jun. Airship Patrol Squadron 14 commissioned at US Naval Air Station, Weeksville.

12 Jun. Contract awarded to the Goodyear Aircraft Corporation for the construction of one ZNP-M type airship for $942,660.00.

21 Aug. Airship training programme authorized by the Chief of the Bureau of Naval Personnel to begin at US Naval Air Station, Moffett Field on 1 October.

15 Sep.	US Naval Air Station, Richmond, Florida, placed in commission.
1 Oct.	US Naval Air Station, Santa Ana, California, placed in commission. Airship Patrol Group 3 commissioned at US Naval Air Station, Moffett Field. Airship Patrol Squadron 31 commissioned at US Naval Air Station, Santa Ana.
31 Oct.	The *K-20* arrives at US Naval Air Station, Moffett Field, as the first of the new K-type airships on the West Coast of the USA.
1 Nov.	US Airship Patrol Group 1 redesignated Fleet Airship Group 1. Airship Patrol Squadron 21 commissioned at US Naval Air Station, Richmond.
1 Dec.	US Airship Patrol Group 3 redesignated Fleet Airship Wing 31. Fleet Airship Wing 30 commissioned at US Naval Air Station, Lakehurst. US Naval Air Station, Tillamook, Oregon, placed in commission.
10 Dec.	Airship Patrol Squadron 33 commissioned at US Naval Air Station, Tillamook.

1943

25 Jan.	US Naval Air Station, Glynco, Georgia, placed in commission.
1 Feb.	Airship Patrol Squadron 15 commissioned at US Naval Air Station, Glynco.
10 Feb.	US Airship Patrol Squadron 51 commissioned.
1 Mar.	Fleet Airship Group 2 commissioned at US Naval Air Station, Richmond.
1 May	US Naval Air Station, Houma, Louisiana, placed in commission.
15 May	The Naval Airship Training and Experimental Command established at US Naval Air Station, Lakehurst. Airship Patrol Squadron 22 commissioned at US Naval Air Station, Houma.
22 May	US Naval Air Station, Hitchcock, Texas, placed in commission.

1 Jun.   Airship Patrol Squadron 23 commissioned at US Naval Air Station, Lakehurst, for operation at US Naval Air Station, Hitchcock.

15 Jun.   Airship Patrol Squadron 41 commissioned at US Naval Air Station, Lakehurst, as Airship Squadron 52.

15 Jul.   Fleet Airship Wing 30 redesignated as Fleet Airships, Atlantic at US Naval Air Station, Lakehurst. Blimp Headquarters Squadron 4 commissioned at US Naval Air Station, Lakehurst. Blimp Headquarters Squadron 1 commissioned at US Naval Air Station, Lakehurst, as a unit of Fleet Airship Wing 1. Blimp Headquarters Squadron 2 commissioned at US Naval Air Station, Richmond, as a unit of Fleet Airship Wing 2. US Fleet Airship Wing 31 redesignated Fleet Airship Wing 3 and Fleet Airships, Pacific. US Airship Squadron 52 redesignated Airship Squadron 41. US Airship Patrol Squadrons redesignated Blimp Squadrons. US Fleet Airship Group 1 redesignated Fleet Airship Wing 1. US Fleet Airship Group 1 redesignated Fleet Airship Wing 2.

18 Jul.   The *K-74* of Blimp Squadron 21 attacks a surfaced enemy submarine off the Florida coast, is damaged by gunfire, and makes a forced landing in the sea. The *K-74* subsequently sinks. All but one of its crew are saved.

1 Aug.   The US airship pilot training program is revised to conduct all primary training at Moffett Field, and all advanced training at Lakehurst.

2 Aug.   Blimp Headquarters Squadron 3 commissioned as a unit of Fleet Airship Wing 3. US Fleet Airship Wing 5 and Blimp Headquarters Squadron 5 commissioned at Edinburgh Field, Trinidad. US Fleet Airship Wing 4 commissioned at Maceio, Brazil.

1 Sep.   US Blimp Squadron 42 commissioned at Lakehurst.

21 Sep.   US Naval Air Station, Houma, made available for heavier-than-air use and administration.

26 Sep.   The *K-84* from Blimp Squadron 41, *en route* from Amapa to Igarape-Assu, Brazil, is the first non-rigid airship to cross the equator.

27 Oct.   *XM-1* christened at Wingfoot Lake, Akron, Ohio.

29 Nov.   *XM-1* delivered to US Naval Air Station, Lakehurst.

1944

6 Jan.   The US Airship Anti-submarine Training Detachment Atlantic Fleet (Blimp Astralant) established at Meacham Field, Key West, Florida.

4 Feb.   The first carrier landing of a non-rigid airship in the Second World War is made by the *K-29* from Blimp Squadron 31 on the CVE USS *Altamaha*.

9 Feb.   Blimp Squadron 24 commissioned at Hitchcock, Texas.

10 Feb.   Airship Utility Squadron 1 commissioned at US Naval Air Station, Lakehurst.

20 Mar.   Fleet Airships Pacific Tactical Unit established at US Naval Air Facility, Del Mar, California, to provide operational training for Blimp Squadrons 31, 32, 33.

21 Apr.   High winds open the north-west door of the hangar at US Naval Air Station, Houma, and result in the *K-56*, *K-57*, and *K-62* being blown out of the hangar and destroyed.

22 May   The major portion of Blimp Squadron 14 is detached from Fleet Airship Wing 1 and the Eastern Sea Frontier and transferred to the US Naval Air Station, Port Lyautey, French Morocco, under operational control of Commander, Eighth Fleet. The remainder of Blimp Squadron 14 designated Blimp Squadron 24, Detachment 1, to operate in Fleet Airship Wing 1.

28 May   The transatlantic ferry flight of 6 ZNP K-type patrol airships to Blimp Squadron 14 commences with the take-off of the *K-123* and *K-130* at US Naval Air Station, South Weymouth, Mass. These are the first non-rigid airships to span the Atlantic Ocean.

6 Jun.   The *K-123* in Blimp Squadron 14 makes the first operational patrol flight of the US Navy airships in the European Theatre of Operations. This flight is made in the Straits of Gibraltar.

10 Jun.   Blimp Squadron 24 is transferred from US Naval Air Station, Hitchcock, to US Naval Air Station (LTA), Weeksville, and absorbs Blimp Squadron 24 Detachment 1. Blimp Squadron 24 is placed under the administrative control of Fleet Airship Wing 1.

1 Jul.   The transatlantic ferry flight of 6 ZNP K-type patrol airships to Blimp Squadron 14 is successfully completed with the landing of the *K-101* and the *K-112* at US Naval Air Station, Port Lyautey, French Morocco.

23 Aug.   Eleven officers and 25 enlisted men of the Brazilian Air Force report aboard the US Naval Air Station, Lakehurst, for lighter-than-air training.

12 Sep.   Blimp Squadron 22 is decommissioned and its operations at Naval Air Station, Houma, taken over by Blimp Squadron 21, Detachment 4.

18 Oct.   US Naval Air Station, Hitchcock, redesignated a US Naval Air Facility.

25 Nov.   Blimp Squadron 51 ordered to Fleet Airship Wing 2 under operational control of Commander, Caribbean Sea Frontier.

25 Nov.   The transfer of eleven ZNP K-type patrol airships to the West Coast of the USA is begun.

2 Dec.   US Blimp Squadron 23 decommissioned and Blimp Squadron 21, Detachment 5, established under operational control of Commander, Eastern Sea Frontier.

7 Dec.   US Blimp Headquarters Squadron 5 decommissioned.

11 Dec.   US Fleet Airship Wing 5 decommissioned.

14 Dec.   The ferrying of eleven ZNP K-type patrol airships to the West Coast of the USA is completed.

20 Dec.   US Blimp Squadron 51 decommissioned.

1945

3 Jan.   First Airship Service Group in US Fleet Airships Atlantic formed in Blimp Squadron 12.

29 Mar.	Blimp Squadron 42 is ordered to be withdrawn to the continental United States for utility employment under Commander Fleet Airships Atlantic.
14 Apr.	US Blimp Squadron 42 with four ZNP K-type patrol airships is ordered to be transferred to Fleet Air Wing 7 for duty.
18 Apr.	Classes are begun for 9 officers and 30 enlisted men of the US Coast Guard for lighter-than-air training at the US Naval Air Station, Lakehurst.
22 Apr.	Blimp Squadron 42 transferred from US Naval Air Station, Richmond, to US Naval Air Station, Weeksville, for further transfer to Fleet Wing 7.
28 Apr.	The *K-89* and *K-114* are ferried from US Naval Air Station, Weeksville, to Kindley Field, Bermuda, on the first leg of a transatlantic flight to Blimp Squadron 14.
1 May	*K-89* and *K-114* arrive at US Naval Air Station, Port Lyautey, French Morocco, for assignment to Blimp Squadron 14.
12 May	Commander in Chief, US Fleet, and Chief of Naval Operations cancels the transfer of Blimp Squadron 42 to the United Kingdom.
16 May	Commanders of US Blimp Squadrons 11, 15 and 24 report to Commander, Air Force Atlantic Fleet, for operational control.
17 May	Commander, US Fleet Airship Wing 2, reports to Commander, Air Force Atlantic Fleet, for operational control.
23 May	US Blimp Squadrons 12 and 21 assigned to Task Group 28.3 (Fleet Airships Atlantic).
27 May	The US Airship Anti-submarine Training Detachment, Atlantic Fleet (Blimp Astralant) is disestablished.
8 Jun.	US Blimp Squadron 11 decommissioned.
9 Jun.	US Blimp Squadrons 15, 24, and 42 and Airship Utility Squadron 1 decommissioned. Transcontinental

movement of 8 ZNP K-type patrol airships to the West Coast of the USA is completed.

15 Jun. US Fleet Airship Wing 2 and Blimp Headquarters Squadron 2 decommissioned.

23 Jun. The Brazilian lighter-than-air programme at the US Naval Air Station, Lakehurst, completed with the graduation of 8 officers, 4 warrant officers, and 28 enlisted men.

27 Jun. Fleet Airships Pacific Tactical Unit at US Naval Air Facility, Del Mar, California, is closed.

12 Jul. The Brazilian Air Minister advises the US Naval Mission in Rio de Janeiro that the Brazilian lighter-than-air programme has been cancelled in its entirety.

15 Jul. US Naval Air Station, Glynco, Georgia, redesignated a US Naval Air Facility. US Fleet Airship Wing 4 and Blimp Headquarters Squadron 4 decommissioned.

6 Aug. The US Naval Air Station, South Weymouth, Mass., redesignated a US Naval Air Facility.

10 Aug. The US Naval Air Station, Weeksville, redesignated a US Naval Air Facility.

15 Sep. Nine airships of Blimp Squadron 21 and the three hangars at US Naval Air Station, Richmond, Florida, and all material within them destroyed in a tropical hurricane which produced winds in an excess of 130 knots. US Naval Air Station, Tillamook, Oregon, reduced to a functional status.

6 Oct. Commander in Chief, US Fleet, directs the decommissioning of Fleet Airships Pacific, Fleet Airship Wing 3, Blimp Headquarters Squadron 3, Blimp Squadron 32 and Blimp Squadron 33.
Commander in Chief, US Fleet, orders Fleet Airships Alantic to be decommissioned effective 20 October 1945.

15 Oct. Four US Coast Guard officers graduated from US Naval Air Station, Lakehurst, and designated naval aviators

(airship). One additional officer graduated as maintenance officer.

20 Oct.   Commander in Chief, US Atlantic Fleet, assumes operational control of all airships operating in the Atlantic Fleet.

26 Nov.   US Blimp Squadron 21 decommissioned.

Select Bibliography

BEUVILLE, A., ed., *85 Récits et Aventures de l'Air*. Gründ: Paris, 1964.

CLARKE, B., *Polar Flight*. Ian Allen: Shepperton, Middlesex, 1964.

Cross and Cockade Journal (various issues).

DENE, S., *Trail-Blazing in the Skies*. Goodyear Tire & Rubber Co., Inc.: Akron, Ohio, 1943.

DUDLEY, E., *Monsters of the Purple Twilight*. George G. Harrap: London, 1960.

ECKENER, H., *My Zeppelins*, tr. D. Robinson. Putnam: London, 1958.

GAMBLE, C. F. SNOWDEN, *The Story of a North Sea Air Station*. Neville Spearman: London, 1967.

HOEHLING, A. A., *Who Destroyed the 'Hindenburg'?* Robert Hale: London, 1962.

HOOD, J. F., *The Story of Airships*. Arthur Barker: London, 1968.

HOOREBEECK, A. van, *La Conquête de L'Air: Chronologie de l'Aérostation et de l'Aéronautique* (2 vols). Marabout: Brussels, 1967.

LAUNAY, A., *Historic Air Disasters*. Ian Allen: Shepperton, Middlesex, 1967.

MEAGER, G., *My Airship Flights, 1915–30*. William Kimber: London, 1970

MIDDLETON, E. C., *The Great War in the Air*, vols 1–4. Waverley Book Co.: London, 1920.

NOBILE, U., *My Polar Flights*, tr. F. Fleetwood. Frederick Muller: London, 1961.

ROBINSON, D. H., *The Zeppelin in Combat*. Foulis: London, 1966.

ROLT, L. T. C., *The Aeronauts: A History of Ballooning, 1783–1903*. Longmans, Green: London, 1966.

SAUNDERS, H. A. StG., *Per Ardua: The Rise of British Air Power, 1911–1939*. Oxford University Press: London, 1944.

SMITH, R. K., *The Airships 'Akron' and 'Macon'*. US Naval Institute, 1950.

SMITH, C. H. GIBBS, *A History of Flying*. Batsford: London, 1953.

SMITH, C. H. GIBBS, *Sir George Cayley's Aeronautics, 1796–1855*. HMSO: London, 1962.

WYKEHAM, P. G., *Santos-Dumont: A Study in Obsession*. Putnam: London, 1962.

Index

© Cassell & Co. Ltd, 1971